RECENT DEVELOPMENTS IN FINANCE

In Honor of Arnold W. Sametz

RECENT DEVELOPMENTS IN FINANCE

Anthony Saunders
Editor

NEW YORK UNIVERSITY SALOMON CENTER
Leonard N. Stern School of Business

BUSINESS ONE IRWIN
Homewood, Illinois 60430

332
R295

Project editor: Karen J. Nelson
Production manager: Mary Jo Parke
Jacket designer: Sam Concialdi
Printer: The Book Press, Inc.

Library of Congress Cataloging-in-Publication Data

Recent developments in finance / Anthony Saunders, editor

    p.   cm.

    "Dedicated to Arnold W. Sametz . . . based on papers presented at a
conference held in his honor on October 5, 1990 . . . [on] his
retirement"—Pref.

    ISBN 1–55623–706–5

    1. Finance—Congresses. 2. International finance—Congresses.
3. Financial Institutions—United States—Congresses. I. Saunders,
Anthony. II. Sametz, Arnold W.
HG63.R43 1992
332—dc20   91–33952

Printed in the United States of America

1 2 3 4 5 6 7 8 9 0 BP 8 7 6 5 4 3 2 1

CONTENTS

PART THREE

U.S. FINANCIAL INSTITUTIONS IN THE 1990s

PREFACE

This book is dedicated to Arnold W. Sametz. It is based on papers presented at a conference held in his honor on October 5, 1990. Arnold was Director of the Salomon Center from 1975 until his retirement in 1990. It was Arnold who built the Center into what it is today, the foremost research center in financial institutions and markets in the country and probably the world. The fact that so many of his colleagues volunteered to write research papers to commemorate his retirement is testament to the superb atmosphere created at the Center during his tenure as Director. The papers enclosed cover a broad range of issues encompassing domestic and international finance. Moreover, the research methodologies range from the institutional to the theoretical. It is this very broadness of perspective and openness to ideas that characterizes the academic career and research of Arnold Sametz.

In putting together this book, I would like to thank the tireless efforts of Mary Jaffier and Jim Cozby in getting the manuscript prepared quickly and efficiently. I hope you enjoy the book.

Anthony Saunders
John M. Schiff Professor of Finance
July 1991

RECENT DEVELOPMENTS IN FINANCE

In Honor of Arnold W. Sametz

INTRODUCTION

A VIEW FROM OUTSIDE

Martin L. Leibowitz

THE SALOMON CENTER AND SAMETZ

Well, Arnie. We've finally reached that point in time. Now, at this ceremony I can tell you *without* ceremony just how we've viewed your stewardship of the Salomon Center over all these years.

Let's start with the conferences and the books they've generated. The list of conferences reads like a leading indicator of the financial hot spots of the past 15 years:

1975 Financial Innovation
1976 Financial Crises
1977 Changing Securities Markets
1978 Deregulation
1979 Exchange Risk
1980 Internationalization of Financial Markets
1981 Problems in Mergers and Acquisitions
1982 Option Pricing
1983 Structural Change in Financial Services
1984 Commercial Bank Penetration of Securities Market
1985 Hedging with Financial Futures
1986 Emerging Markets for Swaps and Options

Martin L. Leibowitz is Managing Director of Salomon Brothers, Inc.

1987   Stabilization Policy
1988   *A vintage year, with an ominous sequence:*
       Leveraged Buyouts
       High-Yield Debt
       Crashes and Panics
1989   Corporate Governance
1990   Institutional Investing

and finally today's Conference in Honor of Arnie Sametz.

We on the outside have been astounded at the range of important topics that have come under the Center's study. We've watched the activities and achievements of the Center grow year by year, paper by paper, conference by conference, book by book.

Plus, how many young careers were nudged and nurtured under your wings?

Arnie, the most amazing thing is what a master of leverage you are! But leverage in a *positive* sense, not in an "Ed Altman" sense. You've done so much with the resources at hand!

Not many of your academic colleagues know your secret. But *I do.* It may take a practitioner to see it so clearly. I know you've studied modern management theory. You know the key to an effectively managed enterprise is a coordinated team of speciality departments—strategy, manufacturing, marketing, purchasing, human resources, finance, shareholder relations, and sales—all tied together by a knowledgeable, hands-on CEO with vision.

Well, Arnie's trick was that he has managed to combine all those functions in one highly motivated (and highly *motivating*) person—himself!

Strategy.   Arnie surely showed his flair for ferreting out the research topics of the future.

Manufacturing.   I've never seen Arnie so proud as when he finally got his desk-top publishing to work.

Marketing.   There is none better at filling seats for a conference—*any* conference!

Purchasing.   As for the make-or-buy decision, Arnie knew how to import just enough high-class talent from other universities so that the program looked ecumenical while still serving as an NYU showcase.

Human Resources.   As far as I know, Arnie was the first to establish a Counseling Service for Assistant Professors—and a Day Care Center for Full Professors.

Finance. Arnie certainly knew how to squeeze fees, contributions, and royalties from all would-be freeloaders—academics and practitioners alike. He was also a recognized master at revealing the costs while quickly reinvesting the proceeds before they saw the light of day.

Shareholder Relations. Arnie was wise in the ways of keeping the wolves from University Administration at bay.

CEO. Arnie was the ringmaster and the rainmaker who put all the wheels in motion and made things happen.

Sales. And last but not least, Arnie demonstrated his consummate salesmanship in conning Ingo Walter into believing that becoming Director of the Salomon Center would really be a desirable career move.

The term "academic leader" may be an oxymoron. But, under the wings of the Salomon Center, Arnie has surely helped to lead other academics forward in their thinking, their research, and their careers.

I am *almost* ready to believe that the Center should be renamed the Sametz Center—almost, but not quite! The guidance and spirit of Arnold Sametz pervades every facet of what the Salomon Center has become. It is a presence that will continue to be felt for many years to come.

GENERAL
INTRODUCTION

ARNOLD SAMETZ AND THE
SALOMON CENTER OVER THE
LAST TWENTY YEARS

Robert A. Kavesh
Lawrence S. Ritter

Arnold W. Sametz was born on Lincoln Road in Brooklyn, New York, on December 4, 1919. He attended James Madison High School, graduated from Brooklyn College, CUNY, in 1940, and went to Princeton University in September of that year to begin graduate study in Economics.

However, graduate work at Princeton was interrupted by World War II. In 1942, he joined the U.S. Navy and served in the Navy until the end of the war, at which time he held the rank of Lieutenant. After leaving the Navy, he returned to graduate study at Princeton and received his Ph.D. in 1951. His doctoral dissertation, on "Secular Stagnation in a Maturing Economy," was written under the supervision of Professor Oskar Morgenstern.

As a new Ph.D., Sametz's first teaching position was at Princeton University, where he was Instructor in Economics from 1948 to 1951 and

---

Robert A. Kavesh is the Marcus Nadler Professor of Finance and Economics at Stern School of Business, New York University.

Lawrence S. Ritter is the John M. Schiff Professor of Finance at Stern School of Business, New York University.

4

Assistant Professor from 1951 to 1957. At Princeton he taught Economics 201-202, the Macro and Micro Principles course that crammed four to five hundred undergraduate students at a time into a lecture section. He also assisted Lester Chandler in teaching the Money and Banking course. Money, banking, the operation of financial markets, and corporate finance became his major interests so that in 1957 he accepted a position at New York University as Associate Professor of Banking and Finance. He was promoted to full Professor at NYU in 1962.

In 1964, Professor Sametz became Associate Director of what was then called the C. J. Devine Institute of Finance, the precursor of today's New York University Salomon Center. The Director of the Institute of Finance at the time was Professor Marcus Nadler. As Associate Director, Professor Sametz assumed editorial responsibility for the Institute of Finance's *Bulletin*, the publication that evolved into today's *Monograph* series. In 1975, Arnold Sametz was appointed Director of the Center for the Study of Financial Institutions, and in 1983 his title became the Sidney Homer and Charles Simon Director of the Center.

INTERVIEW WITH PROFESSOR SAMETZ, APRIL 19, 1990

I came to NYU in 1957. I started out at the undergraduate school, the School of Commerce, Accounts and Finance we called it then. Dean John Prime was there, but he had nothing to do with hiring me. Hobart Carr and Joe Taggart talked with me and convinced me that NYU would be a good place to go to, that it had a bright future. Carr was Chairman of Finance and I think Taggart was an Associate Dean. He wasn't Dean yet. I think his predecessor, Collins, was still Dean of Graduate School of Business Administration (GBA) at the time, but Taggart was making all the academic decisions.

The two schools, graduate and undergraduate, weren't very closely integrated at that time. But already I think they were starting to build for the full-time day program that they in fact started at GBA a few years later. My shift from liberal arts (economics) to business school (finance) felt right but I recognized the risks of joining what was an academic growth venture both for the school and for myself. For insurance, I asked for a commitment that I could regularly teach a graduate economics course in the Graduate School of Arts and Sciences. Manny Stein, the Chairman of Economics at GSAS, agreed that I was to teach the graduate microeconomics course and I did so until 1962 when I went downtown to GBA where I taught some macroeconomics.

At Princeton, there was only one finance course in the whole department. I taught the big macro and micro undergraduate courses—huge lecture sections, 400 or 500 kids. I started to teach, actually, before I had my degree. I loved teaching then, back in 1948 and 1949. I think I was a great teacher at that time, if I do say so myself. I wasn't nervous or anything like that. I got headlines in the student papers and everything. Funny thing, I got much more nervous later on than I ever was when I was just beginning.

This was the immediate postwar period and the students were hard working and very good. I had some outstanding ones, like Gary Becker and Otto Eckstein. That was a good time to take up teaching, because the students were very interesting, mature people.

Then of course I accepted NYU's offer, as I said, and came here in 1957. I wanted to teach finance courses, especially corporate finance, and NYU specialized in that sort of thing. (If I had known how 1920s-like the contents of the finance courses were, I might have been scared off!)

Remember, this was the time when the first great wave of financial theory was building to a crest: Modigliani/Miller's seminal piece was in the June 1958 *American Economic Review*. In effect, the use of micro-finance (growing out of microeconomics) and cost of capital (rather than "the" interest rate of capital theory) describes much of the 1955-1965 decade's great scholarly output.

Also I wasn't happy at Princeton for reasons that had nothing to do with academic subjects. It was a stuffy place then... tea every couple of weeks... Sundays at the chairman's house... I was the first Jew on the faculty in that group and I was aware of that... a very closed community.

But it was a great center of scholarly activity on a beautiful campus in a lovely town, all enjoyed by me at almost no cost while a student. As an instructor pre-Ph.D., however, I was paid $3600 for my first year, 1949. By the time I left, my salary had doubled. NYU found it easy to beat that!

Of course, there were positive aspects too. I met Albert Einstein. He used to walk in the woods behind the Institute, hands clasped behind his back, a very friendly person. And I learned to like (not love) football.

Anyway, I started teaching undergraduate corporation finance at BPA and then in about five years, in 1962, I moved down to GBA. Larry Ritter was there then. He'd just become chairman of the finance department. Kavesh was in the economics department, apprenticing to take Marcus Nadler's place. Soon Gruber, Elton, Engberg, Keenan, Lindsay, Silber, Bloch and a number of others arrived and made GBA a very exciting place to be.

Taggart made me Associate Director of the Institute of Finance— Marcus Nadler was the Director—and for a long time my office was next door to Sipa Heller and Sam Shipman, and next to Nadler, on the eighth floor of Nichols Hall, and my principal, if not only, job was to edit the *Bulletin*, the C. J. Devine Institute of Finance's *Bulletin*. Eventually that turned into our present Monograph Series. Then in 1965, after Marcus died, I became Director of the Institute.

Marcus had been very nice to me. He was very nice to all the young people, as a matter of fact. He went to the doctor for his annual check-up one year—he felt fine but did this just as a matter of course—and that's when they found lung cancer and before you know what happened he died in April of 1965.

Anyway, as I said, after Marcus died I became Director of the Institute of Finance and we started soliciting outside authors and we also started to become less institutional, less current events oriented, and more analytical. Until then almost all the *Bulletins* had been written by Marcus himself. Or really by Shipman and Heller and then edited by Marcus.

Actually, nobody's name was on them as author. I think for a while Dean Taggart's name was on them in some capacity or other. People would stop him and say, "I enjoyed reading your *Bulletin*," and he would say, "Thank you."

With respect to the *Bulletins*, by the way, there was a survey of their importance and impact published as an article in the *Journal of Economic Literature* in 1971 [Vol. IX, No. 1]. It was done by Sam Katz of the Board of Governors. That was an important publication for us because it gave us academic respectability and made it easier to find top-notch people to write monographs for the series.

The Institute's Director's job was little more onerous than editing but my slight fund-raising duties began inauspiciously. C. J. Devine's widow was disinclined to continue C. J.'s exclusive support of the Institute. She chose rather to support her church perhaps to assure the soul of her husband who, after all, was a bond-trader. I did succeed by 1968 in establishing a goodly list of sponsoring subscribers to the *Bulletin*.

I concentrated on developing a scholarly Monograph series in finance out of the Bulletin series by soliciting manuscripts from outside the university and instituting an ad hoc refereeing process. The search was for original studies "too long for the scholarly journals and too short for a book." These basic guidelines still prevail. The early issues (1964–1968) mark the rise of another wave of academic studies, this time in innovation in financial markets and institutions as interest rate regulation and rigidity were eased.

All at once it seems financial research funding began to flow into GBA. First in 1967 came the grant via the Institute from the National League of Federal Savings and Loan Associations to study "Cyclical and Growth Programs Facing the S&L Industry." For example, Silber modeled the mortgage market and Lindsay made the case for capital debenture finance of S&Ls and I tried to separate the cyclical from the structural problems. These papers were published as Bulletin Nos. 46–47, monograph size.

Second and of far greater importance was the large grant to GBA from the Ford Foundation to finance a three-year 1968–1970 series of studies and curriculum development in international trade and finance. Bob Hawkins was the primary director of the project. A portion of the funds were allocated to me to commission and to edit a series of papers to explore the effects of the varied types and stages of financial development on real economic growth. The papers were largely by GBA-IB (international business) professors but Yale and Columbia lent experts on Japan's and the USSR's capital markets. A Symposium was held in January 1970 and the papers were published by NYU Press in 1972 under the title *Financial Development and Economic Growth—The Economic Consequences of Underdeveloped Capital Markets.*

Third, in 1972 the American Life Insurance Association granted the new Salomon Brothers Center $207,600 to study long-run demand/supply conditions in the U.S. capital markets. These studies of long-term financing, modeling and forecasting resulted in three books.

So gradually the Institute of Finance evolved in the Salomon Brothers Center. The first head of the Center was Kalman Cohen, who came from Carnegie Tech in 1972. Kal lasted about two years. He was succeeded in 1974 by Bill Silber, who didn't enjoy the job: it woke him up at night and distracted him from his research. Then I succeeded Bill in 1975. I had a lot of misgivings about taking the position because I really didn't want to be an administrator. However, I had gotten emotionally and intellectually involved in the business of the Center: I had argued a lot with Kal, and I had served as a sounding board for Silber. Also, Dean Dill was urging me to take the job.

And perhaps in the back of my mind was the thought that my own days as a productive researcher were about over. Maybe it was time, in other words, for me to help younger people do their research instead of thinking that I could continue doing substantial, original research of my own.

In my early years of teaching at Commerce and GBA I think I was still a terrific teacher. That's when I realized that you're at your best as a teacher when you're involved with research or a book of some sort or have just finished a book on the subject. I was doing the corporate finance textbook with Bob Lindsay then... that was probably my peak as a teacher at NYU. After 1975 or so I got busy with the Center and I think from then on I really had divided loyalties and it harmed my classroom teaching.

As I say, my best-rated teaching always occurred when I was engaged in new research directions and my best teaching in my opinion occurred in the two to three years following completion of the research. During the years of the 1960s when I was working on capital investment and capital structure articles and portions of books/texts were in process, corporate finance classes were a joy to me and to the students.

Likewise, during the mid-1950s at Princeton my work as co-author of an introductory economics text—*The Economic Order* (Harcourt Brace, 1958) with Paul Homan (micro-systems) and Albert G. Hart (micro-money)—fired up the teaching. That textbook was superb but too stodgy to compete with Samuelson. I think that my three chapters on the role of the price system in socialist and in planned economies still read well and currently provide the analytical framework for Chinese/Eastern European financial economic reform.

With the avalanche of research in finance since 1955, the areas of research concentration in the profession seemed to shift about every seven years: after corporate finance came international corporate finance; and then portfolio analysis, accompanied by work on financial markets and innovation; and currently financial regulation and financial institutions.

I see now that I shifted *both* research and teaching focus. I taught international corporate finance, not corporate finance; then I shifted to the basic financial markets course; and finally I tackled the "financial innovation and regulation" course. These shifts were in good part due to my need to teach in the areas I was trying to master and write.

The routine for me in teaching was always to have a wonderful outline—an annotated outline of about five or six pages. And I knew I was teaching well when I simply didn't need to refer to the outline. You just take a glance at the outline now and then.

In any event, I took the Center job and have never regretted it. In addition to money from Henry Kaufman and Salomon Brothers, we got early generous funding from Ken Wright and the Life Insurance Association and Silber received NSF and HUD support. All that got us off the ground, and by 1980 we had an average of $100,000–$125,000 a year in external funding, and annual endowment income for basic research was rising from $30,000 towards $100,000 plus annual associate funding.

But above all there was (and is) Henry Kaufman. When inflation undermined our endowment income, Henry added to the corpus and agreed to manage the funds so as to assure the real income. (NYU's endowment funds were then invested almost exclusively in bonds.) When in 1986 I began to think about retirement, I told him that to attract the right successor would likely require more money and title; Henry's response was to endow the named Directorship which was indeed fully paid in by 1989.

Early in the game, we published Ernie Bloch's monograph on Eurodollars and that got wide circulation. It is still one of our all-time best sellers. Others in that category were the one on gold by Larry Ritter and Tom Urich, Larry Ritter's monograph on the flow of funds accounts, and Guy Wyser-Pratte's on risk arbitrage.

Many of the monographs, for example Hawawini's "European Equity Markets," serve a real purpose as supplementary books, so to speak, for classrooms all over the country. We don't make any money on most of them but we don't lose much either. After all, these aren't supposed to be money-making propositions. They're supposed to be contributions to knowledge, the output of academic research.

The conferences and the books, many of which come out of the conferences, are just as important as the monographs, of course. Many of them were on the cutting edge of research and practical affairs, such as those on regulation, options and futures, and modern portfolio theory and the "Prudent Man" legal rule, to name just a few that come to mind immediately. And they sell rather well, too... we're currently getting about $15,000 a year royalties on the books.

In the beginning, the books were mainly research volumes. Later, the research found its way into articles and monographs and the books became less specialized—the proceedings of conferences, handbooks, with a research volume every two years or so. And of course the working paper series serves an important function. There are about forty or fifty of them a year.

A few things I learned about administering the Salomon Center are perhaps worth mentioning. With respect to the *structure* of a Center, a successful Center must be a partnership for it requires the active participation of the faculty and the chairmen in Finance, Economics and International Business and the Deans as well. But it is a *limited* partnership. The endowed Center itself has a mission to accomplish which will not please some faculty or some deans. And of course the Center is also a small business on its own account: the annual cash flow through the Center's books exceeds $600,000—one third to research, two fifths for publications and conferences, and one quarter to staff salaries.

With respect to the *functioning* of a Center, its first priority is to support the research activities of the faculty and doctoral candidates. But funds for *basic* research are assured only to the extent that endowment income is available. Almost all additional funding, even from foundations, is available only for applied (tied) research projects.

Fortunately, basic research can frequently be extended indirectly by participating in a "tied" project. More specifically, a rule of the Center was that 20 percent of all contract funding must be earmarked for basic research within the broad area of the project.

One of the Director's principal tasks is to get the faculty to develop research projects for funding. This is a difficult process for all concerned: it is a time-consuming interpersonal process, and even counting only really well-developed projects, only 1 of 3 will be funded in full or in part. I have found it less onerous but more uncertain to raise "untied" endowment and "associate" funding. But much of basic funding depends on the overall impact and reputation of the Center's activities as a whole.

A Center for research benefits from being involved in the dissemination of research findings: symposia, conferences, and publications. These break-even activities interact to generate reputation, and consequently additional research funding. But these activities do add substantially to the Director's task.

I think that on balance the Center has been very beneficial for the school. Thanks to the Center, many people have research funding they might not have otherwise and it has surely helped the chairmen in hiring good people.

There is no way, of course, to satisfy the financial requirements of a finance faculty of stature. Nor can the Director satisfy all the demands of project funders. Somehow we managed, though there were times when I wished a plague on both funders and fundees. Not now.

I am really looking forward to retirement. I think it's time for a change in the leadership of the Center if not in its mission, and there are a number of things I've wanted to do for a long time that now I'll be able to do. I want to do a book on innovative financial regulation and do some lecturing abroad, for instance, and without the time-consuming administration of the Center, I can now get to those things.

APPENDIX 1
CENTER-SPONSORED CONFERENCES AND
SEMINARS, 1975–1990

1975   Conference on Financial Innovation: Portfolio Theory, Implication and Application
1976   Conference on Financial Crises: Forecasting Demand and Supply in the Capital Markets, 1976–1985
        Seminar on Demand and Supply in Capital Markets, 1976–1985
1977   Conference on the National Securities Market: Prospects and Proposals
        Conference on the French Economy and the U.S. Investor
        Conference on Options Trading
        Conference on Issues in Utility Regulation
        Seminar for Executives in the U.S. Securities Markets
1978   Conference on the Crisis in Trading Policy
        Conference on Deregulation of the Banking and Securities Industry
        Quantitative Bond Analysis Group Seminar
        Conference on Space Commerce: New Options for Economic Growth
1979   Conference on Exchange Risk and Exposure: Current Developments in International Financial Management
        Conference on Regulating Securities Activities of Commercial Banks
1980   Conference on Financing Mid-Range Growth Companies in the 1980s
        Conference on the Internationalization of Financial Markets and National Economic Policy
1981   Conference on Mergers and Acquisitions: Current Problems in Perspective
        Conference on Economic and Financial Structure: Bubbles, Busts and Shocks
1982   Conference on Option Pricing: Theory and Application
        Conference on Financing and Investing in Hi-Tech
        Conference on the Emerging Financial Industry—Implications for Insurance Products, Portfolios and Planning
        Conference on the Future of the International Monetary System
1983   Conference on New York and London—Structural Change in Financial Services in the 1980s

Conference on Recent Advances in Corporate Finance: Implications for Corporate Financial Management Practice
Conference on New Opportunities in Financial Service Industries
1984   Conference on Market Making and Structure of the Securities Industry
Conference on Commercial Banks and the Securities Industry—Is the Glass-Steagall Act an Anachronism in the 1980s?
1985   Conference on Technology and the Regulation of Financial Markets
Conference for Institutional Investors on "Beginning a Hedging Program with Financial Futures"
1986   Conference on the ECU Market: Current Developments and Future Prospects
Conference on the Emerging Markets for Swaps and Options
Conference on Modern Portfolio Analysis and the "Prudent Man" Rule for Portfolio Management
1987   Italian Study Group Seminar: Deregulation of Italian Financial Markets
Symposium on Monetary Economics in Memory of Michael Hamburger
1988   Conference on Financial-Economic Perspectives on High Yield Debt Market
Conference on Uses of Financial Options for Institutional Investors
Conference on Crashes and Panics in Historical Perspective
Conference on Management Buyouts
Conference on Information Technology and Securities Markets under Stress
Conference on Off-Balance Sheet Activities
1989   Conference on Corporate Governance and Takeovers: The Market for Corporate Control and Restructuring
Conference on European Banking After 1992
1990   Conference on the Fiduciary Responsibilities of Institutional Investors
Recent Developments in Finance: Conference in Honor of Arnold W. Sametz
1991   Conference on Structural Change in Banking and Bank Regulation
Conference on Deposit Insurance Reform
Conference on Corporate Bankruptcy and Distressed Restructurings: Analytical Issues and Investment Opportunities

APPENDIX 2
CENTER-SPONSORED BOOKS, 1975–1990

1975   *Financial Innovation*, ed. William Silber
1977   *Financial Crises: Institutions and Markets in a Fragile Environment*, eds. Edward Altman and Arnold Sametz
Understanding Capital Markets (Vol. 1), ed. Patrick Hendershott, (Vol. 2), eds. Arnold Sametz and Paul Wachtel
1978   *The Deregulation of the Banking and Securities Industries*, eds. Lawrence Goldberg and Lawrence White
Prospects for Capital Formation and Capital Markets, by Arnold Sametz
1979   *Exchange Risk and Exposure: Current Developments in International Financial Management*, eds. Richard Levich and Clas Wihlborg

Impending Changes for Securities Markets: What Role for the Exchanges?, eds. Ernest Bloch and Robert Schwartz

1980 *Securities Activities of Commercial Banks*, ed. Arnold Sametz
1981 *Crises in the Economic and Financial Structure*, ed. Paul Wachtel
1982 *Mergers and Acquisitions: Current Problems in Perspective*, eds. Michael Keenan and Lawrence White
1983 *Option Pricing: Theory and Applications*, ed. Menachem Brenner
The Emerging Financial Industry, ed. Arnold Sametz
1984 *Market Making and the Changing Structure of the Securities Industry*, eds. Yakov Amihud, Thomas Ho, and Robert Schwartz
Recent Advances in Corporate Finance, eds. Edward Altman and Marti Subrahmanyam
1985 *Deregulating Wall Street: Commercial Bank Penetration of the Corporate Securities Market*, ed. Ingo Walter
1986 *Modern Investment Management and the Prudent Man Rule*, ed. Bevis Longstreth
Technology and the Regulation of Financial Markets—Securities, Futures, and Banking, eds. Anthony Saunders and Lawrence White
Hedging with Financial Futures for Institutional Investors: From Theory to Practice, ed. Stephen Figlewski
1987 *The ECU Market: Current Development and Future Prospects*, eds. Richard Levich and Andrea Sommariva
1988 *Information Technology for the Securities Markets*, eds. Robert Schwartz and Henry Lucas
1989 *Leveraged Management Buyouts*, ed. Yakov Amihud
1990 *European Banking in the 1990s*, ed. Jean Dermine
The Capital Market Effects of International Accounting Diversity, eds. Frederick Choi and Richard Levich
The High-Yield Debt Market, ed. Edward Altman
Financial Options: From Theory to Practice, eds. Stephen Figlewski, William Silber, and Marti Subrahmanyam
Crashes and Panics, ed. Eugene N. White
1991 *The Battle for Corporate Control*, ed. Arnold Sametz
Institutional Investing: The Challenges and Responsibilities of the 21st Century, ed. Arnold Sametz
Off-Balance Sheet Activities, eds. Joshua Ronen, Ashwinpaul Sondhi, and Anthony Saunders

New York University
Leonard N. Stern School of Business
CITATION
Arnold T. Sametz
Professor of Finance and Economics

More than thirty years ago you joined the Faculty of the Schools of Business of New York University. And, since then, you have compiled an impressive record as a teacher, scholar and administrator.

As a teacher you have stood out in the classroom as a perceptive instructor: challenging and inspiring. Students have regularly selected you as "tops."

As a scholar your research record is long and impressive. Ranging over a wide variety of fields, your writings are relevant and incisive.

But if this were not enough, you truly hit your stride as an administrator. As the Sidney Homer and Charles Simon Director of the Salomon Brothers Center for the Study of Financial Institutions, you have charted a course for that organization's development and destiny.

An institution is the lengthened shadow of one man," said Emerson. Your work with the Center reinforces that statement.

Thus, with admiration, respect and gratitude we salute you.
May 14, 1990

Daniel E. Diamond
Dean

Richard R. West
Dean

PART ONE

FINANCIAL MARKETS IN THE 1990s: INSTRUMENTS AND ISSUES

CHAPTER 1

HOW 1989 CHANGED THE HIERARCHY OF FIXED INCOME SECURITY PERFORMANCE

Edward I. Altman

In the mid to late 1980s, the hierarchy of fixed income security returns was consistent with the risk attributes of corporate and government debt. Over the last decade and longer, high-yield "junk" bonds had high arithmetic and compound average returns, whether measured monthly or annually.[1] While individual year returns did not always witness this hierarchy (for example, 1982 and 1984–86), the longer term return spreads favored the more risky securities. But, high-yield bonds clearly possessed greater liquidity risk and default risk than long-term, investment-grade corporate and government bonds. The volatility measures, however, also seemed to favor junk bonds. If you matched portfolios for duration, the volatility measures were fairly similar for all securities.[2]

Many observers questioned whether this seeming anomaly of higher returns and lower or equal volatility could continue. Indeed, some questioned the use of standard volatility measures, such as the variance of return, when the debt contained an embedded put option.[3] Others noted

Edward I. Altman is the Max L. Heine Professor of Finance, Stern School of Business, New York University. He would like to thank Prof. Marti Subrahmanyam for his helpful comments and Kola Luu for computational assistance.

This chapter is reprinted with permission from the *Financial Analysts Journal*, May–June 1990.

that the duration measure should be adjusted in assets that are not free of default risk.[4]

Much has been written about the turmoil in the junk bond market which started in June 1989 and continued throughout the remainder of the year and into 1990. Did this short-run dive in junk bond prices rearrange the hierarchy of returns over the last decade? What are the implications of the record-setting 7.5 to 8 percent yield spreads between junk bonds and Treasuries that existed at the end of 1989 and have continued into the first several months of 1990? And what about the less commonly observed yield spread between investment-grade and low-rated corporate bonds?

We will examine these questions using two measures to analyze performance. First, we'll look at standard risk and return performance from 1980 to 1989, highlighting the changes that have taken place over the last year. This will be accomplished using fixed income index and also average mutual fund performance measures. To complement this standard analysis, we will then analyze risk and return using the mortality rate and mortality return spread analysis techniques.

The results indicate that 1989 was an extremely important year in that the historical hierarchy of fixed income returns changed drastically, with BBB-rated and A-rated investment-grade bonds being favored for the first time. Current yield spreads between BBB and B grades, however, are possibly signaling the market's desire to return to the more typical hierarchy of performance, with risk and return being positively related.

RISK AND RETURN

Despite the potential bias introduced by the unusual skewness of returns on fixed income securities, the standard risk versus return comparison is useful and instructive. Figure 1–1 illustrates monthly arithmetic return relative to monthly standard deviations of return over the period 1980–88. The high-yield composite of low-rated bonds was clearly the dominant fixed income class, with returns on high-yield bonds higher than investment-grade corporate and government bond returns and the volatility about the same for all grades of debt (except short-term governments, where the expected low volatility is manifest). Over this nine-year period, junk bonds also outperformed the

FIGURE 1–1
Average Returns vs. Standard Deviation of Returns—Monthly Data,
January 1, 1980 to December 31, 1988

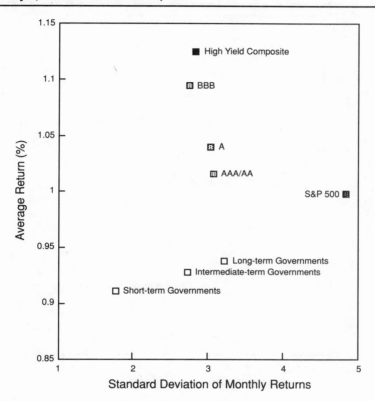

Source: Salomon Brothers Bond Indices & Blume Keim HY Comp.

S&P 500, which registered lower returns and higher risk. Investors who were willing to take on the incremental default and liquidity risk of high-yield bonds were obviously rewarded over this period.

The last year, 1989, changed this hierarchy dramatically. Figure 1–2 shows the risk and return measures for 1980–89. For the first time, BBB-rated bonds outperformed all other fixed income classes, and the S&P 500 also outperformed all the fixed income groups. While the latter relationship conforms with classic risk versus return expectations, the fixed income comparisons do not.

FIGURE 1–2
Average Returns vs. Standard Deviation of Returns—Monthly Data,
January 1, 1980 to December 31, 1989

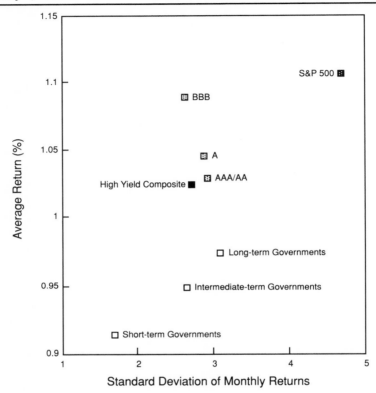

Source: Salomon Brothers Bond Indices & Blume Keim HY Comp.

The high-yield composite fell from number one among all asset classes to last among the corporates, although it still managed to slightly outperform short-, intermediate-, and long-term governments. The average monthly junk bond return fell from about 1.13 percent, through 1988, to about 1.02 percent. BBB returns, however, stayed at about 1.10 percent per month. The monthly returns of the other investment-grade debt levels also changed little. Monthly volatility measures for all debt classes were basically unchanged with long-term governments and AAA/AA-rated corporates still showing slightly higher variability, at slightly above 3.0 percent per month and the other corporates at a bit below 3 percent per month.

FIGURE 1–3
Average Returns vs. Standard Deviation of Returns—Monthly Data,
January 31, 1985 to December 31, 1989

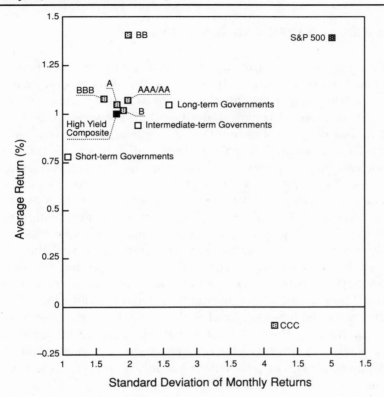

Source: Salomon Brothers Bond Indices & Blume Keim HY Comp.

We were not able to break down the high-yield sector into BB, B, and CCC rating classes over the entire 10-year sample period. Figure 1–3, however, shows the performance of all major bond rating classes over the five-year period, 1985–89. The BB composite vastly outperformed all other fixed income assets and did about as well as the S&P 500. Indeed, the average monthly return on BB debt was almost 1.40 percent per month, compared with the BBBs' 1.10 percent. The BBBs did have slightly lower variability of returns. Finally, the CCCs had a negative average monthly return over the five-year period. The poor performance of the CCCs and, to a lesser extent, the Bs, reduced the high-yield composite to just below the investment-grade bond levels.

Note also the extremely high variability of the S&P 500, with a return about equal to the top-performing BB debt class.

MEASURES OF RISK AND SKEWNESS

Returning to the issue of the distribution of returns on junk bonds, we mentioned that the skewness (non-normality) of returns on individual high-risk bonds might be a problem when using the standard deviation as a risk measure. The potential "long-tail" skewness is due to the limited liability put option implicit in equities; that is, you can only lose a fixed amount, but the upside potential is great. And a high default risk bond behaves more and more like an equity as the risk increases. This is perhaps not a problem in our analysis, however, since we are dealing with performance measures on portfolios of debt issues and not individual issues. Therefore, the option feature is not likely to be as important as it would be for individual securities.

In order to test for skewness, we observed the distribution of returns on the various portfolios of corporate fixed income securities and the S&P 500 stock index depicted in Figure 1–2 for the period 1980–89. We observe that all of the portfolios have significant skewness coefficients at the 5 percent level. This indicates some degree of skewness. The median returns, however, are quite close to the mean, indicating a fairly symmetrical distribution around the mean. And, when we eliminate the two or three outlier monthly returns from the analysis, skewness was not significant in any of the distributions. Simple observation of the various fixed income return distributions indicates fairly symmetrical and normal distributions.

We can conclude that there does appear to be some skewness in our fixed income and stock portfolios, but not serious enough to detract from our return comparisons. Since the focus of this chapter is on returns, any problems of the type discussed are probably not significant.

MUTUAL FUND PERFORMANCE

Index measures are not necessarily indicative of the net performance of all investors. Those who invested in fixed income securities via a more typical vehicle—mutual funds—did not enjoy quite the same performance as our index. Indeed, average mutual fund performance has always fallen short of the average returns to various stock and bond indexes because of transaction costs and management fees. In terms of patterns of return over time, however, mutual fund performance was consistent with the monthly data from our various indexes. The poor 1989 performance of high current yield funds vis-à-vis all other fixed income portfolios is clearly evident in Table 1–1.

Over the most recent 10-year period, 1980–89, investment-grade corporate bond mutual funds (A- and BBB-rated) registered the highest total compound return—about 192.5 percent, compared with 176.9 percent for high current yield funds (junk bonds). Government bond fund returns also outperformed the junk bond average. The 1989 returns clearly make the difference: during 1989, high current yield funds on average lost 0.89 percent, while BBB-rated funds returned 11.44 percent and A-rated funds 12.53 percent. One year before, however, the

TABLE 1–1
Average Fixed Income Mutual Fund Performance—Various Time Periods

1980–1989 Performance

	1 Year 1989	5 Year 1985–89	10 Year 1980–89
High current yield	−0.89%	52.30%	176.88%
Long-term governments	12.85	61.55	186.78
Intermediate-term governments	11.53	61.76	167.51
Short-term governments	10.25	52.44	−
A-rated corporates	12.53	70.58	192.58
BBB-rated corporates	11.44	71.78	192.55

1979–1988 Performance

	1 Year 1988	5 Year 1984–88	10 Year 1979–88
High current yield	12.46%	69.14%	196.74%
Long-term governments	6.90	60.70	170.69
Intermediate-term governments	6.29	58.97	−
Short-term governments	6.81	41.09	145.68
A-rated corporates	7.60	70.89	167.98
BBB-rated corporates	8.24	71.55	167.76

Source: "Lipper—Fixed Income Fund Performance Analysis," Lipper Analytical Services, Inc., Summit, NJ (December 1988 and December 1989)

10-year performance ending December 1988 would have shown exactly the opposite picture: the average high current yield fund recorded a return of 196.7 percent versus about 168.0 percent for both BBB- and A-rated bonds.

The starting and ending points in any statistical compilation are critical to the result. This is clearly the case in comparing mutual fund performance over two overlapping 10-year periods. What a difference one year can make!

MORTALITY RATES

The primary difference between risky corporate debt and risk-free government bonds is default risk. While all the return measurements discussed earlier include default losses and other reasons for changes of price, the *ex post* nature of the returns does not reflect current yield spreads and future expectations. Also, in the prior analyses, the sample period was 10 years for most of the rating classes, but only five years for some. Mortality rates provide an alternative measure of default rates, losses and net return spreads. Mortality rates are default estimates measured over the life of a bond issue in terms of the bond's original rating. Mortality rates are relevant to all rating classes, including investment grade.

Table 1–2 lists   mortality rates over the 1971–89 period for

TABLE 1–2
Cumulative Mortality Rates by Original S&P Bond Rating Covering Defaults and Issues from 1971–1989

Original Rating	Years After Issuance									
	1	2	3	4	5	6	7	8	9	10
AAA	0.00%	0.00%	0.00%	0.00%	0.00%	0.15%	0.20%	0.20%	0.20%	0.20%
AA	0.00	0.00	1.21	1.46	1.63	1.63	1.86	1.86	1.96	2.07
A	0.00	0.34	0.62	0.68	0.68	0.78	0.93	1.00	1.12	1.12
BBB	0.03	0.63	0.97	1.57	1.87	2.22	3.22	3.22	3.40	4.10
BB	0.00	1.08	1.54	4.80	5.23	6.92	12.09	12.09	12.09	15.04
B	1.08	2.58	5.58	8.84	11.56	15.69	20.97	23.76	30.92	32.94
CCC	1.39	3.21	7.63	22.37	24.55	NA	NA	NA	NA	NA

AAA to CCC ratings for up to 10 years after issuance.[5] Compared with data through 1988, all junk bond mortality rates are higher, especially for the BB category. The single-B rate was just under 33 percent for 10 years, up slightly from 31 percent based on data through 1988. These rates are relatively high and consistent with earlier findings.[6] The picture is not complete, however, until we assess return spreads, given these mortality rates.

Table 1–3 lists return spreads over Treasuries for each bond rating class for up to 10 years after issuance. The body of the table is in dollars per $100 of investment and assumes that all cash flows received from coupon payments, calls, sinking funds, maturities and recoveries on defaults are reinvested in the same asset class at the then-prevailing yield spread over Treasuries. The results are net of default losses, including the loss of a coupon payment at default. Figure 1–4 graphs these results. While B-rated bonds did relatively well over most of the 10-year holding period, for the first time the BBB category did best. These results are consistent with the risk-return profiles in Figure 1–2 and the mutual fund comparative results in Table 1–1. Prior to 1989, either the B-rated class (for shorter horizons) or the BB-rated debt (for longer horizons) did best.[7]

TABLE 1–3
Expected Return Spread on Net Investment in Corporate Bonds over Risk-Free Government Bonds, for Years Ended 1989

Years After Issuance	Bond Rating at Issuance						
	AAA	AA	A	BBB	BB	B	CCC
1	$0.46	$0.77	$1.07	$1.70	$3.14	$3.94	$7.04
2	1.01	1.70	2.28	3.33	6.36	8.07	16.06
3	1.67	2.59	3.76	5.60	10.64	11.47	27.27
4	2.49	3.83	5.67	8.67	12.19	15.15	29.65
5	3.46	5.41	7.95	11.94	17.71	20.09	46.98
6	4.51	7.37	10.62	15.72	22.68	24.00	NA
7	5.82	9.40	13.80	19.84	20.75	26.45	NA
8	7.51	12.28	17.80	26.09	30.19	33.09	NA
9	9.56	15.63	22.66	33.43	39.90	27.49	NA
10	12.00	18.51	28.51	41.39	37.80	37.03	NA

Source: Altman (1990)

FIGURE 1–4
Realized Return Spread on Net Investment in Corporate Bonds over Risk-Free Governments

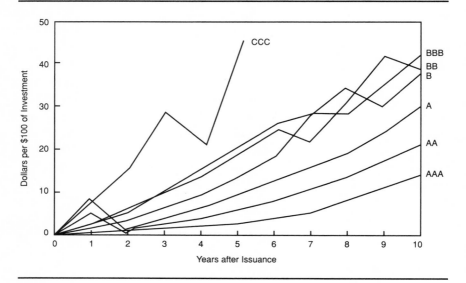

YIELD SPREADS AND THE NORMAL HIERARCHY

That an investment-grade category (BBB) has emerged as the highest-return class over the last 10 years is more surprising than the consistent return spread leadership that junk bonds had held until 1989. Indeed, one would expect that investors need to be compensated for the greater liquidity and default risk inherent in junk bonds.

Figure 1–5 shows the yields-to-maturity of the various rating classes, as well as government bond yields, over the 1973–89 period. Note the relatively constant spread of about 250 basis points between the lowest investment-grade category (BBB) and the primary junk bond category (B) over the 1985–88 period. This yield spread widened considerably in 1989.

The March 1990 BBB-versus-B spread differential was over 575 basis points! Clearly, the market is discounting junk-bond prices at a much higher rate than ever before. The reasons are, in my opinion, a heightened anticipation of default rates and lower recovery values after default, a greater liquidity risk premium requirement (partly due to the

FIGURE 1–5
Yield to Maturity—Long-Term Corporate and Government Bonds, 1980–1989

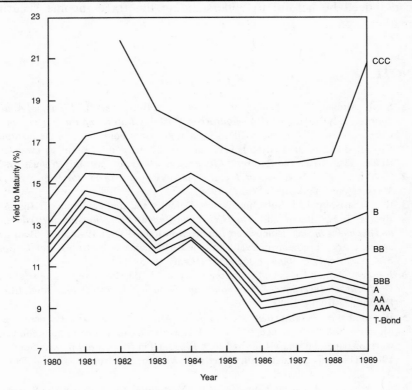

Note: Annual yield is the average for the 12-month period.

Source: Standard & Poor's *Bond Guides,* 1973–1990 and Altman (1990).

large supply of junk bonds that must be liquidated over the next several months), and finally the attempt to restructure the hierarchy of returns between different risk categories of corporate bonds.

How long this restructuring will last is a major unknown at this time. If actual default rates in 1990 and 1991 turn out to be lower than expected, we should see a marked correction in favor of lower rated bonds. Of course, if default rates are equal to or greater than expected, then the restructuring process will be lengthened.

One might also conclude that if the hierarchy of returns can change drastically in one year, the usefulness of historical returns is questionable. On the other hand, we observed that the hierarchy of risk and returns was quite as expected until 1989. Both of these observations can indeed be helpful to understanding the fixed income securities market.

NOTES

1. See E. Altman, "The Anatomy of the High-Yield Bond Market," *Financial Analysts Journal,* July/August 1987; *Default Risk, Mortality Rates, and the Performance of Corporate Bonds* (Charlottesville, Virginia: Research Foundation of the Institute of Chartered Financial Analysts), 1990; and M. Blume and D. Keim, "Lower Grade Bonds: Their Risks and Returns," *Financial Analysts Journal,* July/August 1987.
2. E. Altman and S. Nammacher, *Investing in Junk Bonds: Inside the High Yield Debt Market,* (New York: John Wiley), 1987.
3. R. Ambarish and M. Subrahmanyam, "Defaults and the Valuation of High-Yield Bonds," in E. Altman (ed.), *The High-Yield Debt Market: Investment Performance and Economic Impact* (Homewood, Illinois: Dow Jones-Irwin), 1990; and R. Bookstaber and R. Clark, "Problems in Evaluating the Performance of Portfolios with Options," *Financial Analysts Journal,* January/February 1985.
4. J. Fons, "Default Risks and Duration Analysis," in E. Altman (ed.), *The High-Yield Debt Market: Investment Performance and Economic Impact* (Homewood, Illinois: Dow Jones-Irwin), 1990.
5. We used the mortality methodology in E. Altman, "Measuring Corporate Bond Mortality and Performance," New York University, Stern School, Salomon Center working paper, February 1988 and June 1989, and in *Journal of Finance,* September 1989. This was updated with data from Altman, "Default Risks and Duration Analysis," note 4 above.
6. See Altman, "Measuring Corporate Bond Mortality," note 5 above; and P. Asquith, D. Mullins, and E. Wolff, "Original Issue High Yield Bonds: Aging Analysis of Defaults, Exchanges and Calls," *Journal of Finance,* September 1989.
7. See Altman, "Measuring Corporate Bond Mortality," note 5 above.

CHAPTER 2

THE CHALLENGE OF INSTITUTIONALIZATION FOR THE EQUITY MARKETS

Robert A. Schwartz
James E. Shapiro

Three interrelated forces—deregulation, the introduction of electronic technology, and the institutionalization of the market—are causing dramatic changes in the way equities are traded worldwide. This chapter focuses on institutionalization and the growing importance of mutual funds, pension funds, insurance companies, banks, broker/dealer firms, etc., in the holding and trading of equities.

The implications of institutionalization are profound but imperfectly perceived and poorly understood.[1] The way in which orders are written, submitted to the market, and translated into trades has been fundamentally altered in recent years. The suitability of trading systems such as the New York Stock Exchange and the Over-the-Counter NASDAQ market, both of which were designed to handle a predominantly retail order flow, needs to be reconsidered.

From an academic point of view, institutionalization has generated new problems to grapple with, but in certain respects has also in-

Robert A. Schwartz is a professor of finance and economics at the Leonard N. Stern School of Business, New York University.

James E. Shapiro is the Managing Director, Economic Research, at the New York Stock Exchange.

The authors thank Laura Cohen, Joel Hasbrouck, Randolph Mann, and Fred Renwick for their helpful comments. The views expressed in this chapter are the authors' and, in particular, do not necessarily represent those of the New York Stock Exchange, its members, or its Board of Directors.

creased the applicability of financial theory. Of particular interest, many institutional investors now hold portfolios that replicate a market index. Consequently, many asset managers are less concerned with the attributes of particular companies' shares. Increasingly, the managers are looking at the return, risk, and liquidity profile of baskets. Within such baskets, individual stocks may be interchangeable. A consequence of this trend to indexation is the commoditization of equities.

In this regard, one might argue that the securities industry has caught up with academia. A cornerstone of modern portfolio theory, the Capital Asset Pricing Model, shows that, in a costless environment characterized by homogeneous expectations, equities are commoditized. That is, investors do not select specific stocks; rather, they select specific risk and return configurations. Alternatively stated, it is not specific stocks that are priced in the marketplace, but risk that is priced. If different stocks (or portfolios) have the same risk, then they should sell at the same price.

While the Capital Asset Pricing Model has proved to be a useful analytical tool, price determination in real world markets is a highly complicated process that is only imperfectly understood by academicians and other students of the market. Price discovery appears to be even more difficult in an institutionally dominated environment. This being the case, institutionalization might explain much of the volatility that has been observed in recent years.[2] The purpose of this chapter is to explore this issue and to consider the appropriateness of current trading systems for institutional investors.

THE FACTS

The growth of institutionally owned assets in the United States has been striking. Total assets of domestic institutional investors rose from $89.6 billion, or 31 percent of GNP in 1950, to $4.9 trillion, or 94.3 percent of GNP in 1989. The proportion of these assets that are held in equities has also grown; in 1950, 10 percent of institutional assets were in equity issues; by 1989, the proportion was nearly 30 percent.

As a consequence of institutionalization, the ownership and trading of equity assets have become far more concentrated. At year-end 1989, domestic institutions held equity assets equal to roughly 50 percent of total NYSE capitalization. Institutions and member firms together now account for over 70 percent of the share volume on the NYSE. Block trades (10,000 shares or more), a widely accepted proxy for institutional activity, have grown from 3.1 percent of NYSE share volume in 1965 to 51.5 percent in 1989.

The U.S. market is not the only one experiencing the trend toward greater institutionalization. On the Tokyo Stock Exchange, share ownership by domestic financial institutions has risen from 18.2 percent of outstanding shares in 1952 to 45.6 percent in 1989. Financial institutions together with member firms and nonfinancial businesses accounted for 76.6 percent of total share volume in Japan in 1989. On London's International Stock Exchange, domestic and foreign institutions accounted for 73.3 percent of trading by value in June 1989. Table 2–1 puts these data in comparative perspective for New York, Tokyo, and London, the world's three largest equity markets.

The portfolios held by major institutional investors are enormous. In 1989, the top 200 defined benefit pension funds together had equity assets of $542.4 billion. On average, these funds each managed $2.7 billion worth of equity.[3] If the average sized $2.7 billion portfolio were diversified equally across 100 issues, substantial positions would have to be held in individual stocks: 540,000 shares of each issue at an average price of $50 per share.

TABLE 2–1
Trading Activity in New York, Tokyo, and London, 1989—by Type of Investor (percent of volume for NYSE and TSE; percent of value for ISE)

Exchange	Nonmember Institutions	Member Firms	Retail/ Other
NYSE	46.2	25.7	28.1
TSE	53.4[a]	23.3	23.3
ISE[b]	73.3[c]	n.a.	23.6[d]

[a] Includes shares traded by foreigners and nonfinancial businesses.
[b] June 1989 only.
[c] Includes shares traded by domestic and foreign institutions.
[d] Includes domestic and foreign individuals.

Sources: "Investor Activity Report," Securities Industry Association, May 1990; *TSE Fact Book*, 1990; and "Market Structure: Transaction Survey Results," International Stock Exchange, July–September 1989.

COMMODITIZATION OF EQUITIES

"Commoditization" means that equity issues are selected with reference to statistical estimates of their risk and return attributes, and without regard to other "fundamental" information related to the future value of each stock. Stocks with similar risk-return measures are treated as perfect substitutes for one another, much as agricultural commodities of a particular variety sell at the same price, regardless of the particular farms on which they are grown. With commoditization, it is risk that is priced in the marketplace, and all issues with the same risk sell at the same price, as is the case under the assumptions of the Capital Asset Pricing Model.

Commoditization is largely explained by the growth of index-related portfolios and the development of the market for index-related derivative products. A substantial portion of the institutionally managed assets are now indexed (managed passively). A *Pensions & Investment Age* survey of the top 50 index fund managers located $193.9 billion in indexed funds as of November 30, 1988. Salomon Brothers estimated that, as of December 1988, $177.8 billion, or 25 percent of pension fund (ERISA) assets, were indexed to the S&P.[4] Current estimates conservatively put the amount of indexed assets at between $200 and $300 billion.

The growth of indexation is itself largely explained by:
- The size of financial institutions (being large relative to many of the listed companies forces them to diversify over many issues).
- The inability of the representative institutional investor to achieve superior returns (many studies have shown that institutional investors typically underperform market indexes).
- The increasing intensity with which the performance of asset managers is assessed (developments in modern portfolio theory have shown how the risk-return attributes of a portfolio can be measured and controlled by asset selection, and have facilitated assessing portfolio performance).

Some rejoice at the commoditization of the equities markets, trumpeting the low costs (and higher returns) of passive investing. Others complain that commoditization has eroded the quality of the prices of underlying instruments. In either case, it is clear that commoditization has brought the world much closer to the textbook realm of two assets—a market portfolio and a risk-free asset (or zero-beta) portfolio.

TRADING COSTS AND PRICE VOLATILITY

Explicit trading costs (commissions), along with other costs of monitoring the market and of record keeping, are appreciably lower for institutional investors than for smaller retail customers. Additionally, because of their size, discontinuities due to round lot trading are not a consideration for institutional investors. Institutions can make relatively small quantity adjustments on the margin, even in round lots. Increasingly, the institutions are using scaled orders for individual securities and, of course, do not make all or nothing decisions in the allocation between, for instance, equities, fixed income securities, and cash.[5]

Execution costs (the bid-ask spread and market impact) are greater for institutional investors who concentrate their holdings in specific issues. These costs also induce institutions to trade large baskets on an incremental basis.

Other trading costs may be incurred because the prices of equity issues are highly volatile over brief time intervals (i.e., over one trading day). Table 2–2 suggests the magnitude involved for individual NYSE-listed S&P 500 issues. The table gives daily high-to-low ranges and open-to-close ranges for these issues for the week of July 30 through August 3, 1990 (stocks that went ex-dividend, or split, or for which no trade was recorded by 10:00 a.m. are excluded for the relevant day). Differences in the price levels of different securities are adjusted for by measuring the ranges in percentage terms, and then computing the comparable dollar amounts for a $50 stock.[6, 7]

The bottom row of the table shows the cumulative number of observations that fall in any high-to-low range category or higher. For instance, 36.09 percent of the daily observations had a high-to-low range that, expressed for a $50 stock, was $1.50 or more; 20.92 percent of the daily observations had a range of $2.00 or more.

To assess the magnitude of the price movements involved, consider a stock trading at 50 that is expected to trade at 55 one year hence. Ignoring dividends, the expected return for the stock is 10 percent. If the stock's low for the day is 49.25, an investor buying at the low can expect a return of 11.7 percent; if the stock's high for the day is 50.75 ($1.50 more), the investor can expect a return of 8.4 percent. Therefore, a $1.50 high-to-low range in dollar terms is associated with a high-to-low range of 3.3 percentage points in returns space. This shows that an asset manager can add (or subtract) appreciably to a

TABLE 2–2
Distribution of NYSE-listed S&P 500 Firms by Price Range Expressed in Dollars for a $50 Stock—Week of July 30, 1990, through August 3, 1990

Open to Close Range	High to Low Range									Total	%	Cumulative %
	0.00 to 0.25	0.251 to 0.50	0.501 to 0.75	0.751 to 1.00	1.001 to 1.50	1.501 to 2.00	2.001 to 2.50	2.501 to 3.00	Over 3.00			
0.000 to 0.250	24	116	142	115	86	36	15	9	21	564	24.9	100.00
0.251 to 0.50		52	137	127	101	36	12	3	2	470	20.79	75.06
0.501 to 0.75			62	91	116	51	20	11	9	360	15.92	54.27
0.751 to 1.00				58	104	54	17	10	10	253	11.19	38.35
1.001 to 1.50					114	103	61	22	28	328	14.51	27.16
1.501 to 2.00						63	41	27	23	154	6.81	12.65
2.001 to 2.50							25	17	25	67	2.96	5.84
2.501 to 3.00								8	17	25	1.11	2.87
Over 3.00									40	40	1.77	1.77
Total	24	168	341	391	521	343	191	107	175	2,261	100.00	
%	1.06	7.43	15.08	17.29	23.04	15.17	8.45	4.73	7.74	100.00		
Cumulative %	100.00	98.94	91.51	76.43	59.13	36.09	20.92	12.47	7.74			

fund's performance over an entire year, by properly (or improperly) timing his or her trades within a single day.[8]

The matrix format used to present the distributions suggests that, as one would expect, the high-low range is positively related to the absolute size of the open-to-close price change (many of the observations lie close to or on the diagonal). The extent to which observations are away from the diagonal is striking, however. For instance, of the 343 observations that fall within the high-to-low range category of 1.501 to 2.50, 36 had an open-to-close range of less than $0.25; 36 had an open-to-close range of $0.251 to $0.50, and so forth. As we have learned from other empirical studies, short-run price movements are frequently reversed.[9]

The appreciable short-run volatility suggested by Table 2–2 has three implications for the decisions made by an asset manager:

1. Any change in current prices is a very noisy signal of change in the expectations of end-of-period values. Consequently, a manager should not necessarily revise his or her expectations of future values every time the current price changes in the marketplace.

2. The asset manager must make a trading decision as well as an investment decision. That is, he or she should assess the alternatives of buying (selling) immediately via a market order at a current price, or of posting a limit order at a lower buying price (higher selling price) in the hopes of enhancing an annual rate of return by buying near the low for a day (or selling near the high).[10]

3. An institutional investor should make marginal decisions. That is, unless he or she has independent reason to reassess the value of a company's stock, the manager should be willing to buy additional shares as the price falls in the marketplace and to sell some shares as the price rises.

Posting limit orders to buy or to sell shares incrementally is a *passive* trading strategy. An institutional investor that uses a passive strategy is, in a sense, acting as a traditional market maker (dealer or specialist). The institution brings liquidity to the market and, in so doing, helps to stabilize share prices. Some institutions such as TIAA/ CREF recently started using this type of passive trading.

INVESTMENT ANALYSIS

Typically, institutional investors are risk-averse. The investors they represent are risk-averse, and the asset managers are assessed according to the performance of their portfolios. Being risk-averse, institutional investors typically diversify their portfolios, not just across individual assets, but across broad asset categories—equities, fixed income, and cash.[11]

In this section, we consider an individual's investment analysis with regard to a particular stock or portfolio. We noted in the previous section that institutional investors should not necessarily change their expectations of future share values every time current prices change, and that they should make marginal decisions (that is, buy and sell incrementally, as current prices change). This, along with risk aversion, implies that institutional investors should make investment and trading decisions as if they had downward sloping demand curves to hold shares of a risky asset. If institutions have downward sloping demand, share prices must be set in the marketplace. This makes price discovery an important function of a market center.

The Discounted Cash Flow Model

We start by presenting the well-known Discounted Cash Flow (DCF) model. Assume a risk-averse investor, who seeks to maximize the expected utility of wealth at the end of one year, buys shares of a risky asset at the start of the year, and sells them at the end. The subscript "0" denotes the current point in time, the subscript "1" denotes the end of the investor's one-year holding period, and P is the price per share of the risky asset. Let the investor assess the current value of shares, P_0, using the simple DCF model. Assume that at the end of each year the stock pays a dividend (D), that D is expected to grow at the rate g, and that k is the risk appropriate interest rate for discounting the dividend stream. If a stock has just paid a dividend of D_0,

$$P_0 = D_0 (1 + g) / (1 + k) + \ldots + D_0[(1 + g) / (1 + k)]^\infty \qquad (2.1)$$

which, being the sum of an infinite geometric progression, reduces to

$$P_0 = D_1 / (k - g) \qquad (2.2)$$

Similarly,

$$E[P_1] = D_2 / (k - g) \qquad (2.3)$$

Thus, the stock's expected future share price grows at the same rate as the dividend, the rate g.

Solving equation 2.2 for k gives

$$k = D_1 / P_0 + g \qquad (2.4)$$

where the discount rate, k, and the expected growth rate, g, are assumed to be constant over the one-year holding period.

Equation 2.4 shows that k is an expected return that comprises two components: a dividend yield and capital appreciation. P_0 is set in the marketplace so that the dividend yield, D_1 / P_0, plus the expected future growth, g, is sufficient to give shareholders their required return. This return comprises two components: the risk-free return (r_f) and a risk premium (π).

This standard presentation of the DCF model might seem to suggest that the risky asset's share price can be determined by "objective" security analysis. The analyst need only (1) forecast the rate at which dividends are expected to grow and (2) determine the appropriate discount rate, given the riskiness associated with the growth rate. If all investors have homogeneous expectations regarding future cash flows and if they use the same discount rate, then the market price of a share (P_0) could be calculated at the desks of the security analysts (or so the analysis might thus far seem to suggest).

The Demand Curve Model

The DCF model can also be used to assess any portfolio or commoditized basket, including the market portfolio. Recognizing this, we next show that the individual discounts dividends on the market portfolio at a higher (lower) rate if that individual holds more (fewer) shares of the market portfolio.[12]

Following Ho, Schwartz, and Whitcomb (1985), we can express a risk-averse investor's demand to hold shares of a risky asset as

$$P_0 = E(P_1) / (1 + r_f) - 2bN \qquad (2.5)$$

where

r_f = risk-free rate of interest

b = $\pi / (1 + r_f)$

N = the number of shares held

π = the risk premium = $-1/2\{[U''(W) / U'(W)] \text{Var}(P_1)\}$

$U'(W), U''(W) =$ the first and second derivatives of the investor's utility function defined on wealth

$\text{Var}(P_1)$ = variance of the asset's end-of-period price

The demand curve given by equation 2.5 is downward sloping: if expectations of the end-of-the-period price (P_1) are constant, any decrease in the current price (P_0) will lead the investor to hold more shares, and any increase in the current price will lead the investor to hold fewer shares. This suggests that the investor does not establish a unique share value for the risky asset, but that he or she determines the optimal number of shares to hold, *given* the market determined price of the asset.

Consistent with this, we show in the Appendix, using the demand curve model, that the discount rate at which dividends should be assessed in the DCF model does not reflect a constant risk premium, but a *marginal* risk premium. Moreover, this premium is an increasing function of the number of shares held (see equation 2.A.6). Thus, k is determined endogenously.

Implementation of an Investment Decision

The downward sloping demand curve expresses an investment decision that must be translated into a trading decision. The trading decision in a continuous market environment is complex; the investor will not reveal his or her full demand to the market, but will select a restricted number of points. The order points are selected with reference to the investor's demand curve, current share holdings, expectation of the clearing price that will be established in the marketplace, and knowledge of the structure of the marketplace that determines how orders are handled and translated into trades.

Transaction costs explain why an investor will submit only a discrete set of order points. The cost of buying at every ⅛ of a point as price adjusts from one level to another is formidable. For example, assume a stock has last traded at 50 ⅛, and that an investor would like to buy (in accordance with his or her demand curve) 1,000 shares at 50, or 1,100 at 49 ⅞, or 1,200 at 49 ¾, and so on down to 1,800 shares at 49. To focus on the extremes, the investor could submit a fully scaled order (1,000 at 50, 100 at 49 ⅞, 100 at 49 ¾, ..., 100 at 49), or a single order to buy 1,800 at 49. The cost of selecting the fully scaled order is the higher amount paid for intramarginal purchases if price actually does fall to 49 in the market. Thus, if the possibility of the price decrease is deemed large enough by the investor, the single order point (buy 1,800 at 49) should be submitted and the intermediate order points should not be disclosed.[13]

IMPLICATIONS FOR MARKET STRUCTURE

Our thesis is as follows: institutional investors typically trade commoditized baskets of stocks, for which they have downward sloping demand. A consequence of downward sloping demand is that asset prices must be determined in the marketplace through the interaction of the buy and sell orders of traders. In this environment, price discovery is more complicated than it would be if all participants believed assets have intrinsic values, as is implied by a simple DCF model when the discount rate, k, is taken to be exogenous. This thesis has major implications for the design of a market center.

In the past, reducing the bid-ask spread has been a central objective of market design. This focus on the spread has called much attention to the desirability of increasing inter-dealer competition. Unfortunately, focusing exclusively on spreads may have undesirable consequences for price discovery and, without accurate price discovery, spreads may not, in fact, be minimized.

The formal dealer models in the academic literature fall into two categories. In the inventory models [Demsetz (1968), Garman (1976), etc.], the dealer is assumed to know equilibrium prices. In the asymmetric information models [Glosten and Milgrom (1985), Kyle (1985), etc.], "informed traders" are assumed to know equilibrium prices. In both models, competitive pressures serve to keep prices reasonably aligned with equilibrium values. Unfortunately, in an environment where no one knows the equilibrium value until it is discovered in the marketplace, price may deviate considerably, even under competitive conditions.

From the viewpoint of an institutional investor, accurate price discovery may be a more important objective than tight bid-ask spreads. Although it has not been possible thus far to measure errors in price discovery, one might infer that they are appreciable compared to bid-ask spreads. The intra-day price variability suggested by Table 2–2 is greater than representative bid-ask spreads (high-low differences of $2.50 or more are common for a $50 stock, while spreads rarely exceed $0.50). Thus mistiming or mispricing an order can cut more deeply into returns than does paying the bid-ask spread.

Despite the fact that accurate price discovery may be important for institutional investors (as well as for others), a trading system that provides superior price discovery is by no means assured of success:

- Equilibrium prices are unobservable; thus, unlike posted bid-ask spreads, errors in price discovery are not measurable and the impact on longer term portfolio performance is not clearly perceived. Consequently, asset managers pay less attention to it.

- The bid-ask spread is the price of immediacy, the sale of which is a private good. Price determination, on the other hand, is a public good; the prices established by the subset of investors who participate in a reported trade are important for others, both as an informational signal and for asset evaluation (i.e., mutual fund redemption). Like all public goods, the services that provide accurate price discovery are undersupplied in a competitive marketplace.

- Some market participants (day traders in particular) may profit from mispricing and the excessive short-run volatility that it generates. Their vested interest can block desirable structural change.

The accuracy of price determination depends on the architecture of a trading system, and more accurate, less volatile prices can be realized through improvements in systems design. We stress the importance of taking this into account when assessing the merits of alternative trading systems.

APPENDIX TO CHAPTER 2

THE MARGINAL RISK PREMIUM

The risk premium (π) is the link between the DCF model and the demand curve model. When the investor holds the optimal number of shares of the market portfolio at a market determined price per share, the market price of risk can be related to his or her risk premium. To see how, let us assess the demand curve at the specific price $P_0 = P_{01}$:

$$P_{01} = E(P_1) / (1 + r_f) - 2\pi N_1 / (1 + r_f) \qquad (2.A.1)$$

At P_{01}, the optimal number of shares to hold is N_1. Multiplying equation 2.A.1 by $(1 + r_f) / P_{01}$, rearranging, and recognizing that $[E(P_1) / P_{01}] - 1 = E(r_m)$ is the expected return on the market portfolio, we have

$$E(r_m) - r_f = 2\pi N_1 / P_{01} \qquad (2.A.2)$$

In the DCF model, k is an expected return that the investor requires as compensation for holding N_1 shares of the market portfolio, and $k - r_f$ is the risk premium demanded by the investor. In the demand curve model, the optimal number of shares to hold at each price is obtained by solving for the number that maximizes expected utility. When the optimum number of shares is held, $E(r_M) - r_f$ (the risk premium paid by the market) equals $k - r_f$ (the risk premium demanded by the investor). Thus*

$$k - r_f = 2\pi N_1 / P_{01} \qquad (2.A.3)$$

The right-hand side of equation 2.A.3 can be interpreted. The uncertainty associated with holding one share of the risky asset is $\text{Var}(P_1)$, and π is the risk premium for holding one share. The uncer-

---

*Strictly speaking, in the DCF model the risk premium is for a perpetuity, and in the demand curve model the risk premium is for a one-period return. Consequently, the term structure of interest rates must be flat for equation 2.A.3 to hold exactly.

tainty associated with holding N shares is $\mathrm{Var}(NP_1) = N^2\,\mathrm{Var}(P_1)$; thus, the *total* risk premium for holding N shares is

$$\pi_T = \pi\,N^2 \tag{2.A.4}$$

Differentiating equation 2.A.4 with respect to N gives the risk premium for holding a marginal share,

$$\pi_M = 2\pi\,N \tag{2.A.5}$$

Dividing by P_{01} expresses the marginal risk premium as a percentage of the current price:

$$\pi_{M\%} = 2\pi\,N\,/\,P_{01} \tag{2.A.6}$$

Substituting into equation 2.A.3 and rearranging, we see that

$$k = r_f + \pi_{M\%}, \tag{2.A.7}$$

which completes the demonstration that the discount rate in the DCF model is a *marginal* risk premium.

NOTES

1. For a recent analysis of the impact of institutional ownership on liquidity, see Jones, Lehn, and Mulherin (1990).
2. See, for example, Schwert (1990) and Duffee, Kupiec, and White (1990).
3. *Pensions & Investments*, January 22, 1990.
4. "Global Equity Market Review and Outlook: 1988–1989," Salomon Brothers, Inc.
5. A "scaled order" is an order to buy (or to sell) a relatively small number of shares at each of several prices, rather than one relatively large number of shares at a single price.
6. Changes in the Dow Jones Industrial Average for each of the five days of the sample week were +18.82, −12.13, −5.94, −34.66, and −54.95, respectively.
7. Similar ranges are reported in Schwartz (1991a).
8. The impact on a fund's annual rate of return is even greater—it is possible to buy at the low now and to sell at the high one year later, or to buy at the high now and to sell at the low one year later. Even if there is no systematic tendency to buy (sell) at the low (high), this variability can add appreciably to the variance of annual returns.
9. See, for instance, Hasbrouck and Schwartz (1988).

10. For an analysis of the limit order strategy, see Handa and Schwartz (1991).
11. As noted above, portfolios are to some extent diversified because the size of assets under management is large relative to the size of individual issues.
12. This allows for the possibility that, in a multiasset environment characterized by heterogeneous expectations and noncostless trading, an individual will discount dividends for a specific stock at a rate that likewise depends on his or her shareholdings of the stock.
13. See Schwartz (1991b) for further discussion of the opportunity costs of trading.

REFERENCES

Demsetz, Harold, "The Cost of Transacting," *Quarterly Journal of Economics,* February 1968.

Duffee, Gregory; Paul Kupiec; and A. Patricia White, "A Primer on Program Trading and Stock Price Volatility: A Survey of the Issues and the Evidence," Board of Governors of the Federal Reserve System, January 1990.

Garman, Mark, "Market Microstructure," *Journal of Financial Economics,* June 1976.

Glosten, Lawrence, and Paul Milgrom, "Bid, Ask, and Transaction Prices in a Specialist Market with Heterogeneously Informed Traders," *Journal of Financial Economics,* March 1985.

Handa, Puneet, and Robert Schwartz, "Limit Order Trading: Theory and Empirical Evidence," Stern School, New York University working paper, 1991.

Hasbrouck, Joel, and Robert Schwartz, "Liquidity and Execution Costs in Equity Markets," *Journal of Portfolio Management,* Spring 1988.

Ho, Thomas; Robert Schwartz; and David Whitcomb, "The Trading Decision and Market Clearing Under Transaction Price Uncertainty," *Journal of Finance,* March 1985.

Jones, Jonathan; Kenneth Lehn; and J. Harold Mulherin, "Institutional Ownership of Equity: Effects on Stock Market Liquidity and Corporate Long-Term Investment," SEC working paper, June 1990.

Kyle, Albert, "Continuous Auctions and Insider Trading," *Econometrica,* November 1985.

Schwartz, Robert, "Institutionalization of the Equity Markets: Implications for Price Discovery, Volatility, and Market Structure," *The Journal of Portfolio Management,* 1991a.

Schwartz, Robert, *Reshaping the Equity Markets: A Guide for the 1990s,* New York: Harper Business, 1991b.

Schwert, G. William, "Stock Market Volatility," in *Market Volatility and Investor Confidence,* Report to the Board of Directors of the New York Stock Exchange, June 1990.

CHAPTER 3

COMMUNICATING WITH THE MARKET VIA DIVIDENDS, INVESTMENT AND TRADING BY INSIDERS

Kose John
Teresa A. John

INTRODUCTION

The effect of corporate dividend policy on stock prices has always been an active concern of financial economists. Since the formulation of the "dividend irrelevance" proposition by Merton Miller and Franco Modigliani in 1961, it has been widely accepted that in a world of perfect capital markets, a company's dividend policy should have no effect on the value of a company's shares.[1] In a world of well-functioning capital markets, with no taxes, transactions costs or other "market imperfections," the value of the shares would simply be the present value of the stream of future cash flows from the firm's assets-in-place and future growth opportunities, adjusted for any additional investment required to generate and sustain those flows. Since the optimal investment policy can be sustained

---

Kose John is Professor of Finance and Teresa A. John is Assistant Professor of Accounting at Stern School of Business, New York University.

Helpful discussions with Yakov Amihud, Larry Land, and Bani Mishra are gratefully acknowledged. The authors also appreciate the computational assistance of Camille Hourani at Emory University and Sang-Lyong Joo at New York University.

in such a world independent of the level of dividend payouts, a company's dividend policy affects only the amount of outside financing required to fund new investments. In other words, a firm's dividend policy is essentially a matter of financial packaging determining (a) the division of the firm's financing between internal and external sources of funds, and (b) the division of its shareholder's returns between cash dividends and capital gains. As long as the securities sold to finance any incremental current dividends are fairly priced, a dividend payment is merely a swap of current cash for future cash (possibly with risk) of equal market value. As Miller (1987) states, an incremental current dividend is thus "not much different in principle from withdrawing money from a passbook savings account."[2]

The dividend irrelevance proposition has provided an important starting point in an analysis of the impact of dividend policy on firm value. However, it seems to be inconsistent with some of the stylized facts and empirical evidence on dividends. For example, if capital gains are taxed less than dividends (in an otherwise perfect market), it will be optimal for firms to pay no dividends. Then why do firms pay substantial dividends when they are subject to higher taxation rates than capital gains?[3]

The empirical research documenting the significant impact that dividend announcements have on stock prices is another important challenge to the "dividend irrelevance" proposition. This research shows that announcements of large dividend increases are met with upward price movements while announcements of dividend cuts are associated with price declines. Miller and Modigliani suggest that managers may announce such dividend changes in an effort to move market expectations closer to those management has about future earnings prospects. In the last 25 years, this heuristic "dividend information" proposition has been the backdrop for a large body of empirical studies which attempt to identify what information, if any, is conveyed by dividend announcements.[4] More recently, "dividend signaling" models have been added at a theoretic level which rigorously analyze whether dividends can be used to credibly convey new information to the market[5]. The signaling models assume that corporate insiders have more information about the company's future earnings prospects than do outside market participants. As was the case with preferential tax treatments (discussed above), an "information asymmetry" between management and others is a market imperfection which may perturb the dividend irrelevance propositions of Modigliani and Miller (1961).

Bhattacharya (1979), John and Williams (1985) and Miller and Rock (1985) construct signaling models in which firms with favorable private information optimally distribute larger dividends than firms which do not. These signaling models also yield testable predictions regarding the announcement effect of dividend changes on stock prices, consistent with the empirical evidence mentioned above.

Some recent evidence which focuses on the fine structure of the announcement effect of dividend changes on stock price behavior also seems to imply that dividend policies may be intertwined with the investment policies of firms. The original M&M scenario assumed that transactions costs (including the cost of issuing securities) are immaterial and that all firms have equal access to capital markets in which security prices impound all available information. These assumptions implied that the company's dividend policy decisions (to retain earnings or pay them out in the form of dividends) will not affect or be affected by its investment decisions. The Lang and Litzenberger (1989) study presents evidence that the announcement effect of dividends is affected by the investment policy and investment opportunities of the firm.

In a setting of asymmetric information between corporate insiders and the market, investment choices by firms directly (or, the dividend policies they imply indirectly) may convey private information to the market. Miller and Rock (1985) develop a signaling model in which dividend policies implied by degrees of underinvestment (passing up some positive net-present-value projects) can communicate private information to the market. Ambarish, John and Williams (1987) argue that the firm may not use dividends exclusively to signal its future prospects, but a (least-cost) efficient mix of signals from a larger menu of potential signals. Their efficient signaling equilibrium implies that mature firms will pursue larger payout policies compared to growth firms and that the announcement effect of dividends will be a function of the firm's investment opportunities.

In John and Nachman (1986), the optimality of intertemporal smoothing of dividends is established in a multiperiod model of financing under asymmetric information.

John and Lang (1988) present evidence that the announcement effect of dividend initiations (defined as first-time cash dividend payouts or dividend payouts after a hiatus of five or more years) is significantly affected by the level and nature of insider trading immediately prior to the announcement. John and Mishra (1990) argue that insider trading subject to disclosure requirements may be an important potential signal, along with other corporate announcements. The model makes testable predictions about patterns of insider trading around corporate announcements.

In this chapter, we will explore some of the details of the above studies. We will begin with a brief look at some of the recent theoretical work in the area of financial signaling with dividends, investment and insider trading which will provide a framework for understanding the evidence contained in these studies as well as some of the other evidence which seems to be at odds with the M&M "dividend invariance" propositions.

SIGNALING WITH DIVIDENDS

As mentioned above, the stock price response which accompanies dividend change announcements has been an important challenge to the "dividend irrelevance" propositions, raising questions regarding the validity of the underlying assumptions. The two-day average abnormal return (over and above the required return of the security, which adjusts for market co-movements) is positive (0.9 percent) for dividend increases, positive (3.7 percent) for dividend initiations, and negative (−3.6 percent) for dividend decreases, all statistically significant.[6] It is clear that the dividend announcement conveys to the market some new information which the corporate insiders have that is relevant for the pricing of the firm's shares. Although the idea of dividends signaling information to the market was always present as a plausible heuristic idea, it is only recently that a rigorous logical structure has been provided by the dividend signaling models.[7]

Dividends as a Signal

In the following discussion, the intuition and the essential arguments behind three of the dividend signaling models will be given. The first model, John and Williams (1985) is an example of the basic underlying structure of the dividend signaling argument. In Ambarish, John and Williams (1987), we see that the nature of the investment opportunities of the firm will influence the market response to dividend announcements, e.g., the payout policy of a growth firm may be different from that of a mature firm and the announcement effects will reflect this. In John and Lang

(1988), the informational content of strategic insider trading around dividend announcements is studied.

The intuition underlying the John and Williams (1985) model is rather simple. The setting is one in which the corporate insiders know more than the investors about the future prospects of the firm—the quality of its investment opportunities and future cash flows. While some of the information can be conveyed to the market fairly easily through audited earnings reports and financial statements, other crucial information may be more difficult. Take, as an example, the level of confidence management has in the economic viability of a new high tech product, crucial components of which are still being developed by the R&D department. Here, it may be costly to communicate to investors the true degree of success of the R&D and therefore the level of confidence felt by management. If the management simply makes announcements that the product will be highly successful, there is a high risk of misrepresentation by firms whose R&D is not, in fact, going so well. On the other hand, if the management releases too much detail to back up their claims, it might detract from the competitive advantage that the firm enjoys.

The effect of this informational asymmetry may be crucial when the firm is put in a position to establish its true market value. This may happen when (1) the firm is selling stocks or other risky securities in the market to raise external funds, or (2) the current stockholders are selling existing shares to raise cash on personal account. (It may also happen when the firm is facing a takeover threat.) In either case, current shareholders suffer a reduction (referred to as "dilution") in their fractional ownership of the firm.

When the inside information about firm prospects is very favorable, it may not be adequately reflected in the price paid by the less-informed market. The stocks will then be underpriced relative to their true value and the dilution of the shareholders correspondingly severe. Therefore, reducing this dilution on either corporate or personal account is more valuable to shareholders of firms with more favorable inside information. Consequently, insiders, acting in the interests of their current shareholders, may distribute a cash dividend (even though it may be tax disadvantaged relative to capital gains) if outsiders can convince themselves that it would pay the better firms to distribute larger cash dividends. In this scenario, outsiders bid up the stock price of firms paying larger dividends and thereby reduce the dilution of its current shareholders to such a degree as to warrant the payment of taxable dividends.[8]

To complete the argument, we have to show that the market can convince itself that the firms with more favorable private information will choose to pay larger dividends, given the pricing behavior of the market. Such is the case because the marginal benefit to insiders of distributing dividends differs across firms. For firms with more favorable inside information, the premium paid in the market for stocks with marginally larger dividends, and the reduction in dilution for current shareholders, just compensates stockholders for the incremental personal taxes on dividends. By contrast, for firms with less favorable inside information, the tax costs of the same dividend exceed at the margin the gains from reducing dilution. Consequently, there exists a pricing function for stock which separates firms with more favorable inside information from those with less.

A simple numerical example may be useful to illustrate the underlying intuition. Consider the case of an industry (say, the cosmetic industry) where firm values are crucially dependent on the success of their R&D effort. For simplicity, assume that there are two firms which differ only in the level of success of their R&D effort, and that this information is known only by insiders. If the degree of success is high, the present value of future cash flows is $1,000 million dollars, and if low, it is only $900 million. Also assume for simplicity that the cash flows from current operations are $10 million for each firm and that each firm requires $30 million for optimal investment. The current liquidity needs of the current shareholders have been estimated to be $20 million, which will be satisfied either by cash dividends paid by the firm, or by current shareholders selling their stock on personal account. The incremental personal tax on cash dividends is 25 percent. Currently, each firm has 1 million shares outstanding.

Let us consider the case of the firm with the higher quality R&D (referred to as the "better firm") following a policy of no dividend payout. To invest optimally at $30 million, the better firm needs to raise $20 million from external sources. Since they receive no dividends, current shareholders will liquidate stock to raise $20 million on personal account. Together, $40 million worth of the firm is being sold in the market. The market, being unable to decipher the quality of the firms, assigns a value based on an average (expected value). Let the probability of having a high quality R&D, as assessed by the market, be 1/20. The average value will be 1/20 ($1000) + 19/30 (900) = 905. Now for equity funds of $40 million, the market will require 40/905 of the total outstanding shares of the firm. If they make this equity issue, the current shareholders of the high quality firm will have a total wealth of

$$20m + (1 - 40/905)1000m = 975.84m$$

Clearly, this is a losing proposition for them.

Now, assume that the insiders of the good firm decide to pay out an aggregate dividend of $16.04 million. For simplicity, assume that the shareholders will raise the additional $3.96 million on personal account to satisfy their liquidity demand of $20 million. But they incur an additional tax liability of $4.01 million (25 percent of each dollar of cash dividend received) which they will pay at the end of the year. Now, it is necessary for the firm to raise an additional amount ($20m + $16.04m) = $36.04m at firm level and $3.96m at investor level, i.e., a total of $40m again. If the above dividend policy cannot profitably be mimicked by a poor firm, then the market can assign a value (to that signal) of a high quality firm, i.e., $1,000m. In other words, if the market imputes a value of $1,000m to any firm paying $16.04m of dividends and $900m to any firm paying less, would it in fact be justified by the optimal behavior of firms?

The wealth of shareholders of high quality firms paying dividends of $16.04m is

$$20m - 4.01m + (1 - 40/1000)\ 1000m = 975.99m$$

They are better off than they were before. It pays for them to signal.

Now does it also pay a poor firm to signal? All we need to do is to compare the wealth effects of dividend policies of $D = \$0m$ and $D = \$16.04m$ for the poor firm. Note, given that the market will price all firms paying dividends less than $16.04 million equally (as worth $900m), it does not pay to use an intermediate dividend policy. For $D = \$0m$, the wealth of the current shareholders of the poor firm will be

$$20m = (1 - 4/900)\ 900 = 880m$$

For $D = 16.04m$

$$20m - 4.01 + (1 - 40/1000)\ 900 = 879.99m$$

The poor firm is better off not mimicking the dividend policy of the better firm.

We have just shown the following: if the market prices firms based on their dividend payouts (i.e., $1000 million for firms paying no less than $16.04 million in dividends and $900 million for others), the optimal dividend policy chosen by the high quality firm will be to pay out $16.04 million while the low quality firm will choose zero payout. Thus, a signaling equilibrium with taxable dividends exists.

The simplifying assumptions made above for expositional ease are relaxed in the general model of John and Williams (1985). Some of the noteworthy results are: (1) In the signaling equilibrium, firms expecting higher future cash flows optimally pay larger dividends. (2) The optimal dividend function derived involves smoothing with respect to future cash flows such that the dividend variability is lower than that of earnings variability. The optimal dividend is decreasing in the tax disadvantage of dividends relative to capital gains. (3) The firm may find it optimal to pay cash dividends and raise new equity financing or repurchase stock in the same planning horizon. The intuition for the simultaneity of dividend payouts and new financing is that dividends are paid to reduce the underpricing of the securities issued to raise new outside financing. When the cash from operations is sufficient to meet the investment needs of the firm and partially satisfy the liquidity needs faced by current shareholders, the firm may repurchase shares and pay cash dividends in the same planning period.

Dividends and Investment

The John and Williams (1985) model predicts an increase in stock prices for announcements of increases in dividends and a stock price decrease for dividend cuts.[9] This is largely consistent with the documented evidence on the announcement effect of dividends. However, by specifying the optimal investment policy as exogenously given, this model does not consider many interesting aspects of possible interaction of dividend policy and investment policy. It also does not explain the differential dividend policies pursued by growth firms and mature firms.[10]

Recent studies, such as Ambarish, John and Williams (1987), do not designate dividends to be the only mechanism for conveying private information to the market. Dividends are only one of the multiple signals allowed and firms optimally choose an optimal mix of signals to convey their private information in a least-cost manner. Dividends, investments, stock repurchases or new issues of equity are in the menu of signals allowed in Ambarish, John and Williams (1987). The nature of the firm's investment opportunities determines the optimal blend of signals used in equilibrium. Mature firms use large payouts as their primary signal, whereas growth firms de-emphasize dividends and use investments as their main signal. The announcement effects of dividend changes and new issues of equity also reflect this dichotomy. The model predicts for announcement of dividend increases larger price increases for the stock of mature firms than for that of growth firms. Similarly, for seasoned issues of equity, the model predicts larger decreases in stock prices for mature firms than for growth firms. The following section contains some evidence from Lang and Litzenberger (1989) which seems to be largely consistent with these predictions for dividend changes.

Insider Trading as a Signal

There is gathering evidence of insider trading around corporate announcements of dividends, capital expenditures, equity issues and repurchases and other capital structure changes. Although signaling models have been used to explain the price reaction of these announcements, a usual assumption made in these models is that insiders cannot trade to gain from such announcements.[11] An innovative feature of the John and Mishra (1990) paper is to model trading by corporate insiders (subject to disclosure regulation) as one of the signals. Detailed, testable predictions are described for the interaction of corporate announcements and concurrent insider trading. In particular, such interaction is shown to depend crucially on whether the firm is a growth firm, a mature firm, or a declining firm. Empirical proxies for firm technology are developed based on measures of growth and Tobin's Q ratio. In the underlying "efficient" signaling equilibrium, investment announcements and net insider trading convey private information of insiders to the market at least cost. The paper also addresses issues of deriving intertemporal announcement effects from the equilibrium (cross-sectional) pricing function. Other announcement effects relate the intensity of the market response to insider trading, variance of firm cash flows, risk aversion of the insiders, and characteristics of firm technology (growth, mature or declining).

Dividends and Free Cash Flow

Another recent concept which relates dividend payouts to the investment opportunities of the firm is the agency costs of free cash flow. This was formulated in Jensen (1986), extending the work of Berle and Means (1932) on the separation of ownership and control. Jensen (1986) argues that many firms generate cash flows in excess of what is required to fund all projects with nonnegative net present values. He calls this excess cash "free cash flow." These firms have assets in place generating substantial rents or quasi-rents, but have very limited amounts of positive NPV projects to fund. Jensen gives as examples oil companies in the 1970s, tobacco, cable system, broadcasting and food processing companies.

Paying out free cash flow reduces the size of the firm and can reduce the manager's power and market value. Consequently, Jensen argues, managers have an incentive not to pay out free cash flow to shareholders even though a payout increases shareholder wealth (by avoiding investment in negative net present value projects). This potential agency problem and the resulting costs of overinvestment have been called the agency costs of free cash flow. If managers are overinvesting, an increase in the dividend will, ceteris paribus, reduce the extent of overinvestment and increase the market value of the firm, and a decrease in the dividend will have the opposite effect. Jensen (1986) views the empirical evidence of a positive association between announcements of dividend changes and stock price response as supporting the free cash flow hypothesis. But it will be argued that an important modification in the free cash flow hypothesis is required before it can yield predictions of announcement effects. However, Lang and Litzenberger (1989) agree with Jensen (1986) and formulate an "overinvestment hypothesis" arguing that dividend increases would elicit a larger response from overinvesting firms than from others. The same criticism will be applicable to the Lang and Litzenberger (1989) hypothesis and their interpretation of empirical evidence. Details of this are given below.

DIVIDENDS AND INVESTMENT OPPORTUNITIES

In this section some interesting new evidence which examines the fine structure of the dividend announcement effect is examined. The punchline of this evidence, presented in Lang and Litzenberger (1989), is that the announcement effect of large dividend changes (increases as well as decreases) is significantly affected by the investment opportunity set of the firm. More specifically, the announcement effect is significantly larger for overinvesting firms than for other firms. The evidence is argued to be consistent with the predictions of an "overinvestment hypothesis" implied by the free cash flow hypothesis discussed in "Insider Trading as a Signal" (above, page 54).

Tobin's Q and Overinvesting Firms

Tobin's Q is a measure of the marginal efficiency of capital, computed for any asset or investment project as the ratio of the market value of the asset to its replacement cost. Value maximizing firms which invest optimally will choose all projects with Q ratios of at least 1. Firms which choose projects with Q ratios less than 1 are overinvesting (i.e., they are investing in projects with a negative net present value) to the detriment of the wealth of the shareholders.

Data on the Q ratios of individual assets of a firm is not readily available. Lang and Litzenberger (1989) use empirical estimates of the average Q ratio of firms to determine a group of overinvestment firms. If it is assumed that a firm's investments exhibit decreasing marginal productivity of capital, an average Q less than unity implies overinvestment with a high likelihood. If a firm is undertaking the value-maximizing level of investment, and has always done so in the past, its average Q will exceed unity. Lang and Litzenberger (1989) argue that the announcement effect of sizeable dividend changes will be larger for overinvesting firms than for value maximizers.

The signaling equilibrium in Ambarish, John and Williams (1987) also makes differential predictions for announcement effects of dividend changes for different classes of investment opportunities. For mature firms (with firm average Q ratio less than unity), the predicted announcement effect is larger than that for growth firms (with average Q ratio exceeding unity).

Empirical Tests

Tobin's Q for the firm is computed as the ratio of the market value of the firm's equity and debt to the replacement cost of its assets.[12] Common stock prices are taken from the Center for Research in Security Prices (CRSP) return file. Daily risk adjusted returns are measured as unadjusted returns minus (beta) × (market return). The market index used is the equally weighted CRSP index returns.

Before examining the systematic evidence presented in Table 3–2, it may be useful to examine the stock price behavior of a few firms (some with very high Q ratios and others, very low Q ratios) in response to a sizeable dividend change announcement.

Table 3–1 contains data on dividend change, price change, Q ratio, and the market adjusted return on the day of announcement of the divi-

TABLE 3–1
Market Adjusted Returns Associated with Announcements of Sizeable Dividend Changes for High-Q and Low-Q Firms

Company/ Date	Prior Dividend	Dividend Change	Q Ratio	Price on Day before Announce- ment	New Price	Market Adjusted Return on Announce- ment Day
Amax, Inc. 4/1/82	0.60	−75%	2.39	25 ¼	26 ⅛	+1.56%
Dun & Bradstreet Corp. 4/21/82	0.50	+17%	3.87	65 ¾	65 ⅝	−0.31%
Brystol Myers Co. 1/17/83	0.45	+16.7%	2.57	65 ½	65 ½	−0.17%
Chesebrough Ponds, Inc. 1/18/84	0.375	+13%	2.30	38 ¾	38 ¾	−0.18%
Weis Market, Inc. 7/6/82	0.25	+16%	3.46	37 ½	37 ½	+0.21%
Bethlehem Steel Corp. 1/26/83	0.25	−40%	0.28	20 ¾	19 ⅝	−5.41%
Ford Motor Co. 4/12/84	0.30	+33%	0.29	34	35 ¾	+3.05%
Fruehauf Corp. 8/19/82	0.35	−71%	0.50	17 ⅛	15 ¼	−11.12%
Exxon Corp. 7/27/83	0.75	+6.6%	0.33	35 ⅝	36	+2.16%
Moore, McCormack Res. 4/28/82	0.25	+8.0%	0.54	20 ½	22	+7.90%
PPG Industries, Inc. 7/21/83	0.60	+8.0%	0.68	62	64 ½	+4.03%

dend change for an arbitrary set of firms with either very high Q ratios (at least 2.3) or low Q ratios (0.7 or below). For the high Q firms (in the top half of the table), the market adjusted return is typically small and often opposite in direction to that of the dividend change. For low Q firms (in the lower half of the table) the stock price response is significant and in the same direction as that of the dividend change.

Displaying only a few of the firms with extreme Q ratio values, Table 3–1 is only meant to be suggestive. The evidence presented in the Lang and Litzenberger (1989) study is based on a final sample of 429 dividend change announcements from 1979 to 1984, which meet two criteria: (a) the dividend change is at least 10 percent, (b) the average Q for the firms could be computed. The total sample was divided into 2 groups using a cut-off point of Tobin's Q = 1. Returns for dividend increases are averaged with the negative of returns of firms for dividend decreases. The average daily returns on dividend announcement days for firms with average Q's less than unity and for firms with average Q's greater than unity are reported below.

The average abnormal returns for firms with average Q's less than unity is more than three times as large as that for firms with average Q's greater than unity. The difference is significant at the 1 percent level. Lang and Litzenberger also present evidence to show that the differential announcement effect between Q > 1 firms exists in a similar fashion for dividend decreases and dividend increases, when examined separately.

Interpretation of Evidence

Lang and Litzenberger (1989) extend the free cash flow hypothesis (see "Dividends and Free Cash Flow," page 54) to formulate the following

TABLE 3–2
Market Adjusted Returns Associated with Announcement of Sizeable Dividend Changes for Firms with Q > 1 and Firms with Q < 1

	Q > 1	Q < 1	Difference (Q < 1) - (Q > 1)
Average Return	0.003	0.011	0.008
p-value	(0.021)	(0.000)	(0.000)

Source: Lang and Litzenberger (1989)

"overinvestment hypothesis." An increase in dividend by overinvesting firms (here, those with Q < 1) will decrease the size of the firm's future investment in negative net present value projects. Consequently, an increase in dividend will, all else equal, lessen the overinvestment and increase the market value of the stock. For value maximizing firms (say, Q = 1) the above effect will not be important. From this, Lang and Litzenberger argue the differential effect on stock prices on announcement of dividend changes for firms with Q < 1 versus firms with Q > 1, which is supported by the evidence they present.

The free cash flow hypothesis, as it stands, assumes symmetric information between managers and the market. To obtain announcement day effects of the type documented in the evidence, the free cash flow hypothesis will need to be modified to incorporate some private information possessed by managers which is revealed through the announcement of the dividend change. If the managers and the market have the same information, the extent of the current suboptimal level of free cash flow, the optimal level of free cash flow and the increase in value which would result from implementing the dividend change necessary to switch to the optimal level are all common knowledge prior to the actual announcement of the dividend change. Since the market is privy to all relevant resolutions of uncertainty as they occur (given symmetric information), at the point of managerial announcement of dividend change there should be no price effect. Therefore, unless you have irrational investors who wait to act until they receive the same information from managerial announcements at quarterly intervals, it is hard to obtain announcement effects from these hypotheses. Of course, the overinvestment hypothesis may be adapted by incorporating private information on the part of the managers (e.g., their own taste for free cash flows). But then the issues of asymmetric information and signaling come into play. In fact, Ambarish, John and Williams (1987) present a signaling model where the nature of the investment opportunity set affects the dividend and investment strategies of firms when corporate insiders have information that the market does not have. The announcement of dividend change is differentially interpreted by the market based on what it knows about firm technology. The detailed announcement effects derived predict larger stock price response for low-Q firms than for high-Q firms. The evidence is consistent with these predictions.[13]

In summary, the evidence presented by Lang and Litzenberger (1989) shows an inverse relationship between the Q-ratio and the dividend change announcement effect. The evidence is consistent with the predictions of the Ambarish, John and Williams (1987) signaling model.

SIGNALING WITH INSIDER TRADING

This section will examine in some detail aspects of insider trading around corporate announcements. John and Mishra (1990) contains a theoretical model of strategic insider trading around capital expenditure (investment) announcements. John and Lang (1988) study insider trading around dividend announcements and provide empirical evidence in support of their predictions using data on insider trading around announcements of dividend initiations.

In the John and Mishra (1990) model, the firms' insiders can signal simultaneously with investment announcements and levels of insider holdings. The nature of the mix of signals efficiently chosen can depend on the class of firms signaling. In particular, how the private information attribute influences the productivity of new investment determines whether firms will choose to underinvest (compared to full-information levels) or overinvest in the efficient signaling equilibrium. For ease of reference, we will categorize firms into three suggestive classes based on the relationship of the marginal productivity of new investments and the private information attribute: for growth firms this relationship is increasing; for declining firms, it is decreasing; for mature firms, no relationship exists. In the efficient signaling equilibrium, in all three classes of firms, insiders hold underdiversified positions in their own holdings in the firm. However, only growth firms and declining firms deviate from their full-information optimal levels of investment; mature firms invest at full-information optimal levels, growth firms overinvest, and declining firms underinvest. More interestingly, the announcement effect of investment increases is shown to be positive for the stocks and bonds of growth firms, whereas it is negative for the securities of declining firms, and neutral for mature firms.

The model yields detailed empirical implications for the announcement effect of changes in investment and changes in insider holdings for prices of stocks and bonds. The derived announcement effects relate the intensity of the price response to measures of insider trading, variance of earnings, and the characteristics of the technology of the firm (growing, mature or declining). Empirical proxies for firm technology can be constructed from measures of growth and Tobin's Q ratios. Currently available data on capital expenditure announcements, insider holdings and insider trading can be used to test these predictions.

Empirical Implication

Dividend initiations are commonly held to be unambiguous signals of good news. Contrary to this, the John and Lang (1988) model predicts that the initiation announcement will elicit a positive stock price response only when there has not been any intense insider selling prior to this announcement. The model predicts a significant difference in the stock price response to dividend initiation between firms with prior insider selling and others. Using data on dividend initiations and concurrent insider trading, John and Lang (1988) test the above prediction of their model. By categorizing firms based on insider trading activity immediately prior to the dividend initiation announcement, differential predictions are developed for the stock price response.

Empirical Evidence

The dividend initiation data came from the 1988 Compustat data base. The procedure for selecting the sample is to search for firms paying a cash dividend following at least 5 years of no cash dividend payments. The dividend initiation announcement dates are taken from the 1987 Daily Master Tape and the *Wall Street Journal Index*. Officers, directors and principal stockholders who hold more than 10 percent of total common stocks outstanding are defined as insiders. The data on their trading records for this study come from the Securities and Exchange Commission (SEC) insider trading tape. The tape contains all transactions by insiders from January 1975 to October 1985.

It may be instructive to examine the stock price behavior of a few firms with intense insider trading in the quarter prior to announcement of initiation. In Table 3–3, the first five firms had intense insider buying and the remaining seven firms had intense insider selling.

The upper half of the table (5 firms) had intense insider buying in the quarter prior to the initiation of cash dividends. The average abnormal return over two days (announcement day and the next) is positive in all cases except for Mattel, Inc. The second half of the table (7 firms) had intense insider selling in the previous quarter. The two-day average ab-

TABLE 3–3
Market Adjusted Returns Associated with Announcements of Initiation of Dividends for Firms with Intense Insider Trading in the Previous Quarter

Company/ Date	Initial Quarterly Dividends	Abnormal Return Day 0	Abnormal Return Day +1	Average Abnormal Return over Days 0, +1	Stock Price on Day −1	Stock Price on Day 0	Stock Price on Day +1
Brown Co. 1/28/76	7 ½ ¢/share 25% stock divd.	7.24%	1.31%	4.28%	12 ⅜	13 ¼	13 ½
Mattel, Inc. 6/8/78	7 ½ ¢/share	−5.16%	3.06%	−1.05%	11 ½	11	11 ¼
Seabord World Airlines, Inc. 1/4/78	7 ½ ¢/share	−1.92%	8.80%	3.44%	5	4 ⅞	5 ¼
United Nuclear Corp. 3/10/78	20 ¢/share 50% stock divd.	2.83%	3.14%	2.99%	36 ⅛	37 ¾	39
Varo, Inc. 12/8/76	10 ¢/share	3.99%	3.81%	3.90%	7 ¼	7 ⅝	8
Hazeltine Corp. 1/19/77	5 ¢/share	−3.02%	−2.06%	−2.54%	11 ⅝	11 ⅜	11
Levitz Furniture Corp. 5/26/77	20 ¢/share	−5.74%	−4.49%	−5.12%	4 ⅝	4 ⅜	4 ⅛
Pickwick International, Inc. 7/24/75	8 ¢/share	−5.63%	4.67%	−0.48%	14 ½	13 ⅝	14 ⅛
Savin Business Machines, Inc. 9/15/76	5 ¢/share	1.50%	1.74%	1.62%	14 ¾	15	15 ⅜
Tosco Corp. 7/1/82	$1 /share Special Divd.	−0.35%	5.35%	2.50%	13 ⅛	12 ⅞	13 ⅜
Winnebago Industries, Inc. 1/22/82	10 ¢/share	1.46%	−2.93%	−0.74%	11	11 ⅛	11 ¾
Xtra, Inc. 12/16/76	8 ¢/share	7.78%	−0.98%	3.40	13 ¾	14 ¾	14 ½

normal return is negative for four firms and positive for the remaining three. Averaging across firms, the announcement day abnormal return is 1.4 percent for the first group of firms (with insider buying) and –0.6 percent for the second group (with insider selling). The average two-day abnormal return is 2.71 percent for the buying firms and –0.192 percent for the selling firms. The difference between the two groups, in both cases, is statistically significant.

Displaying only 12 of the firms with extreme insider buying or selling, Table 3–3 is only meant to be suggestive. The reader is referred to the John and Lang (1988) study for more systematic evidence based on 265 firms. The abnormal returns of the group of firms with net selling by insiders are compared with the abnormal returns of all others. The average announcement day excess return for the selling group is significantly lower than that for the other group (by about 2.5 percent).[14]

Dividend initiations are a particular example of dividend increases where the change in dividends is mostly unexpected. Therefore, the above evidence can be interpreted in the context of the John and Lang theoretical model and its predictions for dividend increases. The evidence presented indicates that the announcement effect of dividend initiations is significantly affected by the extent and direction of insider trading activity during the quarter prior to the announcement. Contrary to the existing notion from earlier studies, all dividend initiations do not convey "good news." The evidence is consistent with the main predictions of the John and Lang model: (1) the informational content of dividend increases has to be read in conjunction with the second signal, i.e., insider trading; and (2) the announcement effect of dividend increases for firms with net insider buying should be significantly different from that for those with net insider selling.

CONCLUSION

The dividend policy of a firm can be entirely independent of its investment policy in the idealized setting of perfect markets. However, if corporate insiders or managers have information about the firm's prospects and its investment opportunities that is superior to that of the investors, then independence may not hold.[15] Dividend policies of firms and the behavior of stock prices around announcements of dividend changes may be affected in important ways by the investment policies and investment opportunities of firms. This chapter contains a survey of some recent theoretical work and empirical evidence on the relationship between dividends and investments.

In the first part of the chapter some of the relevant models of signaling with dividends were examined. The least-cost blend of signals chosen by a firm, and the dividend component in it, can be shown to be determined by the investment opportunity set of the firm. Ambarish, John and Williams (1987) characterize the differential dividend policy implemented by growth firms and mature firms. They generate the prediction that announcement effects of dividends for low-Q firms will be larger than those for high-Q firms. John and Mishra (1990) also predict differential announcement effects based on the investment technology. The John and Lang (1988) model yields testable implications relating the announcement effects for dividend changes to the extent and direction of insider trading immediately prior to the announcement.

Interesting evidence presented in Lang and Litzenberger (1989) shows that the announcement effect of dividend changes is significantly larger for Q < 1 firms than Q > 1 firms.

John and Lang (1988) present evidence of differential announcement effects of dividend initiations as a function of insider trading in the previous quarter. The evidence seems to suggest that the market is using its information about the direction and extent of insider trading in interpreting whether or not a dividend initiation is "good news" or "bad news." Treating the concurrent insider trading as an additional signal seems to provide a useful perspective for understanding the informational content of corporate announcements and concurrent insider trading.

NOTES

1. "Dividend Policy, Growth, and the Valuation of Shares," *Journal of Business*, October, 1961, pp. 411–33.
2. See Miller (1987).
3. For an early discussion of the dividend puzzle, see Black (1976). For a recent detailed discussion of the dividend puzzle, see Miller (1986).
4. For example, see Asquith and Mullins (1983), Aharony and Swary (1980), Woolridge (1983), Pettit (1972), Lang and Litzenberger (1989) and John and Lang (1988), to cite a few.
5. See Bhattacharya (1979), John and Williams (1985), Miller and Rock (1985), Ambarish, John and Williams (1987), John and Nachman (1986), John and Lang (1988), to mention a few.

6. See, for example, Copeland Weston (1988) *Financial Theory and Corporate Policy* (Third Edition), Addison-Wesley, New York, pp. 521–23.
7. See Miller (1987) for an excellent discussion of some of these issues.
8. Different signaling models have focused on differential potential costs of paying cash dividends. John and Williams (1985) and Ambarish, John and Williams (1987) focus on the personal tax disadvantage of cash dividends. Miller and Rock (1985), Woolridge and Ghosh (1985) and John and Lang (1988) study models where dividend payouts are tied to suboptimal investments by the firm. In John and Mishra (1990), unsystematic risk of insider holdings and suboptimal investment drive the signaling costs.
9. Also see other dividend signaling models, e.g., Bhattacharya (1979), Miller and Rock (1985).
10. See, for example, Rozeff (1982) who documents that dividend payouts of firms are decreasing in measures of growth.
11. Under SEC Rule 144(e)-1, "insiders" are prohibited from liquidating more than the minimum of (i) 1 percent of the outstanding shares of the class of securities, or (ii) the average weekly trading volume in the class of securities, within any three month period, unless a (secondary distribution) registration of the offering is filed with the SEC. In addition, Sections 16(a) and 16(b) of the Exchange Act require that changes in "insider" ownership positions be reported to the SEC within ten business days of the close of the month in which the change takes place. These rules make it illegal for "insiders" to secretly change their holdings in the firm.
12. Details are omitted. See Lang and Litzenberger (1989) for a summary of the individual calculations and data sources.
13. Lang and Litzenberger (1989) argue that the signaling models imply a larger announcement effect for dividend decreases than for dividend increases. This is certainly not the case for the recent signaling models, e.g., John and Mishra (1990) and John and Lang (1988).
14. For details, see the John and Lang (1988) paper.
15. Such dependence could also result from high costs of accessing capital markets or issuing securities or other market imperfections.

REFERENCES

Aharony, J., and I. Swary. "Quarterly Dividend and Earnings Announcement and Stockholders' Returns: An Empirical Analysis." *Journal of Finance,* 35 (March 1980), 1–12.

Ambarish, R.; K. John; and J. Williams. "Efficient Signaling with Dividends and Investments." *Journal of Finance,* 42 (June 1987), 321–44.

Asquith, P., and D. Mullins. "The Impact of Initiating Dividend Payments on Shareholder's Wealth." *Journal of Finance,* 56 (January 1983), 77–96.

Bhattacharya, S. "Imperfect Information, Dividend Policy, and 'The Bird in the Hand Fallacy.'" *Bell Journal of Economics,* 10 (Spring 1979), 257–70.

Black, F. "The Dividend Puzzle." *Journal of Portfolio Management,* 2 (Winter 1976), 5–8.

Brickley, J. A.; J. L. Coles; and M. S. Nam. "Investment Opportunities, the Reluctance to Cut Dividends and Corporate Payout Policy: The Case of Annual Extra Dividends," University of Rochester Working Paper, MERC 87-01, (January 1987).

Finnerty, J. E. "Insiders and Market Efficiency." *Journal of Finance,* 31 (September 1976), 1141–48.

Finnerty, J. E. "Insider's Activity and Inside Information: A Multivariate Analysis." *Journal of Financial and Quantitative Analysis,* 11, pp. 205–16.

Givoly, D., and D. Palmon. "Insider Trading and the Exploitation of Insider Information: Some Empirical Evidence." *Journal of Business,* 58 (1985), 69–87.

Jaffe, J. F. "Special Information and Insider Trading." *Journal of Business,* 47 (1974), 410–28.

Jensen, M. C. "Agency Costs of Free Cash Flow, Corporate Finance and Takeovers." *American Economic Review: Papers and Proceedings* (May 1986), 323–29.

Jensen, M. C., and W. Meckling. "Theory of the Firm: Managerial Behavior, Agency Costs, and Capital Structure." *Journal of Financial Economics,* 3 (1976), 305–60.

Jensen, M. C., and C. W. Smith, Jr. "Stockholder, Manager and Credit Interests: Application of Agency Theory." In E. Altman, and M. Subrahmanyam (eds.), *Recent Advances in Corporate Finance*, Homewood, IL: Irwin, (1985), pp. 93–131.

John, K., and L. Lang. "Strategic Insider Trading around Dividend Announcements: Theory and Evidence." New York University Working Paper (1988).

John, K., and B. Mishra. "Investment Announcements, Insider Trading and Market Response: Theory." *Journal of Finance,* 45 (July 1990), 835–55.

John, K., and D. C. Nachman. "On the Optimality of Intertemporal Smoothing of Dividends." New York University Working Paper (1986).

John, K., and J. Williams. "Dividends, Dilution, and Taxes: A Signaling Equilibrium." *Journal of Finance,* 40 (September 1985), 1053–70.

Lang, L., and R. Litzenberger. "Dividend Announcements: Cash Flow Signaling vs. Free Cash Flow Hypothesis." *Journal of Financial Economics,* 24 (December 1989), 137–54.

Miller, M. H., and F. Modigliani. "Dividend Policy, Growth and the Valuation of Shares." *Journal of Business,* 34 (October 1961), 411–32.

Miller, M. H. "The Information Content of Dividends." In R. Dornbusch, S. Fischer, and J. Bossons (eds.), *Macroeconomics: Essays in Honor of Franco Modigliani.* Cambridge, MA: MIT Press (1987).

Miller, M. H. "Behavioral Rationality: The Case of Dividends." *Journal of Business,* 59 (1986) 8451–68.

Miller, M., and K. Rock. "Dividend Policy under Asymmetric Information." *Journal of Finance,* 40 (September 1985), 1031–51.

Myers, S., and Majluf. "Stock Issues and Investment Policy when Firms Have Information that Investors Do Not Have." *Journal of Financial Economics,* 13 (June 1984), 187–221.

Pettit, R. "Dividend Announcements, Security Performance, and Capital Market Efficiency." *Journal of Finance,* 27 (December 1972), 993–1008.

Rozeff, M. S. "Growth, Beta and Agency Costs as Determinants of Dividend Rates." *Journal of Financial Research,* 5 (1982), 249–59.

Rozeff, M. S., and M. A. Zaman. "Market Efficiency and Insider Trading: New Evidence." *Journal of Business,* 61 (January 1988), 25–35.

Securities and Exchange Commission. *Official Summary of Security Transactions and Holdings.* (1975–81), Washington, DC: U.S. Government Printing Office.

Seyhun, H. N. "The January Effect and Aggregate Insider Trading." *Journal of Finance,* 43 (March 1988), 129–42

Seyhun, H. N. "The Information Content of Aggregate Insider Trading." *Journal of Business,* 61 (January 1988), 1–24.

Woolridge, J. R. "Dividend Changes and Security Prices." *Journal of Finance* (1983).

Woolridge, J. R., and C. Ghosh. "Dividend Cuts: Do they Always Signal Bad News?" *Midland Corporate Finance Journal,* 3 (Summer 1985), 20–32.

PART TWO

INTERNATIONAL FINANCE
IN THE 1990s

CHAPTER 4

THE ROLE OF STRATEGIES AND CULTURAL FACTORS IN INTERNATIONAL TRADE: EXPERIENCE OF JAPAN

Ryuzo Sato
Rama Ramachandran
Shunichi Tsutsui

INTRODUCTION

One of the proudest achievements of classical and neoclassical economics is the derivation of the superiority of free trade. While the models of international trade differ in specifics, this result is common to all of them and is obtained by assuming constant returns to scale, perfect competition and absence of externalities. The empirical validity of these assumptions has been questioned for some time, but the construction of theoretical models incorporating alternate assumptions began only within the last decade and a half.

Ryuzo Sato is the C.V. Starr Professor of Economics and Director, Center for Japan-U.S. Business and Economic Studies at Stern School of Business, New York University.

Rama Ramachandran is a clinical professor of economics and Associate Director at the Center for Japan-U.S. Business and Economics Studies, New York University.

Shunichi Tsutsui is a research associate at the Center for Japan-U.S. Business and Economics Studies, New York University.

In the earlier models, there are no ambiguities in the benefits of trade as determined by exogenous differences in endowments or technology while, in the new models, they are open to strategic manipulations. This realization leads to a new line of research on the welfare implications of possible national policies. Even neoclassical models accept that the existence of externalities will make it desirable to impose tariffs or subsidies but, in their discussion, the extent of the problem is exogenously determined. Recent theories identify at least one source of externalities: the incomplete appropriability of the results of R&D.[1]

The challenge to the neoclassical tradition has moved to a deeper level. The new models are able to endogenize technology only by simultaneously abandoning all three assumptions on which traditional trade theory is anchored. Derivations of welfare results are complicated by a host of factors that must be taken into consideration. Further, the separation between "economic" and "non-economic" factors in the neoclassical economic theory, based as it is on the methodological position that consumers and production units can be treated as black boxes, requires reexamination.

Technology is the core of the production process and the mastery it provides of material surroundings determines most aspects of the economic and some aspects of the non-economic structure of a society. While all this was evident from the time of the industrial revolution, the study of the dynamics of technology evolved slowly along three separate lines. The chronicling of the transformation of society by economic historians is supplemented and supported by studies in the history of technology. Industrial organization studies of technological change can be traced back to the seminal works of Hicks (1932), Schumpeter (1942) and Arrow (1962). The first examined the cost motives; the second, the influence of the market structure; and the last, the problem of appropriability. This last tradition arose in studies of international trade and development; it examines whether the historical factors that determine the directions of trade through comparative advantage can be modified by natural evolution of economies and through deliberate policies to promote economic development.

At any point of time, economies which are comparatively poorer are also exporters of raw materials and importers of finished goods.[2] Many of these economies strive to improve their economic condition by "industrialization". Their ability to achieve the same with or without assistance from other nations, the appropriate methodology for doing so, and its consequences are all hotly debated in economic and political literature.

Even confined to the technological aspects of industrialization, the Gerschenkron thesis[3] is that the greater the backlog of innovations that a country can take over from another, the larger the gap between economic potential and actualities of that economy and the greater the speed with which it can go through the development process. Of course, those nations whose technologies are being imitated do not view this process with equanimity. The Germans have criticized the English and were criticized in turn. The Western nations have, in the post-World War years, tried to circumscribe the ability of the Soviet Union and its allies to acquire Western technology. In this case, at least it was accepted that basic research in the Soviet Union was up to Western standards. When it comes to Japan, the criticism is that the country has utilized the results of basic research which are in the public domain to generate applied technology and out-compete the nations that funded the basic sciences. In the third section, we use recent strategic trade theory to model the effect of such externalities on the share of international markets.

Once the rate of generation of technology is recognized to have an effect on national welfare, the factors that determine it are subject to strategic manipulation. These factors frequently involve characteristics that are outside the purview of traditional economic analysis. In a recent survey,[4] the following are discussed: life expectancy, nutrition, willingness to bear risks, geographical environment, path dependency, labor cost, science and technology, religion, values, property rights, resistance to innovation, politics and the state, war, openness to new information, and demographic factors. A similar set of factors is considered to determine the ability of one nation to learn from the economic systems of others. The early European explorers beheld with awe the Eastern civilizations that they discovered. But as the industrial revolution progressed, the Atlantic economies began to overtake all others and soon European travelers seemed able to identify, in the visiting countries, the cultural, intellectual and physical deficiencies that explained their backwardness.[5] The growth of the Pacific basin reset the balance once more. As Japan joined the ranks of international economic powers, the criticisms that one European nation leveled against another that was catching up were collectively directed against the Eastern competitor.

The paradigm of modern economics subsumes under individual preferences much of the cultural and sociological factors that influence human behavior; by treating the preferences as given, any discussion of these influences can be avoided. However critical one may be of such an approach, it would be blind not to recognize the vitality of the neoclassical tradition; the insights obtained from it have a great degree of validity. The recent realization, however, that appropriability of R&D is the source of the externality in trade models necessitates a conscious examination of those influences that determine the generation and diffusion of technology. An analogy can be made with the revolution in value theory at the turn of the last century. The then prevalent labor theory assumed that prices were determined by costs, and costs by labor input. In rejecting the anchoring of prices on given costs, the marginalist tradition had to base their model on demand, specified by exogenous tastes, and on supply specified by known technology. Today, we realize that both technology and tastes are subject to strategic manipulations, and we are compelled to look for forces that determine the degree of their manipulability. The following section reviews some current discussions that are relevant to Japan.

JAPAN AND WESTERN TECHNOLOGY

The international diffusion of technology is the result of two reinforcing factors. The existence of differences provides an opportunity, as Gerschenkron pointed out, for nations that are lagging behind to accelerate their development. On the other hand, no nation has, all by itself, developed all the relevant technologies internally. If all the production sectors within a diversified economy are to remain efficient, then the economy has to import some of its technologies.

The diffusion, however, cannot be understood solely in terms of a technological gap. Even within a nation, the best technology frequently coexists with the less efficient ones. An industry, adjusting to the continuous evolution of techniques, should be best pictured as a moving spectrum; at any point it permits a variety of processes, but the least productive ones are abandoned and more advanced ones added as the focal point of the spectrum shifts over time.

What is true within an economy is even more so for diffusion across national boundaries. Hence it is not surprising that we notice that even England at the height of her industrial revolution failed to adopt the latest technology.[6] The interplay of the technologies of European nations is recorded and analyzed by historians of technology. Early Western travelers to non-European countries tended to speak eloquently about the splendor of some of the nations they visited or to deprecate the backwardness of others. In contrast, the earliest comments on Japan noted the willingness of its citizens to learn from foreigners. The Chinese influence on the cultural and political development of Japan is well known.

In an historical study, Sugimoto and Swain (1989) divides the successive waves of cultural influx into Japan before the Meiji restoration into Chinese Wave 1, semiseclusion, and Chinese Wave 2 (which overlaps with Western Waves 1 and 2). In Chinese Wave 1, direct contact with China was established though Kentoshi missions and followed by the institutes under the ritsuryo system. The earliest of the eighteen missions were of a diplomatic nature but soon it became a means for the absorption of the T'ang culture with the student priests as the main conduit. The four institutions that were set up under the ritsuryo system were the University, the Institute of Divination, the Institute of Medicine, and the provincial colleges.

The three hundred years of cultural absorption (600–894 A.D.), however, were followed by five centuries of semi-seclusion (894–1401 A.D.). The University ceased to be a means for appointment to the higher administrative posts and was not rebuilt after it was destroyed by fire. Alternative educational institutions that arose included the departments of the University which became private institutions and the hereditary professorships that became houses of learning. Under the new arrangements, learning became a formalistic preservation of the earlier knowledge derived from Chinese sources. In the latter part of this period, some contacts were permitted by the Kamakura regime and through pirate traders. The New Buddhism also encouraged medical studies along Chinese lines.

Chinese Cultural Wave II began when Japan signed the Tally Trade Agreement of 1401. The Ming Court in China at that time was not interested in expanding foreign contact, but only in limiting the wako trade. The Japanese merchants and Buddhist priests showed more initiative. Within the country, the rise in the power of the daimyo (local lords) and their decision to move samurais to the castle towns had a profound effect both on the towns and on the surrounding villages.

Merchants and craftsmen followed the militia to the towns, leaving the villagers to provide raw material and foodstuffs. Soon there arose a pragmatic culture in the towns that encouraged secularization and specialization. Each daimyo had an interest in the expansion of mining and crafts within his realm and this encouraged an expansion of commodity production and exchange. The social conditions were favorable to the use of innovative techniques, and the importation of books from China facilitated the acquisition of new skills.

The arrival of the Jesuits, with Portuguese backing, in 1543 opened the first contact with the West. The leaders of various military factions welcomed the foreigners as they saw the benefits of obtaining firearms. Japan used its skills in making sword steel to master the manufacture of Western arquebus (gun with a hook) and soon began to export it. The Japanese recognized the superiority of Western ship architecture and navigational methods and were quick to adopt them; by 1610 local ships were only marginally smaller than contemporary Western ships. Similarly, imported mercury was used to improve metallurgic refining.

The Jesuits introduced new educational institutions, but they did not have a lasting impression due to the ban on books in 1630 and the reintroduction of the isolation policy. While Japan was learning techniques at a practical level, its native educational institutions did not absorb the Western intellectual developments of the Renaissance era, and the reimposition of the isolation policy in the seventeenth century resulted in losing much of the gain from Western contacts.

The next period, 1639 to 1720 A.D., showed a flowering of Confucian scholarship and the rise of indigenous astronomy and mathematics. The Chinese influence was almost solely through the import of books, foreign travel being limited. The Confucian academies offered an attractive career for those without hereditary status, and the new learning spread more as a result of private initiatives than through official patronage as in the earlier Chinese wave. The Western influence disappeared altogether except in medicine, where it was kept up by the Dutch. Techniques, particularly in shipbuilding and mining, regressed.

The pedantic traditions of the official Confucianism soon lost their vitality and led to the reintroduction of Western learning in the last period, 1720 to 1854 A.D., before the opening up of Japan. The period began with the partial lifting of the ban on books by Shogun Yoshimune (1716–1745). Like many other leaders during times of cultural revolution, Yoshimune had an ambivalent attitude toward new science and culture. A Confucian consultant to the shogun, Arai Hakuseki, had interrogated the Jesuit priest, Giovanni Sidotti, who smuggled himself into Japan in 1708, and was impressed by his knowledge. In a memorandum circulated among high officials, Hakuseki recommended a general relaxation on the ban on Western books, but this was rejected by the shogun.

Meanwhile, Yoshimune considered it among his traditional responsibilities to reform the calendar, and it became clear to him that this could not be achieved without importing books on Western astronomy written in Chinese by Jesuits. Hence, he was convinced to permit importation of books not connected with Christianity. Ironically, the first partial calendar reform incorporating Western knowledge could not be achieved until 1798 and full reform not until 1842; this was due to the delay in learning Newtonian mechanics.

As in Europe at the end of Scholasticism, so in Japan in this period we see a multi-faceted response to the new cultural threat. Some scholars tried to incorporate the new studies into the Confucian tradition. Others, like the schools of National Learning, sought to develop an indigenous tradition marrying classic Japanese texts with Shinto religion and rejecting everything foreign. The clearest break with the past can be said to have come in the field of medicine. Two Edo doctors performed a dissection on a woman who was executed in 1771 and noticed the superiority of a Dutch anatomical atlas over the Confucian texts. Translations which they and their followers brought out led to an integrated western tradition in medicine, the *Rangaku* movement.

The pull and counterpull between the old and the new continued for some years. The ban on all but the official school of Confucianism in 1790 was soon followed by the establishment of the "Office for the Translation of Barbarian Texts" in 1811; the Office became the "Center for Western Learning" in 1863. The peasant revolts that became common at the end of the Tokugawa shoganate, the arrival of the British frigate in Nagasaki in 1808, and the British victory over the Chinese in the Opium War of 1840–42 paved the way for the Third Western wave with the arrival of Commander Perry.

The changes that took place after the Meiji Restoration and the reconstruction of the Japanese economy after the Second World War are well recorded and need not be repeated here. The point to note is that the response and methods for transmission of the culture and technology into Japan differed from time to time. Study in China was the most important means for assimilation during the First Chinese Wave, while imported books were the major channel in the Second Chinese Wave. Books were the main source of information on the developments in the West, though Jesuit missionaries and Dutch tradesmen played a catalytic role. All this was interspersed with periods of isolation which provide historical counterexamples to widely held beliefs on the nature of Japanese society. The Meiji Restoration increased both the channels and the inflow of foreign information.[7]

The multiplicity of channels and their varying importance have been noted for other countries also. Myllyntaus (1990) lists six factors and ranks their importance for six countries in the nineteenth century (see Table 4–1). Ichimura (1990) considers the recent experiences of three East Asian nations.

Sweeny (1987) stresses information flows in Japanese companies. 66.6 percent of small and medium enterprises (SME) and 75.4 percent of large firms (LF) use business and technical periodicals as a source of technology. Other significant sources (used by 20 percent or more of firms) of similar information for SMEs are parent companies, enterprises in the same business, and sample fairs. Parent companies and sample fairs are listed as important sources by LFs. Porter (1990) notes that Japanese companies have long invested heavily in attending foreign conferences, visiting friendly overseas companies, studying the literature, and licensing good technologies rather than attempting to duplicate them.

Dosai (1989, p. 1122) shows that both Japan and the United States spent about the same percentage of GNP on R&D, but the growth rate of R&D in Japan during the years 1969 to 1983 was well in excess of that of the United States. Another noticeable difference is in the percentage of business-financed and business-performed R&D. It may partly reflect the manner in which the two governments subsidize research; in Japan, tax subsidies play a greater role than direct subsidies.

Sato (1988) breaks up the R&D expenditure into basic, applied and development expenditures. He notes that the level of expenditure on basic research in Japan declined from 1973 to 1975, remained flat until 1979, and then grew at a fast rate to the 1973 level by 1981. Since the percentage of GDP spent is the same in both countries, the cumulative expenditure on basic research as a percentage of the GDP for the period 1973 to 1983 must be substantially less in Japan than in the

TABLE 4–1. Main Channels of Technology Transfer

	United States[a]	Russia[a]	Germany[a]	Japan[a]	Sweden[a]	Finland[a]	The Philippines[b]	Thailand[b]	Indonesia[b]
1. Importing foreign machinery and equipment	★	★	★	★	★	★	★	☆	
2. Receiving direct foreign investment	★	☆							
3. Acquiring foreign licenses	★		☆		★				
4. Recruiting abroad or permitting mass migration	☆			★	★	★			
5. Encouraging educational travel	★	★	★		★	☆	☆		★
6. Trade and scientific publications and analyzing foreign products	★	★		☆	☆	★	★	★	★
7. Trading companies							☆		

a For nineteenth century.
b Recent years.
★ Most important channels.
☆ Other important channels.

Source: Myllyntaus (1989), pp. 627 and 638; Ichimura (1990), p. 3

U.S. In this sense, Japan can be said to have benefited from the public goods nature of basic research in the U.S. Bernstein and Nadiri (1989) argue that the spillover effects reduce R&D investment by the receiving firms. On the other hand, Deolalikar and Evenson (1988) have estimated that Indian firms' elasticity of their R&D investment with respect to the flow of technology from U.S. firms is unity in light industries, greater than two in chemical industries and not significantly different from zero in engineering industries. It is therefore clear that quantitative studies do not give, at this stage, a conclusive answer on the nature of the spill-over effects.

STRATEGIC TRADE AND R&D: AN INTRODUCTORY ACCOUNT

This section is divided into two subsections. In the first subsection, we discuss the factors which are not consistent with traditional theories but play an important role in explaining two-way trade (the exchange of similar goods), which is a large and growing part of current trade among industrialized countries. In the second subsection, we discuss three strategic trade models developed by Spencer and Brander (1983), Beath et al. (1989), and Sato and Tsutsui (1987) in order to deepen our insight into the complex issues of technological innovation in trade. In the first model, we discuss the role of R&D subsidies, focusing on how R&D subsidies change the outcome of trade under duopolistic competition. In the second model, we investigate the incentive of R&D investment and the role of R&D policy when firms are engaged in a R&D race to be the first to introduce new technology. In the third model, we study the effect of diffusion of technology in the framework of a continuous time differential game, paying particular attention to the information structures.

Departure From Traditional Theories

It is not difficult to see that the non-interventionist stance of trade policy has its foundation on one of the important results in economic thought: perfect competition is efficient. In other words, a system of private markets, when each market is perfectly competitive, can achieve the most (Pareto) efficient allocation of resources.

There are a number of conditions which have to be met for a perfectly competitive market to prevail. They include access to relevant information and the absence of externalities and public goods. In addition, each firm is required to takes prices as exogenously given by the market, believing that it has no influence on market prices so that it can sell whatever amount it wants to. Furthermore, free entry and free exit are required so that no excess profits will be reaped by firms.

The assumption of perfect competition and its workable derivative that markets do not deviate very much from perfect competition have been the core assumptions used in most of traditional economic analysis. Of course, no one denies that such assumptions remain a good approximation for some markets and industries. However, as noted before, the recent pattern of international trade makes it increasingly difficult to accept them as appropriate working assumptions. A large and growing part of current trade, as evidenced by the extensive two-way trade among industrialized nations, seems to be generated by factors which are not quite consistent with the conditions of perfect competition. Among them are the advantages of large-scale production, the advantages of cumulative learning and experience, the temporary advantages created by technological innovation, and imperfect competition. These factors are important characteristics of many manufacturing industries and are easily found in the real world. It is instructive as well as informative to consider how the incorporation of these factors affects our understanding of trade.

First, we need to take into account a dynamic aspect of trade. The advantages of cumulative learning and experience, and the advantages generated by technological innovation not only describe how the cost structure of a firm changes over time, but also allow the possibility that the firm can actively influence its cost structure over time through some kinds of economic activities. We consider R&D one of the most important among those activities.

The incorporation of a dynamic dimension into trade makes a stark contrast with the traditional static view on this matter, and consequently, at least in the short run, there arises the possibility that firms earn excess profits above the normal return. But the presence of such excess profits need not be regarded as a manifestation of inefficient resource allocation since it can assume a new role of financing R&D to further cost reduction in the future—the view that was vigorously advanced by Schumpeter (1942).

Second, the consideration of imperfect competition opens up the possibility that firms can act *strategically*. Under imperfect competition, an individual firm faces a few identifiable rivals in the market or industry and no longer acts as a price taker because it knows what it does affects the market price and thus the behavior of rival firms in the same market. Thus a firm can act strategically in the sense that it takes into account how its behavior affects the behavior of its rivals and how the behavior of the rivals affects its behavior.

The incorporation of strategic interaction makes it necessary for us to adopt the game theory approach as in industrial organization in which oligopoly—an intermediate case between perfect competition and pure monopoly—plays an important role.

A game is classified in a number of ways, depending on what aspect of the game's structure one looks at. For example, static vs. sequential games; games with perfect information vs. games with imperfect or incomplete information; continuous time vs. discrete time games; deterministic vs. stochastic games. In a static game, every player (the term for a decision maker in game theory) moves simultaneously and only once, while in a sequential game, some or all players are allowed to move sequentially or more than once in the course of play. In a game with perfect information, every player can perfectly observe all of the past moves including chance moves, while in a game with imperfect or incomplete information, some or all players cannot. In a continuous time game, moves can be made continuously in time, while in a discrete time game, moves can only be made discretely in time. In a deterministic game, no random element is present in the relationship between moves and payoffs, while in a stochastic game, there are some elements which affect players' payoffs randomly. The choice of a particular type of game, of course, depends on what the researcher regards as the most important element in the strategic interaction in question.

Game theory has proved to be very powerful in the analysis of strategic interaction, being applied to many areas of economic study including industrial organization, macroeconomics and resource economics. However, it is worth noting that the game theory approach is not without problems. One problem is concerned with the limitations of game theory. As Binmore (1990) discusses, the standard assumptions used in game theory regarding common knowledge and rationality of players have difficulties in their relevance to reality, yet play a crucial role in solving games. Another problem is concerned with the modeling of strategic interaction. It matters greatly what elements one incorporates into the game. Adding new elements such as sequential moves and imperfect or incomplete information makes the game more realistic, but can give rise to significantly different results.[8] As a result, great care has to be taken in modeling strategic interactions and interpreting the results of the game.

Three Models

R&D Subsidies
We first discuss the model of Spencer and Brander (1983).[9] This model illustrates the important and interesting role of R&D subsidies in the setting of strategic international trade in the simplest possible framework.

Suppose that there are two firms, one domestic and one foreign, producing a homogeneous product and selling all of their output in a world market which is entirely contained in other countries. Note that with this assumption, we can equate the domestic firm's profits to the domestic country's welfare, and hence the objective of the domestic government is reduced simply to promoting the domestic firm's profits, assuming that the domestic government is concerned only with the national welfare.

With only two firms in the market, each firm acts strategically, recognizing that its profits depend significantly on what its rival does— the emergence of strategic interaction. To proceed with the analysis, more has to be specified. We first suppose that output is a firm's choice or strategic variable. In this case, the situation facing the firms is called a quantity-setting (Cournot) game. The consideration of output as a strategic variable, however, is not the only way to model the strategic situation. It may be appropriate if quantities are set by physical capacity constraints but inappropriate if firms can choose prices as their strategic variables. We also suppose that the firms set their output once and for all. This amounts to neglecting the possibility that the firm can change its output at a future time and thus any possibility that the firm can induce collusion with its rival by means of future retaliation. Finally, it is assumed that both firms make their output decisions simultaneously.

Under these assumptions, we consider our quantity-setting game. Each firm knows that it could earn greater profits if it could persuade or force its rival to cut back on output, since the output contraction of its rival firm raises the market price, and thus the firm's profits, even without any change in the firm's output. So the firm might try to induce the contraction of output or, for that matter, the exit of its rival from the market by threatening to produce a large output. However, it is difficult to see why one firm, intimidated by such a threat, should be forced to contract its output, since the other firm is well aware that by simply matching the increase, it can induce a price war—an outcome which is not in the best interest of the threatening firm. This argument shows that it is necessary in equilibrium that no aggressive threat by one firm should not be believed by the other. In the terminology of game theory, it implies that we need to consider a Nash equilibrium of the quantity-setting game. Formally, Nash equilibrium requires that at this equilibrium, a unilateral deviation of the firm does not strictly improve its profits.

Now we modify the quantity-setting game; we consider that both firms are engaged in R&D activities as an effort to improve their production efficiency. Suppose that only the domestic firm succeeds in such a way that the cost of producing an additional unit of output is now substantially reduced (i.e., lowered marginal cost). Suppose further that the foreign firm knows its rival's success. We are interested in how the Nash equilibrium will be affected by this. It is straightforward to see that it is in the best interest of the domestic firm to expand its output. In fact, given the output of the foreign firm, the marginal profit, the difference between the additional revenue from selling an additional unit of output (i.e., marginal revenue) and the marginal cost, is now positive for the domestic firm due to the lowered marginal cost. This gives the first firm an incentive to increase its output. The process of output expansion continues as long as marginal profit is positive.

The next question is how the foreign firm reacts to this output expansion. For this firm, the central issue is whether this output expansion constitutes an aggressive threat. However, knowing the success of the domestic firm and thus its underlying incentive, the output expansion by the domestic firm is no longer mistaken as an aggressive threat to the foreign firm. The domestic firm's success induces the foreign firm to contract its output. To see this, suppose on the contrary that the foreign firm does not respond to the output expansion. Since the output expansion reduces both firms' marginal revenue, the foreign firm's marginal profit becomes negative (note that the foreign firm's marginal cost remains the same as before). This gives the foreign firm an incentive to contract its output. Combined with these two effects, we can conclude that the domestic firm produces more and the foreign firm produces less in the new Nash equilibrium than in the original Nash equilibrium.

Suppose now that both firms are not engaged in R&D originally, but the domestic government could always entice the domestic firm to engage in R&D by providing R&D subsidies. Moreover, suppose that there is no uncertainty in the link between R&D subsidy and the outcome of R&D, so that the domestic government can make it possible to reduce the domestic firm's marginal costs through R&D subsidies. There are two effects of R&D subsidies. One effect is the trivial cost savings, which is essentially just a transfer from taxpayers to shareholders of the domestic firm. Thus, this has no impact on national welfare. But there is another effect to be taken into account. The R&D subsidies, in the eye of the foreign firm, have exactly the same effect as the marginal cost.[10] Hence, the expansion of output by the domestic firm is credible to the foreign firm.[11] As a result, the domestic firm earns more profit and the foreign firm earns less profit, the net effect of subsidizing subsidies—a phenomenon known as profit shifting.

R&D Competition and Uncertainty

We now consider the model of Beath et al. (1989). This model focuses on the nature of R&D investment and its relationship to the success of R&D. In essential ways, R&D investment is different from ordinary capital investment in that the success of R&D is not a deterministic function of R&D investment. Moreover, firms are frequently engaged in an R&D race to be the first to introduce some new technology or product. These factors significantly affect the incentive of individual firms to do R&D investment. The model examines the relation between R&D subsidies and the outcome of the R&D race when these factors are taken into account.

It is necessary to consider two forces that drive the firm's R&D investment. One is the profit incentive which arises from the firm's desire to increase profits through R&D investment. The important point is that this profit incentive remains even if there is no rival. The second force is the competitive threat which stems from the difference between the firm's profits if it innovates before its rival, and the profits it would make if its rival innovated first. The competitive threat motivates the firm to become the first to invent.

A main determinant of the relative magnitude of these forces is the ease of imitation. If imitation is impossible due to a highly effective patent, then the competitive threat dominates the profit incentive. On the contrary, if imitation is very easy, then the profit incentive outweighs the competitive threat.

Suppose that the competitive threats dominate the profit incentives for both firms due to the difficulty of imitation. Then both firms are trying to become the first to invent, resulting in too much R&D even in the absence of R&D subsidies. In this case, subsidizing the domestic firm is matched by the expansion of the foreign firm's R&D investment. Thus, R&D subsidies do not necessarily give rise to (expected) profit shifting as in the basic model.

Suppose now that profit incentives dominate competitive threats due to the easiness of imitation. Then the domestic firm wants to encourage the foreign firm to do more R&D. But this is not achievable through the use of R&D subsidies, since the foreign firm relaxes its R&D investment and tries to let the domestic firm bear the costs. Hence R&D subsidies cannot increase the national welfare any more.

Diffusion of Technology

Finally we consider the model of Sato and Tsutsui (1987) (see also Sato (1988)). The model pays special attention to the dynamic aspect of R&D investment and the effect of spillovers of newly created knowledge. Here R&D activities are considered to create new knowledge. As newly created knowledge, the outcome of R&D investment has all the complicities that are associated with information goods. One of them is its strong tendency to spill over, benefiting not only the producer of the new knowledge but also those who are not directly engaged in knowledge production. As a result, the presence of spillovers affects the firm's incentive to do R&D investment. The model examines the long-run competitiveness of the firms in this environment.

R&D process is divided into basic and applied knowledge production processes. The firms are engaged in both basic and applied knowledge production. Basic knowledge is characterized as having a strong tendency to spill over, while applied knowledge, regarded more as firm specific knowledge, has a weak tendency to spill over. The production of knowledge as well as output is assumed to take place continuously. In order to focus on the impact of the spillover effect of basic knowledge, it is assumed that only the domestic firm is engaged in the production of basic knowledge. But the model allows for the possibility that the costs of basic knowledge production are shared by both the domestic and foreign firms. Moreover, the model allows for the possibility that the efficiency of producing applied knowledge can vary between the firms. Note that this last assumption tries to capture the reality that some countries are known to excel in applied knowledge production. Both the domestic and foreign firms maximize their discounted sum of instantaneous profits over an infinite horizon; i.e.,

$$jD = \int_0^\infty \exp(-r\,t)[P(qD + qF)qD - aDqD - S(aD, uD, b)$$
$$- (1 - s)\,T(b, v)]dt,$$

$$jF = \int_0^\infty \exp(-r\,t)[P(qD + qF)qF - aFqF$$
$$- eS(aF, uF, db) - sT(b, v)]dt.$$

Here r is a common discount rate; q_i is firm i's output; A_i is firm i's effective marginal cost (the inverse of the level of applied knowledge); B is the level of basic knowledge; u_i is the rate of change in A_i; v is the rate of change in B; s is the cost-sharing parameter of basic knowledge production; d is the diffusion parameter of basic knowledge; e is the efficiency parameter of applied knowledge production; P is the inverse demand function; S is the cost function in terms of u_i; T is the cost function in terms of v.

The game considered in the model constitutes a differential game. In general, differential games are distinguished from sequential games in that the evolution of states is described by differential or difference equations and that the objective of each player is given by the discounted sum of instantaneous payoffs over a horizon. However, the same equilibrium concept (i.e., Nash equilibrium) is applied to solve this game.[12]

What remains is the specification of the information structure of the game. A type of information structure has to be specified to describe the extent to which firms can observe the current level of basic and applied knowledge. It is conceivable that in some instances, the firms may make only partial observation, while in other instances, the firms may make full observation. The importance of observation, of course, is that it is deeply related to a firm's ability to tell whether a particular action of the other firm is credible or not. It is customary in the literature that a firm is said to have a closed-loop information structure when it makes full observation, while a firm is said to have an open-loop information structure when it does not.

The outcome of the game is measured by steady-state market shares of output. Of course, it is dependent upon the type of information structure, the cost sharing and the difference of efficiency in applied knowledge production between the firms. Figure 4–1 shows the iso-share curve in the e-d parameter space when both firms have open-loop information structures (compared to closed-loop, Figure 4–2). Upward-sloping iso-share curves show that in order to maintain the equal market share, the domestic firm's efficiency in applied knowledge production relative to the foreign firm's has to increase to compensate for the adverse effect caused by the increased basic knowledge diffusion. It is interesting to note that the domestic firm can capture more than 50 percent market share regardless of the rate of basic knowledge diffusion, as long as the domestic firm is more efficient in applied knowledge production (i.e., e is greater than unity).

Figure 4–3 shows the iso-share curve for the case where the domestic firm has a closed-loop information structure, while the foreign firm has an open-loop information structure. We observe again that these iso-share curves are upward-sloping. Perhaps what is interesting in this case is that even if the domestic firm's efficiency in applied knowledge production is higher than that of the foreign firm, its market share can be less than 50 percent when the rate of basic knowledge

FIGURE 4–1.   **FIGURE 4–2.**

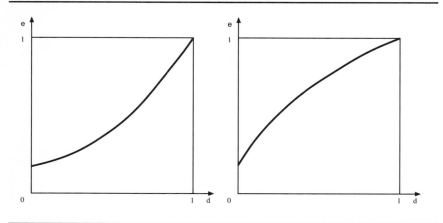

FIGURE 4–3.

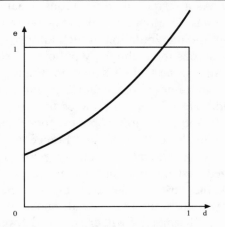

diffusion is sufficiently high. In other words, the diffusion of basic knowledge permits the foreign firm to compensate for the inefficiency in applied knowledge production. The reason is the following. This information structure endows the foreign firm with an ability to commit to the pre-planned R&D. Thus, the foreign firm is no longer forced to react to the domestic firm's R&D, unlike in the case of the basic model. As a result, a kind of negative strategic effect, caused by the foreign firm's forced reaction to the domestic firm's action, does not appear any more. It is to be noted that another interesting case arises if the domestic firm has an open-loop information structure, while the foreign firm has a closed-loop information structure.

CONCLUSION

The theory of technological competition is a new branch of economics but, apart from its infancy, it suffers from the intellectual incompatibility of its progenitors. Until recently, the dominant paradigm of international trade was that of laissez-faire. In contrast, the theory of innovation recognizes the need to internalize the benefits from R&D investments; the possibility of market failure became widely recognized and the need for government intervention vehemently argued. Strategic trade theory recognizes that one of the sources of externalities that nullifies the assumptions of traditional trade theory is the incomplete appropriability of R&D. As a result, an acrimonious debate has arisen as to whether any nation has developed an advantageous position in international trade through the manipulation of technology policy.

Ergas (1987) divides the technology policies of six Western countries—the United States, the United Kingdom, France, Germany, Switzerland, and Sweden—into two categories: "mission oriented" and "diffusion oriented." He relates the policies to two possible purposes, national sovereignty and provision of public goods. He argues that the technology policies of the U.S., U.K. and France are mission oriented and have close links to national sovereignty goals. The decision process is concentrated and the projects which receive funding are few and biased towards industries in the early stages of the technology lifecycle. Further, they concentrated on radical innovations.

Ergas considers Germany, Switzerland, and Sweden to be diffusion-oriented countries where centralized policy-making is rather limited and funds are widely distributed to industry associations or cooperative research groups. These benefit a large number of small and medium-sized firms. Moreover, these countries emphasize education. The chemical and electric industries, which were highly concentrated, needed a high quality university system which in turn needed a superior school system, and lobbied for these objectives. In contrast, the mechanical industry was highly decentralized and lobbied for vocational training, product standardization, and cooperative research. The German-speaking countries developed a comprehensive system of vocational apprenticeship and skill certification. The government provided subsidies to firms to hire research scientists; the program was administered through industry organizations and had very precise eligibility rules to prevent arbitrary selection. Overall, the diffusion-oriented policy leads to quick dissemination of incremental technologies, but firms tend to be conservative in adopting radical alternatives.

The Japanese system seems to be an amalgam of the two approaches. Sato (1988) notes that the government plays a dual role. In supporting a mission-oriented policy, it selects a small number of important and powerful companies in the industry so as to protect them from domestic and foreign competition. In the early stages, these are the only companies permitted to import foreign technologies, and they are encouraged to develop a cooperative research program and receive tax credits and subsidies. But some aspects of Japanese policy are best characterized as diffusion oriented. Once a technology is developed, the government encourages competition. The public school system is well-known for its emphasis on science education at secondary school levels, and the universities graduate a high percentage of engineers.

The debate as to whether government intervention is needed to correct market failure or would only lead to market failure is not confined to strategic trade theory alone. The probability is that the debate will not be resolved in the near future. But one has to be careful when inconclusive arguments are used to evaluate the performance of a nation or, even more, if they are used to compare two nations. Without proper care, any desirable conclusion can be derived depending on a careful marshaling of assumptions and data.

Much of the debate on Japan has concentrated on whether Ministry of International Trade and Industry has superior signaling abilities in directing technology trade by firms and whether this requires a response from the Western nations. We seek to show that the channels of transfer of technology to Japan and its method of utilizing this technology differ at best only in degree from what prevails in other countries. This will not resolve the debate but hopefully it can bring some perspective to it.

NOTES

1. See Krugman (1987) for a review of the implications of the new theories of trade.
2. The oil-rich nations are, of course, an exemption to this generalization.
3. Gerschenkron (1962) p. 8.
4. Mokyr (1990) pp. 151-92.
5. See Adas (1989), who gives an excellent review of the evolution of the concept of Western superiority.
6. Hollister-Short (1976) notes that the lag was surprisingly in coal mining though England was dependent on coal for energy.
7. See, for example, Burks (1985).
8. See Kreps and Wilson (1982), Milgrom and Roberts (1982) for example.
9. Strategic trade has attracted much attention of many economists lately: Many issues have been investigated in international trade in the framework of strategic trade. The recent studies include Brander (1986), Brander and Spencer (1984), Clemenz (1990), Dixit (1984), Fung (1989), Krugman (1984), Levinsohn (1989), Meza (1989), Ono (1989) and Tsutsui (1989). This is only a partial list and is not meant to be inclusive.
10. For this to happen, it is necessary that both firms make full observation of the domestic government's R&D subsidies. Therefore, it is to be noted that if the foreign firm makes no such observation, its reaction to R&D subsidies cannot be the same.

11. The domestic government's R&D subsidies essentially provide the domestic firm with first-mover advantages.
12. See Tsutsui and Mino (1990) for the derivation of a Nash equilibrium in a differential game with an infinite horizon.

BIBLIOGRAPHY

Adas, M. (1989). *Machines as the Measure of Men: Science, Technology and Ideologies of Western Dominance.* Ithaca, New York: Cornell University Press.

Arrow, K. (1962). "Economic Welfare and the Allocation of Resources for Invention" in R. R. Nelson (ed.), *The Rate and Direction of Inventive Activity.* Princeton, New Jersey: Princeton University Press.

Beath, J., Y. Katsoulacos, and D. Ulph (1989). "Strategic R&D Policy," *Economic Journal, 99,* 74–83.

Bernstein, J. I., and M. I. Nadiri (1989). "Research and Development and Intra-Industry Spillovers: An Empirical Application of Dynamic Duality," *Review of Economic Studies, 56,* 249–69.

Binmore, K. (1990). *Essays on the Foundations of Game Theory.* Oxford, United Kingdom: Basil Blackwell.

Brander, J. A. (1986). "Rationales for Strategic Trade and Industrial Policy" in P. R. Krugman (ed.), *Strategic Trade Policy and the New International Economics.* Cambridge, Massachusetts: MIT Press.

Brander, J. A., and B.J. Spencer (1984). "Tariff Protection and Imperfect Competition," in H. Kierzkowski (ed.), *Monopolistic Competition and International Trade,* Oxford, United Kingdom: Oxford University Press.

Brander, J. A., and B.J. Spencer (1984). "Export Subsidies and International Market Share Rivalry," *Journal of International Economics, 18,* 83–100.

Burks, A. W. (ed.) (1985). *The Modernizers: Overseas Students, Foreign Employees and Meiji Japan.* Boulder, Colorado: Westview Press.

Clemenz, G. (1990). "International R&D Competition and Trade Policy," *Journal of International Economics, 28,* 93–113.

Deolalikar, A. B., and R. E. Evenson (1988). "Technology Production and Technology Purchase in Indian Industry: An Econometrics Analysis," Harvard Institute of Economic Research, Harvard University.

Dixit, A. (1984). "International Trade Policy for Oligopolistic Industries," *Economic Journal, 94,* 1–16.

Dosai, G. (1988). "Sources, Procedures, and Microeconomic Effect of Innovation," *Journal of Economic Literature, 26,* 1120–69.

Ergas, H. (1987). "The Importance of Technology Policy," in P. Dasgupta and P. Stoneman (eds.), *Economic Policy and Technological Performance,* Cambridge, United Kingdom: Cambridge University Press.

Fung, K. C. (1989). "Tariffs, Quotas, and International Oligopoly," *Oxford Economic Papers, 41*, 749–57.

Gerschenkron, A. (1962). *Economic Backwardness in Historical Perspective.* Cambridge: The Belknap Press.

Hicks, J. R. (1932). *The Theory of Wages.* London: Macmillan.

Hollister-Short, G. (1976). "Leads and Lags in Late Seventeenth Century English Technology," *History of Technology, First Annual Volume.* London: Mansell Information/Publishing Ltd.

Ichimura, S. (1990). "Institutional Factors and Government Policies for Appropriate Technologies in Southeast Asia," Institute of International Relations, Osaka International University.

Kreps, D., and R. Wilson (1982). "Reputation and Imperfect Information," *Journal of Economic Theory, 27*, 253–79.

Krugman, P. R. (1984). "Import Protection as Export Promotion: International Competition in the Presence of Oligopoly and Economies of Scale," in H. Kierzkowski (ed.), *Monopolistic Competition and International Trade.* Oxford, United Kingdom: Oxford University Press.

Krugman, P. R. (1987). "Is Free Trade Passe?," *Journal of Economic Perspectives, 1*, 131–44.

Levinsohn, J. A. (1989). "Strategic Trade Policy When Firms can Invest Abroad: When are Tariffs and Quotas Equivalent?," *Journal of International Economics, 27*, 129–46.

Meza, D. D. (1989). "Not Even Strategic Trade Theory Justifies Export Subsidies," *Oxford Economic Papers, 41*, 720–36.

Milgrom, P., and J. Roberts (1982). "Limit Pricing and Entry Under Incomplete Information: An Equilibrium Analysis," *Econometrica, 50*, 443–59.

Mokyr, J. (1990). *The Lever of Riches: Technological Creativity and Economic Progress.* New York: Oxford University Press.

Myllyntaus, T. (1990). "The Finnish Model of Technology Transfer," *Economic Development and Cultural Change, 38*, 625–43.

Ono, Y. (1989). "Foreign Penetration, New Entry and National Welfare Under Oligopoly," *Journal of Japan and the World Economy.*

Porter, M.E. (1990). *The Competitive Advantage of Nations.* New York: The Free Press.

Sato, R. (1981). *Theory of Technical Change and Economic Invariance.* New York: Academic Press.

Sato, R. (1988). "The Technology Game and Dynamic Comparative Advantage: An Application to U.S.-Japan Competition," in A. M. Spence and H. A. Hazard (eds.), *International Competitiveness.* Cambridge, Massachusetts: Ballinger Publishing Company.

Sato, R., and S. Tsutsui (1987). "Information Strategies, Market Barriers and Trade Performance," New York University, Stern School of Business, Center for Japan-U.S. Business and Economic Studies mimeo.

Schumpeter, J. A. (1942). *Capitalism, Socialism and Democracy.* New York: Harper and Row.

Spencer, B. J., and J. A. Brander (1983). "International R&D Rivalry and Industrial Strategy," *Review of Economic Studies, 50,* 707–22.

Sugimoto, M., and D. L. Swain (1989). *Science and Culture in Traditional Japan.* Rutland, Vermont: Charles E. Tuttle Company.

Sweeny, P. (1987). *Innovation, Entrepreneurs and Regional Development.* New York: St. Martin's Press.

Tsutsui, S. (1989). "Cost Differential and Welfare Effects of Interventionist Trade Policies in Oligopolistic International Trade," *Journal of Japan and the World Economy.*

Tsutsui, S., and K. Mino (1990). "Nonlinear Strategies in Dynamic Duopolistic Competition with Sticky Prices," *Journal of Economic Theory, 52,* 136–61.

CHAPTER 5

RECONFIGURATION OF GLOBAL FINANCIAL MARKETS IN THE 1990s

Roy C. Smith
Ingo Walter

During the 1980s world financial markets experienced change as never before. These were years of explosive growth in all types of financial transactions. The U.S. bond and stock markets entered a boom period early in the decade that continued until nearly its end, alongside a torrent of financial innovations and aggressive trading operations, the fourth wave of mergers and acquisitions of the twentieth century, and a new focus on international investment management. The decade also saw extraordinary growth in the issuance and trading of Euromarket securities, radical deregulation of financial markets in the U.K. and several other countries, a flurry of privatization share issues by governments, as well as the EC 1992 initiatives and the launching of the first great mergers wave to envelop the whole of Europe—where industrial restructuring more or less along American lines was seen to be necessary and unavoidable. Meanwhile, Japan emerged during the period as the world's most solvent nation, pumping its excess savings into foreign securities, real estate, and control of corporations.

Roy C. Smith is Professor of Finance and International Business, New York University, and Limited Partner, Goldman, Sachs & Co.

Ingo Walter is the Charles Simon Professor of Applied Financial Economics and the Sidney Homer Director of New York University Salomon Center.

Although propelled by a certain degree of serendipity, these developments were hardly accidental. They were the result of more or less simultaneous policy shifts toward the free market on the part of governments of the OECD countries, shifts that reflected sharply different philosophies of economic governance than had prevailed before. This policy redirection also reflected a broad realization that global economic forces cannot be ignored or resisted, and indeed must be accommodated.

The further evolution of world financial markets will continue to be highly sensitive to such basic policy developments, and can be discussed in terms of the implications for each of the three principal regional marketplaces—Europe, the United States, and Japan. Just as the oil price rise which so affected international finance in the 1970s was unforeseeable at the beginning of that decade, or as the impact of Reaganomics and the changing role of Japan were unforeseeable at the beginning of the 1980s, the full consequences for financial markets of new developments such as the political and economic reforms in Eastern Europe or events in the Middle East remain unforeseeable today. Some probable directions, however, can be identified based on an assessment of underlying policy vectors and the changing capabilities of the markets themselves.

In this chapter, we review the salient financial market developments in Europe, the United States, and Japan, and suggest that they represent a confluence of forces that will lead up to "seamless" markets for many securities and derivatives by the end of the 1990s, in much the same way as a seamless market in foreign exchange exists today. This prognosis, if correct, has major implications for the competitive positioning and performance of all kinds of financial institutions as well as for public policies toward the financial services industry as competition continues to intensify between firms as well as across national financial centers.

EUROPE

The European financial and industrial deregulation and privatization already under way, and those additional developments associated with the EC single market initiatives, will help sustain a long overdue restructuring of industry in Europe. This restructuring is occurring through mergers, corporate recapitalizations, strategic alliances and minority investments, leveraged management buyouts, and other free-market responses. In addition, the restructuring has been aided by the availability of financial resources, somewhat more aggressive attitudes about business takeovers that have accompanied capital market liberalization, and the availability in continental Europe of the U.S. and U.K. takeover know-how (Walter and Smith, 1989). Nevertheless, there are persistent differences between the Anglo-Saxon and Continental European market traditions in how industrial restructuring is carried out. This, in turn, has a great deal to do with the structure of relationships between business firms and their investors and creditors.

Changing Banking Relationships

The differences between corporate restructuring in continental Europe and the Anglo-American experience reflects the fundamental differences that have existed in national financial systems. In much of continental Europe, corporate finance traditionally has been heavily bank-oriented. Universal banking institutions are dominant in corporate lending as well as securities issuance. The banks also make equity investments for their own and fiduciary accounts, and retain voting rights on shares held in trust. Such practices provide banks with both nonpublic information and (indirectly and through external board memberships) considerable influence over management decisions involving corporate restructuring activities. Firms that do not meet bank performance expectations find themselves under pressure to restructure (Rybczynski, 1989). When such restructuring is to be accomplished, it is usual for the company's main bank (*Hausbank*) to carry it out. Historically, continental European banks have periodically been called upon to push through industrial restructurings in the absence of well-functioning capital markets, especially following periods of war or economic collapse, and so are accustomed to this role.

In the United States and the United Kingdom, on the other hand, banks have not had a comparable tradition since the early 1930s, and capital markets have played a large role in industrial finance for most of this century. Corporate debt financing has relied much more heavily on the securities markets, with bondholders exerting limited influence on managerial decisions. Nor have shareholders exerted much influence over management in recent years. Neither U.S. nor U.K. banks have been able to effectively exercise surveillance and influence on management even remotely comparable to that of some of their continental European counterparts.

Consequently, changes in corporate control have been effected through the capital markets, frequently contested by incumbent management and justified by a need to replace that management so as to improve the performance of the company. Even when such efforts are unsuccessful, management may choose to carry out its own restructuring of the company, often resulting in changes not dissimilar from those sought by the challenger. Some observers of the U.S. and U.K. merger scene over the past several years believe that self-restructurings to escape or avoid takeovers have been more numerous than the takeover attempts themselves, arguably enhancing corporate profitability and efficiency (Jensen and Ruback, 1983).

Others worry about the impact of increased leverage on the stability and competitive viability of firms—especially in times of recession—redistribution of wealth to shareholders from bondholders, employees, and other interest groups, and the sort of managerial short-termism and distraction from conduct of the underlying business that takeover activity may entail. They point to the lack of empirical evidence that companies and countries exposed to intensive takeover activity outperform those exempt from such pressures over the long term, for example, UAL, Inc. (United Airlines) versus AMR Corp. (American Airlines) or the United Kingdom versus Germany. Definitive conclusions, of course, remain elusive given the impossibility of running the world twice, that is, how things went as against how they might have gone under different takeover market conditions.

The merits and demerits of the two systems have been widely debated. Bank-oriented systems are said to be less crisis-prone, to favor long-term as opposed to short-term views in corporate decision-making, and to provide superior continuous monitoring of corporate performance leading to preemptive structural adjustment. Market-oriented systems are credited with greater efficiency, financial innovation and dynamism, superior resistance to inherent conflicts of interests among the various stakeholders involved, and (through better transparency) less susceptibility to major uncorrected industrial blunders.

In the 1990s there is likely to be some degree of convergence between the two approaches. Financial liberalization and wider use of the securities markets by continental European corporations—together with increasingly performance-oriented portfolio management on the part of European mutual funds, insurance companies, and other institutional investors—is leading to a gradual shift away from bank finance, and the introduction of unwanted takeover attempts through acquisition of shareholdings by unaffiliated (perhaps foreign-based) investors. At the same time, easing restrictions on bank activities in the United Kingdom and the United States is beginning to allow them to play a larger role in industrial restructuring transactions, and to exploit some of the information and relationship advantages they have as lenders.

The Unfolding European Merger Wave

Of the $329 billion of non-U.S. mergers and acquisitions recorded between 1985 and 1989, $196 billion, or 60 percent, were intra-European (Smith and Walter, 1989). An additional $156 billion (80 percent of the intra-European total) involved Europe–non-Europe transactions. European corporations were entering the M&A field more aggressively, with transaction volume growing far more rapidly than anywhere else in the world during the 1985–1989 period. This expansion was occurring simultaneously on two fronts—within Europe and in other regions of global importance to European corporations, mainly the United States. Intra-European transactions increased by a factor of 9 during the five-year period, and Europe–non-Europe deals (in which 73 percent of the transactions by volume involved European acquisitions of non-European corporations) grew 5.4 times, as shown in Table 5–1. Overall, European transactions rose from 8 percent of the world M&A volume in 1985 to 32 percent in 1989 and made further gains in 1990.

Although it is difficult to predict how long the growth in European M&A volume will continue, it appears that—barring any unexpected reversal of government policies affecting market-driven transactions or a substantial deterioration of economic prospects in Europe—there remains a great deal more to be done. Most of the M&A activity in Europe during the period 1985–1989 (about 58 percent by volume) has involved United Kingdom corporations, which have a long history and familiarity with such transactions. French and Italian corporations (together accounting for 22 percent of intra-European transaction volume) have been the next most active M&A participants, followed by German corporations, which—despite the size of the German economy—accounted for only 5 percent of intra-European transaction volume during 1985–1989.

Most of the continental European countries do not have a tradition of, or substantial experience with, market-driven domestic M&A activity. As a result, only a comparatively small percentage of enterprises in continental European countries have so far participated in such transactions. As more of them become involved, and the benefits of doing so become

TABLE 5-1
Volume of Completed International Merger and Corporate Transactions[a,b] (1985-89)[c]

Year	Domestic U.S. (No.)	($M)	Cross-Border U.S. Buyer from U.S. (No.)	($M)	Seller from U.S. (No.)	($M)	Total Cross-Border (No.)	($M)	Outside U.S. (No.)	($M)	Global Totals (No.)	($M)
1985	778	181,544.6	28	4,799.1	72	9,732.6	100	14,531.7	82	16,296.5	960	212,372.8
	852[d]		*60*		*104*		*164*		*90*		*1,106*	
1986	1,145	201,745.8	35	2,905.4	147	27,280.1	182	30,185.5	132	28,728.5	1,459	260,659.8
	1,253		*59*		*138*		*197*		*161*		*1,611*	
1987	1,273	199,878.2	46	7,669.4	172	35,481.7	218	43,151.1	310	70,706.7	1,801	313,736.0
	1,178		*102*		*123*		*225*		*279*		*1,771*	
1988	1,510	286,918.8	72	5,886.6	226	60,915.9	298	66,802.5	1,115	97,798.4	2,923	451,519.7
	1,178		*135*		*168*		*303*		*789*		*2,270*	
1989	1,489	200,330.6	124	17,500.0	324	44,615.5	448	62,115.5	1,459	115,306.5	3,396	377,752.6
	1,331		*184*		*183*		*367*		*1,275*		*2,973*	
Totals 1985-89	6,195	1,070,418.0	305	38,760.5	941	178,025.8	1,246	216,786.3	3,098	328,836.6	10,539	1,616,040.9
	5,881		*540*		*716*		*1,256*		*2,594*		*9,731*	

[a] Completed transactions include: mergers, tender-mergers, tender offers, purchases of stakes, divestitures, recapitalizations, exchange offers, and LBOs.

[b] The volume data are classified according to the announcement date of a transaction—not taking into consideration when a transaction is completed.

[c] Million dollars of purchase price—excluding fees and expenses—at current exchange rates. The dollar value includes the amount paid for all common stock, common stock equivalents, preferred stock, debt, options, assets, warrants, and stake purchases made within six months of the announcement date of the transaction. Liabilities assumed are included if they are disclosed in press releases or newspaper articles.

[d] Numbers in italics represent completed transactions with undisclosed dollar values.

Source: Securities Data Corporation, Mergers and Corporate Transactions database.

TABLE 5–2
Volume of Completed International Merger and Corporate Transactions[a, b]—Europe (1985–89)[c]

| | Intra-Europe Transactions | | Europe/Non-Europe Transactions | | | | | |
| | | | Buyer from Europe | | Seller from Europe | | Total Cross-Border | |
Year	(No.)	($M)	(No.)	($M)	(No.)	($M)	(No.)	($M)
1985	31	8,326.0	40	6,083.2	22	2,441.0	62	8,524.2
	32[d]		*44*		*40*		*84*	
1986	59	11,911.4	85	17,752.0	34	3,523.2	119	21,275.2
	76		*54*		*33*		*87*	
1987	189	38,335.0	111	27,825.9	45	8,307.5	156	36,133.4
	61		*67*		*72*		*139*	
1988	835	63,431.6	179	35,978.9	104	8,433.6	283	44,412.5
	559		*134*		*125*		*259*	
1989	1,090	74,432.9	255	33,367.1	180	12,671.0	435	46,038.1
	874		*134*		*211*		*345*	
Totals 1989–89	2,204	196,436.9	670	121,007.1	385	35,376.3	1,055	156,383.4
	1,702		*433*		*481*		*914*	

[a] Completed transactions include: mergers, tender-mergers, tender offers, purchases of stakes, divestitures, recapitalizations, exchange offers, and LBOs.
[b] The volume data are classified according to the announcement date of a transaction—not taking into consideration when a transaction is completed.
[c] Million dollars of purchase price—excluding fees and expenses—at current exchange rates. The dollar value includes the amount paid for all common stock, common stock equivalents, preferred stock, debt, options, assets, warrants, and stake purchases made within six months of the announcement date of the transaction. Liabilities assumed are included if they are disclosed in press releases or newspaper articles.
[d] Numbers in italics represent completed transactions with undisclosed dollar values.

Source: Securities Data Corporation, Mergers and Corporate Transactions database.

more visible (such as utilizing an efficient market for corporate control to dispose of shares in family-owned or closely held businesses that have limited liquidity), participation in M&A activity should continue to penetrate further.

The patterns of intra-European M&A volume for the 1985–1989 period can be observed by sorting transactions by the nationality of buyers and sellers (see Table 5–3). The average annual rate of growth in all intra-European M&A volume was 120 percent, an exceptionally high growth rate. U.K. activity in the European merger marketplace was by far the greatest—64 percent of all reported intra-European transactions in-

TABLE 5–3
Volume of Completed Intra-European M&A Transactions by Country,
1985–1989 (in Millions of U.S. Dollars)

Country of Buyer Company		Country of Seller Company					
		U.K.	France	Italy	Germany	Other European	Totals Buyer
U.K.	1985	6,747.4	0.0	0.0	0.0	12.2	6,759.6
	1986	7,713.7	0.0	0.0	0.0	60.0	7,773.7
	1987	21,671.3	4.3	100.0	0.0	236.6	22,012.2
	1988	27,391.7	1,085.0	149.0	139.8	741.7	29,508.1
	1989	44,035.9	1,163.7	257.1	293.5	2,048.3	47,798.5
	Total	107,560.0	2,253.0	507.0	433.3	2,098.8	113,852.1
	CGR	59.8%					63.1%
France	1985	0.0	10.7	0.0	0.0	0.0	10.7
	1986	0.0	176.0	520.9	0.0	0.0	696.9
	1987	316.7	1,324.2	0.0	0.0	0.0	1,640.9
	1988	2,897.6	6,860.5	98.7	310.2	3,253.7	13,420.7
	1989	4,896.5	5344.0	392.4	0.0	248.3	10,881.2
	Total	8,110.8	13,715.4	1,012.0	310.2	3,502.0	26,650.4
	CGR		372.7%				464.7%
Italy	1985	16.8	0.0	165.0	0.0	0.0	181.8
	1986	0.0	0.0	1,199.4	71.0	0.0	1,270.4
	1987	0.0	20.4	7,876.3	0.0	1,050.8	8,947.5
	1988	0.0	710.0	1,292.7	0.0	887.7	2,890.4
	1989	99.0	90.9	3,344.3	63.1	0.0	3,598.2
	Total	116.7	821.3	13,877.7	134.1	1,938.5	16,888.3
	CGR			112.2%			110.9%
Germany	1985	0.0	0.0	0.0	898.5	0.0	898.5
	1986	425.0	0.0	887.4	0.0	0.0	1,312.4
	1987	159.6	330.6	0.0	251.0	0.0	741.2
	1988	59.2	154.0	627.4	1,231.8	44.8	2,117.2
	1989	170.0	1,176.1	37.5	1,803.0	1,457.4	4,644.0
	Total	813.8	1,660.7	1,552.3	4,184.3	1,502.2	9,713.3
	CGR				19.0%		50.8%
Other European	1985	0.0	0.0	0.0	0.0	475.4	475.4
	1986	563.9	0.0	0.0	0.0	294.1	858.0
	1987	382.0	153.4	0.0	239.0	4,218.8	4,993.2
	1988	6,673.8	0.0	1,759.5	0.0	7,061.9	15,495.2
	1989	1,729.0	20.3	305.9	149.7	5,306.1	7,511.0
	Total	9,348.7	173.7	2,065.4	388.7	17,356.3	29,332.8
	CGR					82.8%	99.4%
Totals Seller	1985	6,764.2	10.7	165.0	898.5	487.6	8,326.0
	1986	8,702.6	176.0	2,607.7	71.0	354.1	11,911.4
	1987	22,529.6	1,832.9	7,976.3	490.0	5,506.2	38,335.0
	1988	37,022.3	8,809.5	3,928.2	1,681.8	11,989.8	63,431.6
	1989	50,931.3	7,795.0	4,337.2	2,309.3	9,060.1	74,432.9
Grand Total		125,950.0	18,624.1	19,014.4	5,450.6	27,397.8	196,436.9
	CGR	65.7%	419.5%	126.4%	26.6%	107.6%	72.9%

Source: Securities Data Corporation, Mergers and Corporate Transactions database.

volved British seller companies. British seller volume grew at an average annual rate of 66 percent, consistent with the overall intra-European growth rates. Transactions involving British sellers to British buyers grew at a somewhat slower rate of 60 percent during the period.

French and Italian companies, however, were acquiring other European companies (including British companies) at a more rapid rate of increase. Especially active on the buy-side in the intra-European market, French buyer-transactions grew at a rate of 465 percent per annum, and purchases by Italian companies grew at 111 percent annually during the same period. French buyers acquiring French companies totaled $13.7 billion (out of a total of $26.7 billion of French intra-European acquisitions) during the five-year period, and reflected an annual growth rate of 373 percent. Italian companies acquired other Italian companies worth $13.9 billion during the period, a growth rate of 112 percent.

Although much less active in intra-European volume terms during the period ($9.7 billion), German companies, whose rate of growth in intra-European buyer transactions was 50.8 percent annually during 1985–1989, substantially lagged British, French, and Italian acquirers. German sell-side activity grew even more slowly, only 19 percent per annum. It has evidently become much easier for French and Italian companies to use the merger market for seller-initiated transactions than it has been for German companies, which are the least accustomed to domestic M&A activity among all those engaging in European mergers and acquisitions. Sellers from these four countries made up about 86 percent of aggregate intra-European transaction volume during the period, although German sellers accounted for only 2.7 percent of all seller activity.

Assuming Eastern Europe's political and economic changes maintain direction and momentum, further and perhaps more extensive and entirely different restructuring patterns may lie ahead. These include the need to carry out large-scale privatizations and the development of new debt and equity markets in an environment where valuation of enterprises is exceedingly difficult, where property rights and legal business structures are yet to be fully defined, and where the role of foreign investment remains highly uncertain—in national economic settings subject to a high level of macro-risk.

Capital Market Integration

European industrial restructuring will require impressive amounts of financing. This should be available primarily, if not entirely, from European sources. European corporations should no longer find it necessary to rely largely on bank lending or to arrange their capital market financings in non-European currencies or in non-European markets. Domestic financial markets in Europe have benefited considerably from increased transaction volumes, greater liquidity, and more competition in recent years, although the percentage of such financings arranged by nonfinancial (i.e., industrial) borrowers remains far lower than in either the United States or Japan (see Table 5–4).

With the elimination of all barriers to cross-border transactions going into effect for both issuers and investors (as well as financial intermediaries) in the coming years, it can be expected that a large, single European capital market will emerge. This integrated market will reflect the consolidation of previously separate domestic capital markets, serviced mainly by local banking institutions, with the existing Eurobond and European "foreign bond" market structures.

TABLE 5–4
Volume of Corporate Sector Capital Market Financing by Regional Corporations in Their Respective Home Markets[a]—1988 ($ Billions of Proceeds at Average Exchange Rates)

	U.S.[b]			Europe[c]			Japan		
	Financial	Non-Financial	Total	Financial	Non-Financial	Total	Financial	Non-Financial	Total
Equities[d]	28.8	13.6	42.4	9.5	42.3	63.0	25.1	40.8	65.9
Bonds[e]	141.1	221.9	363	155.2	26.3	181.4	287.7	137.9	425.6
Total	169.9	235.5	405.4	164.7	68.6	244.4	312.8	178.7	491.5
GNP ($ trillions)			4.88			5.27			2.9
Financing per dollar of GNP	$0.03	$0.05	$0.08	$0.03	$0.01	$0.05	$0.11	$0.06	$0.17

[a] Issues by domestic firms outside of their bond country are excluded.
[b] Because the U.S. 1989 equities' breakdown into financial and nonfinancial corporations is only given for first two quarters, the breakdown given above was estimated from proportions evident in those quarters: Total 22.7, NF 7.3.
[c] European figures are aggregated from Germany, France, Greece, Italy, Norway, Netherlands, U.K., Switzerland, Finland, Spain, Belgium, Portugal, and Luxembourg.
[d] Equities include public and private enterprise issues (lines A.1.a+b for nonfinancial; lines A.1.c for financial).
[e] Nonfinancial corporate bonds are taken from line B.1.1.e (or lines B.1.1.e.1 + e.2).

Source: OECD Financial Statistics Monthly Domestic Markets December 1989 (earlier months where not updated).

In essence, the new market will derive from the integration of financial competition in Europe. Under the EC Second Banking Directive a German bank, for example, may open branches or buy local banks in France and in Italy. In Germany, however, the bank will itself be subject to new competition for the business of its traditional clients from German branches of French and Italian banks. The German bank may propose an ordinary traditional *hausbank* financing for an old customer, only to discover that better terms under a more imaginative structure are offered by a German branch of a foreign bank, or by a U.S. investment bank operating out of London.

The German bank may match the terms to keep the client's business. The financing could then become a capital market operation, because the cheapest financing for borrowers tends to emanate from the issuance of securities rather than from bank loans, especially in those situations in which the rates have to be sharpened to fully competitive levels. The German bank would take the client to the market for the necessary funds, perhaps using the domestic bond market structure and prospectus, if this is convenient. If it is not—for example, if it involves translating the prospectus into all EC languages—the bank could instead offer a Eurobond structure, even though the ultimate investors may in either case be the same—partly local nationals who know the issuer well, partly other Europeans who will be offered the new paper through the bank's branches or affiliates throughout the EC. Some French investors may subscribe to a German domestic issue, just as they might to a Eurobond issue, and German investors may subscribe just as they might to a domestic private placement. Before long, all such issues will be structured to find the most receptive investors, wherever they may be located in Europe, or outside Europe.

The Stimulating Effects of Competition

The simultaneous activities of financial market competitors throughout Europe—by banks and securities firms from EC member countries, as well as from Switzerland, Japan, and the United States—will force the markets to conform to the most efficient transactions structure possible. The result should be similar to the introduction of the "bought deal" to the Eurobond market in the early 1980s, which opened all clients to the competitive offerings of capable securities houses with whom no prior relationship existed. Indeed, the competition-enhancing influence of the bought deal was so strong that the Securities and Exchange Commission took it into account when proposing and later adopting Rule 415 ("shelf registration") in the United States, which likewise led to a marked increase in competition for the new issue business involving corporate debt securities.

The emerging, consolidated European market will be characterized by comparably free-wheeling competition, pressure for financial innovation, and proliferation of sophisticated financial services. The large European issuers will be the first to benefit from these changes, but certainly not the last. Soon U.S. and Japanese issuers will likewise be attracted to a large and more efficient pan-European financial market. And financial firms marketing these services will certainly attempt to reach beyond large blue-chip companies to capture as well the business of middle-market companies that previously did not think themselves capable of capital market access.

UNITED STATES

In remedying a structure of financial regulation that has become increasingly obsolete and uncompetitive, major changes in U.S. banking laws—especially in the Glass-Steagall separation of banking and securities activities, and restrictions on interstate banking—can be anticipated early in the 1990s. These will result in far-reaching, possibly radical restructuring of the U.S. commercial and investment banking industries.

Market Interpretation

A dozen or so large banks will enter the domestic securities business as important competitors, particularly in the underwriting of new debt and equity issues. Few in number but including some of the premier money center and regional banking entities, they will attempt to introduce a version of universal banking to the United States. Some of these institutions view investment banking as the preferred vehicle for escaping the destiny of large, unwieldy and bureaucratic institutions trapped in an overcrowded industry with depressingly low margins and questionable credits. They expect that universal banking will be a business they can assimilate—in the manner of the large German or Swiss banks, for example—more easily that they could assimilate the aggressive, free-wheeling business of a Morgan Stanley or a Shearson Lehman. Other banks will prefer to pursue opportunities in interstate banking and/or possibly insurance. These efforts will be focused on middle-market lending and retail financial services, as the viability of classic wholesale banking activities continues to erode.

The choice of direction is not an easy one, and both will be expensive. Nationwide financial services offer much appeal to banks hemmed in by regulatory geography. But the cost of putting together a first-rate nationwide banking network may well exceed the $1 billion or so that many observers think is the minimum needed for a comparable investment banking commitment.

These challenges will arrive at a time when bank capital has been depleted by various LDC charge-offs, bond ratings have been lowered throughout the banking industry, share prices are at historic lows, and tough new capital adequacy standards have been adopted by the Federal Reserve and the other bank regulators. Banks also enter the 1990s with problems in their HLT (highly leveraged transactions) portfolios and troublesome prospects for real estate loans in a market likely to remain soft throughout the savings and loan workout and a macroeconomic slowdown.

It nonetheless seems probable that among the U.S. banks most adept at money market, government securities, and foreign exchange dealing, there will emerge several that will attempt to become leaders in global securities markets. Initially at least, these banks could be expected to concentrate on all types of debt financing, in all of the major currencies, using all of the latest swapping and synthetic securities techniques.

Foreign banks operating in the United States will find these market developments ideal—they can continue to attempt to increase their penetration of the traditional commercial banking businesses (where their superior credit standing has provided a decided advantage over many U.S. banks), and they can improve their international securities business by placing U.S. issues in their home markets or in other foreign markets.

Globalizing the U.S. Bond Market

Bond market operators will be taking advantage of the opportunities presented by SEC Rule 144A, which became effective April 1990 and offers a safe haven to any issuer (domestic or foreign) offering securities to qualified institutional investors on an unregistered basis. Whereas SEC Rule 415 earlier permitted qualified issuers to sell securities under a shelf-registration procedure, Rule 144A omits registration requirements altogether, thereby greatly simplifying new-issue procedures for international borrowers unwilling to submit to the trouble and cost of preparing a registration statement (SEC, 1988). By eliminating the two-year holding period for qualified investors in privately placed securities, it adds significantly to the liquidity of these securities and therefore reduces the yield penalty to borrowers as against public issues—even as it significantly cuts issuing costs—and for the first time qualifies such securities for purchase by mutual funds marketed to the public. For all practical purposes, Rule 144A has transformed the U.S. institutional market for debt securities into an equivalent of the self-regulated and highly innovative Eurobond market.

Rule 144A contemplates a substantial increase in the number of non-U.S. debt and equity financings done in the American capital market, many of which will be offered not only to domestic investors but also, simultaneously, to investors in Europe and Japan. Figure 5–1 illustrates

FIGURE 5–1
Potential Market Structure after the Adoption of Rule 144A

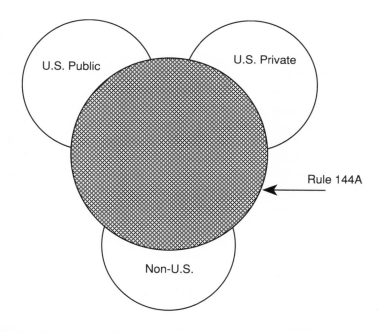

the market overlaps that are expected as a result. Debt issues brought to European and Japanese markets—whether by U.S. or other corporate issuers—may also be offered to institutional investors in the United States under Rule 144A. From a regulatory viewpoint, it has eliminated virtually all remaining obstacles to full international market integration. Issuers will, as always, choose the lowest-cost market for the securities they wish to offer—which may or may not be in the United States—regardless of regulatory considerations.

Rule 144A also permits banks to broaden and perfect their distribution of loans. During the 1980s, many U.S. banks adopted the practice of "selling down" loan participations to other banks. This process could be made more efficient by securitizing the loans through Rule 144A provisions that would permit liquid markets to develop and extend the group of investors to whom they are offered to encompass nonbank financial institutions as well. Should such practices become widespread, the market for bank loans would come to be substantially integrated with the bond market, thereby facilitating the development of meaningful placing power by banks in the securities field—and raising questions as to how such loans/securities should be treated for accounting and regulatory purposes.

Adjusting to Overcapacity

Competition in the securities market from the banking industry is occurring just as the U.S. securities industry is recovering painfully slowly from a substantial overcapacity problem that developed after the October 1987 crash. Trading volume declined and profitability and returns on capital fell dramatically for most investment banks and brokers.

Many traditional U.S. securities firms, having adjusted to intense competitive conditions at home and abroad during the fifteen years since negotiated commissions were first introduced on "Mayday" in 1975, may decide to reconsider the desirability of life as large, full-service players subject to shrinking margins and growing overheads, and opt instead for smaller, more profitable niches that offer the sort of rapidly changing "windows" of rewards and opportunities that investment bankers as a species have always sought. Some firms, such as Morgan Stanley, Kidder Peabody, and Salomon Brothers, have already reduced their commitments to certain debt underwriting and market-making activities, leaving room for newer competitors such as banks and foreign institutions eager to expand in the business.

American equity markets will no doubt experience similar competitive restructuring. Most firms have diversified away from plain institutional block trading or retail sales activities in search of more profitable areas, such as money management, program trading and foreign securities brokerage. The equities markets in general, however, should be buoyed by greater international involvement in the 1990s as overseas portfolio investors—especially those from Japan—develop professionally and become more active. Greater volume will not, of course, relieve the pressures on margins caused by new domestic and foreign-based market entrants.

Growing Foreign Presence

Foreign corporations, attracted by strategic requirements and relatively low stock prices in the U.S., have continued to be active as acquirers of U.S. companies. This continuing foreign investment volume could offset somewhat the downward pressure on equity prices that the ending of the U.S. merger boom and adverse environmental developments might be expected to have on the market. Permanent foreign participation in U.S. portfolio investments and acquisitions will become more welcome and should, by the end of the 1990s (perhaps much sooner), begin to alleviate American anxieties over "excessive" foreign ownership. It will become clear that foreign capital injections are beneficial and that foreign shareholders are no more threatening to Americans than American stockholdings, now long in place, have been in European and other foreign companies.

U.S. and foreign equity trading may also become integrated on an expanded NASDAQ/SEAQ electronically linked system, which could result in a substantial increase of American institutional ownership and trading of foreign equities. Such linkages could, by the end of the 1990s, offer lower trading costs, simpler clearing systems, and ultimately lead toward a greater standardization of accounting, disclosure, and regulatory procedures, all of which tend to encourage still greater international financial market activity.

JAPAN

Japanese financial markets are likely to experience substantial additional deregulation in the 1990s, which in turn should lead to major changes in the competitive dominance of capital markets by Japanese banks and brokers.

The basic business of the Japanese banks has changed rapidly—the surplus cash of Japanese companies has substantially paid down all but the barest minimum of bank debt owed by manufacturing companies. Table 5–5 shows the dramatic decline of net interest costs as a percentage of Japanese corporate profits. The traditional influence and power of the banks over their industrial customers is becoming a thing of the past. Banks, however, continue to have large balance sheets, which are partly inflated by cosmetic loans maintained for the sake of appearances (i.e., loan proceeds that are subsequently redeposited in the same bank). Increasingly, however, loans and other new business are coming from banking transactions outside Japan.

Pressures on Article 65

As in the United States, Japanese banks need to find a new domestic business, and many believe the greatest promise resides in securities ac-

TABLE 5–5
Net Financial Costs (Interest Charges) as a Percent of Operating Profits, Tokyo Stock Exchange First-Section Companies, Fiscal 1975–1988E

Year	All Companies	Manufacturing Sector
1975	62.8%	69.0%
1976	39.6	44.4
1977	41.5	42.2
1978	44.7	30.8
1979	36.7	23.9
1980	33.3	30.0
1981	35.5	28.6
1982	35.8	28.0
1983	35.9	24.5
1984	28.6	16.1
1985	27.0	13.3
1986	26.5	11.8
1987	18.9	4.4
1988	0.0	0.9
		(0.6) [a]

[a] Net financial *receipts*—i.e., investment income—exceeded interest charges in manufacturing.

Source: Tokyo Stock Exchange

tivities. Similarly, Japanese brokers want to be able to move into lucrative areas that have traditionally been set aside for banks, if possible without giving up their exclusive hold on their extremely profitable securities business. The question of reforming Article 65 (the Japanese law which closely resembles the U.S. Glass-Steagall provisions), however controversial and locked into immovable opposition it may appear, will have to be resolved during the 1990s—presumably soon after or perhaps even leading any legislative changes to the U.S. Glass-Steagall Act. Otherwise, the Japanese market will be entirely out of alignment with markets in Europe and the United States. American and European banks and securities firms will use every opportunity (as they have over matters of Tokyo Stock Exchange membership) to force roughly equivalent Japanese deregulation and substantial equality of market access. Failure to change Article 65 sets up the question in both the EC and in the U.S. of imposing sanctions under existing or proposed reciprocity provisions.

Repeal of Article 65 will dramatically alter the competitive structure of financial intermediation in Japan. In the United States there are a dozen or so large securities firms preparing to face competition from a handful of large and adequately capitalized banks with the demise of Glass-Steagall. In Japan four large securities firms face sixteen large city banks, three long-term credit banks, and a dozen trust banks and cooperative banks with major aspirations in the securities field. Certainly, the coming battle between the traditionally well-capitalized and well-connected banks and the big securities firms will have a number of important competitive consequences for Japanese and non-Japanese players alike.

Negotiating Commissions

Fixed commission rates in Japan are required by the Tokyo Stock Exchange—virtually the last major exchange in the world that does not mandate negotiated commissions between customer and broker—although in recent years there have been a number of authorized institutional discounts from standard rates for large orders. It is inevitable in the 1990s that the Japanese commission structure will collapse, after which competition for securities transactions will—as in the case of Mayday in the United States, Big Bang in Great Britain, and virtually everywhere else negotiated rates have been introduced—will become very bloody indeed. This will be true especially if the big banks are allowed into the game at the same time, as was the case in the United Kingdom.

Japanese brokers trace virtually all of their profitability to domestic brokerage commissions. They are reluctant block traders, offer little else in the way of service beyond taking orders against the latest stock ideas, and are heavily overstaffed for what they do. Profit pressure could be exceedingly tough for these firms for some time, especially if competent, smaller-sized foreign brokers are nicking off their clients with block tradings and research services. Several foreign firms operating in Tokyo have been able to demonstrate their ability to do this, and a few have introduced U.S. program trading techniques and other derivatives-related business into Tokyo and have become very profitable in the process. It is certainly not unthinkable for foreign firms to develop a significant share of securities activities business in Japan, assuming a fully level playing field and large commitments of time and resources.

New-Issue Market Reforms

Japan must also bring its domestic new-issue capital market access conditions into line with those of the United States and Europe. This has not been the case in the past, new securities issues being subject to substantial regulations that have limited market usage to a comparatively small number of blue chip companies, queueing delays, interest rate controls, collateralization requirements, and approval of "commission banks" (city banks acting as trustees for bondholders). Accordingly, most Japanese corporations have preferred to utilize the Eurobond market, where none of these obstacles exist, even when the investors in their securities are overwhelmingly Japanese. During 1987–1989, for example, in excess of $100 billion of Japanese debt issues with equity purchase warrants attached were offered to Euromarket investors, although most of these securities (perhaps 70 to 80 percent) were ultimately sold back to investors in Japan. The round-tripping to escape confining new issue conditions in the domestic market was motivated almost entirely by financial arbitrage on the part of the issuers.

The authorities finally began to act in 1989 to bring this business back to Japan by liberalizing the standards to be met by Japanese companies seeking to use the domestic public bond markets, by introducing shelf registration procedures to provide quicker access to markets, and by proposing that securities issued abroad bought predominantly by Japanese investors be registered in Japan. These steps, along with fewer opportunities for gain in financial arbitrage, should substantially curtail the use of the Euromarket for the purposes of Japanese round-tripping. An important result of recapturing this business for Japan, however, would be the continued liberalization of market-access rules, in turn increasing further the volume of corporate new issues in the Japanese market. Many of these issues, like Rule 144A issues in the United States and Euromarket issues, could well be sold on a global basis to foreign investors.

MARKET REALIGNMENTS IN THE 1990s

Most capital market issues, wherever they originate, will be capable of being offered simultaneously to investors worldwide by the middle of the 1990s. Those investors will continue to differ significantly as to their preferences for names of issuers, for the form of the issue (e.g., bearer form, as opposed to registered form), for maturities, and for currencies— although the latter can be easily and cheaply accommodated through currency swaps and hedging instruments. Institutional investors will emerge as the dominant buyers, even in Europe, as more individuals switch to performance-oriented investment funds. Issuers shopping for the lowest-cost financing opportunities will find substantial investment capacity in the emerging integrated European market, the post-144A U.S. market, and in a newly unrestricted Japanese domestic bond market.

The development of a global, "seamless" fixed-income securities market may begin to resemble the global, "seamless" market in foreign exchange and certain commodities. The resemblance will be greater as the volume and spread characteristics of the bonds markets fall into line with those of the foreign exchange market. Competitive skills in the foreign exchange markets, with related activities in swaps and hedging, may indeed become a model for what it takes to succeed as leaders in the debt markets of the 1990s. Such changes in world bond markets will substantially alter the character of the marketplace for debt securities and those competing in it.

The markets for equity securities have never been the same as debt markets; the volume of activity is much less and each individual stock is different from all the others. But as volume increases, as electronic trading and settlement takes over from the traditional floor-traded markets, as commission rates become very low (as in the U.S. and London), and as technology encroaches on individual trading skills, the market in equities too will change along the same lines as the bond markets. Banks will see opportunities to move in alongside securities firms and competition will be intensified greatly, particularly in continental Europe and in Japan.

There should thus develop during the 1990s powerful capital market centers in the United States, Europe, and Japan that are predominantly regional but nonetheless global in operation. These markets will be extremely competitive, internally and with each other, forcing some well-known players to retire to other pursuits or to market niches. The three principal hubs will adopt essentially similar principles of market governance: (1) universal banking will be permitted; (2) commission rates will be negotiated; (3) foreign banks and brokers will gradually approach market access equal to locals, although in some environments it will require a long, sustained effort; (4) cross-border investment demand will become a major factor in all securities trading; and (5) similar, if not standardized, trading rules, disclosure requirements, settlement procedures, and capital requirements will apply to securities firms (as they do now to banks).

Changes in government policies, of course, could once again substantially alter these conclusions. Protectionism could undo much of the real-sector market integration already achieved. The Middle East crisis of 1990 could have unforeseen and long-lasting repercussions. The 1992 initiatives in Europe could give way to internal squabbling and foot-dragging or be derailed by developments in Eastern Europe or by disputes over alignment of monetary and tax policies. Japan or the United States could further delay the deregulation needed to assure all markets and competitors a level playing field. Capital controls could be reimposed. Policies affecting savings rates and capital formation, mergers and acquisitions, leveraged transactions, enforcement of securities laws, foreign direct investment, and competition could likewise force reversals in market evolution. Other setbacks could range from major environmental developments, such as fallout from the 1990 crisis in the Middle East, to such specific problems as adjusting to overcapacity in various parts of the financial services industry.

Barring such developments, however, the configuration of the financial markets at the end of the 1990s could in many ways constitute a global modernization of financial capacity, which in turn could help to lower the cost of capital, including all of its agency costs, and provide a basis for sustained world economic growth during the next century. As such, the financial markets of the future will not be government-dependent. They will constitute independent sources of funds provided by the private sector, and the role of the market itself will dominate. Thus, it may resemble the global financial market of the period prior to World War I, when the role of governments was slight as against that of the private sector, and the market played the dominant role in allocating capital. In that context, perhaps the world of finance will exit this century much as it entered it.

REFERENCES

Arthur Andersen & Co., *European Capital Markets: A Strategic Forecast,* London: Economist Publications (1989).

Bank for International Settlements, *Recent Innovations in International Banking,* Basel: Bank for International Settlements (1986).

Bloch, Ernest, *Inside Investment Banking* (2d edition), Homewood, IL: Dow Jones-Irwin (1989).

Dermine, Jean (ed.), *European Banking in the 1990s,* Oxford: Basil Blackwell (1990).

Hayes, Samuel, III; A. M. Spence, and D.v.P. Marks, *Competition in the Investment Banking Industry,* Cambridge, MA: Harvard University Press (1983).

Jensen, Michael C., and Richard S. Ruback, "The Market for Corporate Control: The Scientific Evidence," *Journal of Financial Economics,* vol. II (1983).

Kallberg, Jarl S., and Anthony Saunders, *Direct Sources of Competitiveness in Banking Services,* New York University Salomon Center mimeo (1986).

Levich, Richard M., "Financial Innovation in International Financial Markets," in M. Feldstein (ed.), *The United States in the World Economy,* Chicago: University of Chicago Press (1988).

Office of Technology Assessment, U.S. Congress, *International Competition in Banking and Financial Services,* Washington, DC: OTA mimeo (July 1986).

Organization for Economic Cooperation and Development, *Trade in Services in Banking,* Paris: OECD (1983).

Pastré, Olivier, "International Bank-Industry Relations: An Empirical Assessment," *Journal of Banking and Finance* (March 1981).

Rybczynski, T. N., "Corporate Restructuring," *National Westminster Bank Review* (August 1989).

Securities and Exchange Commission, Securities Act of 1933, Rule 144A and Amendments to Rule 144 and 145, *Federal Register,* 53 F.R. 44016, 1 November 1988.

Smith, Roy C., and Ingo Walter, "European Industrial Restructuring and the Market for Corporate Control," in Karel Cool, Damiel Neven, and Ingo Walter (eds.), *Economic Restructuring in Europe,* London: Macmillan (1991).

Walter, Ingo (ed.), *Deregulating Wall Street,* New York: John Wiley & Sons (1985).

Walter, Ingo, *Global Competition in Financial Services,* Cambridge, MA: Ballinger–
Harper & Row (1988).

Walter, Ingo, and Roy C. Smith, *Investment Banking in Europe: Restructuring for
the 1990s,* Oxford: Basil Blackwell (1989).

CHAPTER 6

ACCOUNTING FOR GLOBAL FINANCE

Frederick D. S. Choi

Accounting historians are likely to describe the present decade as one of "globalization." During the next ten years, more and more institutionalized structures, based on structural linkages between national markets, will evolve as financial managers attempt to exploit imperfections in world product, factor and financial markets. These linkages will, in turn, significantly increase the volume of international transactions, so much so that international financial statistics for the previous decade will pale in comparison. International accounting and reporting issues, formerly regarded as interesting but peripheral concerns, will move to the forefront and command the attention of financial managers and accountants the world over.

What follows is a sampling of trends that are occurring in the global economy, and their likely impacts on international corporate finance, financial markets and related accounting information systems during the 1990s. The trends I will describe relate to a changing competitive environment, continuing macro-economic volatility, a deepening of financial technology, deregulation/re-regulation of financial markets and internationalization.

Frederick D. S. Choi is a Research Professor at the Stern School of Business, New York University.

GLOBAL COMPETITION AND MACROECONOMIC VOLATILITY

There are a number of trends which will necessitate a global perspective on the part of financial managers, investors and accountants. Most are closely interrelated, making it difficult to order them sequentially or to gauge their relative importance. Hence, we discuss some of them in combination.

A major element in the changing competitive context of multinational enterprises is the phenomenon of global competition. Continued reduction in national trade barriers, the emergence of Europe as a unified market, convergence of consumer tastes and preferences, and a growing sophistication of business firms in penetrating foreign markets, either directly or indirectly through strategic alliances, joint ventures and other cooperative arrangements, means that uninational approaches to the production and marketing of goods and services (including their financing) are no longer sufficient (Bartlett and Ghoshal, 1989).

Increasing parity in the development and exploitation of basic and applied technology in Asia and Europe, as well as in North America, is also contributing to enhanced competitive pressures.

Market and product interpenetration is not confined, however, to the non-financial sector. Financial innovation, securitization of international capital flows and continued evolvement of offshore capital markets are also inducing significant competitive pressures in the financial services industry, both internationally and within various national financial markets (Walter, 1989).

The challenge of global competition is made more difficult by continued macroeconomic volatility. The absence of coordinated macroeconomic policies among nation-states, together with structural pressures, account for continued gyrations in the relative prices of commodities, interest rates and foreign exchange rates. In preserving bottom lines, financial managers are developing in-house capabilities that will enable them to directly access capital suppliers. They will also perform more of their own trading operations in foreign exchange, money markets and commodities, functions which were previously shared with financial intermediaries. These trends mean that the finance function will increasingly be viewed as a business in its own right. This does not necessarily mean that finance departments will remain "islands unto themselves." On the contrary, in responding to interest rate and exchange volatility, firms must confront entities with differing geographic configurations and, consequently, differing exposures to environmental uncertainties. This will necessitate risk management policies that integrate both financial and operating stratagems (Lessard, 1989).

Consider the area of exchange risk management. Traditional hedging policies have revolved around the conversion of foreign currency earnings into the reporting currency of parent companies. For example, under extant currency translation methods in the United States, a foreign subsidiary's balance sheet exposure is measured by the difference between its exposed assets and liabilities. A foreign currency asset or liability under this framework is considered exposed if a change in the exchange rate causes its dollar equivalent to change. Assessment of the future direction of exchange rate movements, in turn, leads to identifiable foreign exchange gains and losses. Under SFAS No. 52, these gains or losses are taken directly to shareholders' equity if the firm utilizes the current rate translation method; they are taken to earnings if the firm chooses the temporal method. Management concern over the equity or earnings impact of exchange rate changes would lead to appropriate hedging practices.

Enhanced global competition, however, will require greater attention to the local currency earnings effects of exchange rate changes in light of potential competitor price and sourcing responses. Thus, a U.S. parent company with a wholly-owned German subsidiary would book an exchange gain should the deutsche mark appreciate in value relative to the dollar. Moreover, the parent might conclude that the mark revaluation would have no effect on its German subsidiary as the latter sources itself, and sells its output locally. Yet, a local German competitor may be purchasing factor inputs from Italy and indeed gain from a mark revaluation, giving it a competitive advantage over the U.S. parent's German operation.

These kinds of effects that focus on the effects of exchange rate changes on future costs and revenues are less easily measured, but are critical. Accordingly, exposure measurement will require financial managers to engage increasingly in "what-if" scenarios that will require inputs from several operating departments, i.e., finance, marketing, planning, production and accounting. As these operating exposures tend to be longer in duration, less certain in terms of measurable outcomes and not based on explicit commitments, newer hedging technologies will be relied on. Appropriate operating responses to exchange rate changes will also require greater cooperation among a greater number of operating departments.

These and related developments will pose new challenges for accountants. The use of newer option-like products to hedge certain operating exposures, discussed in more detail in the next section, will call for accounting treatments that depart from traditional "hedge" accounting. Firms will need to account for both credit and market risks associated with the newer hedge products they are employing. This, in turn, will increasingly call into question the use of traditional accruals-based accounting for hedge products in favor of mark to market methods which recognize changes in the value of a particular instrument resulting from changes in interest rates, exchange rates and counterparty credit risk. Complicating these measurements is the fact that markets in which many of these instruments are traded may be thin or appropriate pricing formulas proprietary in nature. In designing systems that will assure optimal operating responses to environmental risks, accountants will have to provide information that spans several operating functions and time frames. The information will be less precise, less structured and have a much shorter "shelf-life." In short, traditional measures of risk exposure based on conventional accounting numbers and static time frames will no longer suffice.

Conventional accounting measurements will also be increasingly questioned as a basis for planning and controlling foreign operations. Thus, for example, how does one evaluate and manage the performance of foreign operations that are domiciled in environments where rates of inflation exceed those in the parent country? Owing to the inverse relationship between local inflation and exchange rates, assets carried at, or restated to, historical costs prior to consolidation and translated at current exchange rates produce parent currency equivalents that distort asset values and income. An ironical result is that affiliates located in highly inflationary, devaluation-prone countries often appear better than those in strong currency countries. Accounting principles in most countries largely ignore the problem. While explicit inflation adjustments were proposed in several countries during the decade of the seventies, these were criticized for producing accounting numbers that were less than objective. This argument, however, is less germane when designing contemporary management information systems.

DEEPENING OF FINANCIAL TECHNOLOGY

A likely response to increased macroeconomic volatility during the 1990s will be an acceleration in the design and marketing of innovative financial products. At the same time, banks and other financial intermediaries are experiencing the phenomenon of "disintermediation," whereby credit suppliers and borrowers increasingly bypass them in favor of direct transactions with one another. This development together with heightened competition within the industry has eroded profit margins to razor-thin proportions. To retain their client base, and indeed to survive, financial institutions have looked to the development of corporate finance related products which link lenders and borrowers around the globe as a necessary structural response. The ability of the financial services industry to respond in such fashion has been facilitated by advances in computer and telecommunications technology. These advances have accelerated transactions processing and settlement, facilitated around-the-clock trading in a variety of complex financial instruments and increased the liquidity of financial markets around the world.

   This deepening of financial technology has made possible the unbundling of financial attributes. These attributes include the principal amount, repayment term, currency of denomination, coupon rate, repricing interval, conversion feature, call provision, risk exposure, and options based on contingent events. Given this state of affairs, financial managers must increasingly decide on the optimum combination of financial attributes to hold and how to adjust these attributes over time. Hedge products such as currency or interest rate swaps and other contingent contracts that transfer risks through financial intermediaries also increase the risks of default. As many of these instruments are presently accorded off-balance sheet treatment, the burden of credit evaluations is increased both in terms of magnitude and scope. Another problem set facing financial managers is the question of whether or not a financial product can or should be used to hedge real operating decisions (Levich 1989).

   The effects of new financial technology on financial management have a direct bearing on accounting policies and practices. To begin, optimal choices among the range of financial attributes that exist suggests a substantial information requirement that management accountants must be prepared to satisfy. In addition, many of the newer instruments have evolved so rapidly that accounting principles have not been able to keep pace. Issues that will need to be addressed relate to recognition, measurement and disclosure.

The issue of recognition centers on the question of whether or not hedging instruments should be recognized as assets or liabilities in the body of the financial statements. One factor which makes this choice difficult is that most of the newer financial instruments are "derivative" as opposed to "basic" in nature. Basic financial instruments, such as repurchase agreements (receivables), bonds, and capital stock, are those which meet the conventional accounting definitions of assets, liabilities, and owners' equity. Derivative instruments constitute formal agreements to transfer risk from one party to another without transferring the underlying basic instrument. Many are based on contingent events and, therefore, do not share the same characteristics as the basic instrument to which they relate. An example would be an interest rate swap which transfers interest rate risk without transferring the underlying debt instrument being hedged. Thus, an important issue is whether the derivative product should receive the same accounting treatment as the basic instrument to which it relates. Another hurdle faced by statement preparers is that little guidance is currently available in the form of definitive accounting standards for these newer financial instruments.

Closely related to the recognition issue is the question of measurement. Thus, how should a derivative instrument be valued? Should it take on the same measurement basis as the basic instrument to which it relates? Or, should it reflect an independent valuation? If it be the latter, which valuation model—historical cost, market value, the lower of cost or market, net realizable value, or discounted present value—is preferable? How should gains or losses related to the derivative instrument be reflected in the income statement? Should they be reflected in income at all? Can and should risks associated with financial instruments be recognized and measured? This question is especially relevant as risks attached to many of the newer financial instruments, such as options and interest rate caps, are nonsymmetric; i.e., someone's gain is another's loss.

Until uniform guidelines are established, pressures will be exerted on financial managers to disclose more about the financial innovations to which they are a party. Even here, however, questions remain. Thus, to what extent should buyers and sellers of financial instruments detail the nature and amounts of financial instruments they employ? What attributes of financial instruments should be disclosed in general—as opposed to special—purpose financial statements? How much disclosure is necessary to sufficiently apprise readers of the magnitude of off-balance sheet risks associated with corporate financial innovations?

Deregulation/Reregulation/Harmonization

Uniformity in regulation has not been a hallmark of the world's securities markets. New bond issues have historically been subject to regulatory controls regarding the size and maturity of individual issues, the quality of borrowers, the number and amount of issues per calendar period, and so forth. While rationalized on grounds of fostering macroeconomic policy objectives, they have often been used to protect domestic financial institutions from foreign competition (SEC, 1987).

This situation has changed. U.S. initiatives during the 1970s to deregulate its capital markets in the interest of spurring competition were followed in the 1980s by a wave of regulatory reforms in Europe and Japan (SEC, 1987). The acceleration of this trend during this decade will be a major factor contributing to the globalization of the world's capital markets. It will not be the only factor, however. Deregulation which improves market access will not necessarily improve a market's competitive position unless a regulatory scheme is developed that will promote and preserve investor confidence. Thus "reregulation" which seeks to govern conduct in more accessible and restructured markets is required (Warren, 1990).

As countries vie for greater competitive positions in global markets, the major fear is that corporate issuers, listers and market makers affected by reregulation will migrate to the jurisdictions with the least onerous disclosure and other investor protection requirements (Smith, 1991). As "regulatory arbitrage" may have negative consequences for market growth, markets may compete among themselves to attract or retain the objects of regulation. At worst, such competition could work to the detriment of investors as market regulators gravitate toward the least burdensome investor protection requirements. On the other hand, market regulations that are too lenient discourage international investors from participating in such markets.

Where lies the answer? Harmonization of regulatory requirements, which eliminates regulatory disparities, is increasingly viewed as a promising remedy. The development of a common set of regulatory requirements limits opportunities for firms to scour the world for regulatory "bargains." It also assures a minimum threshold of investor protection.

At the present time, two general approaches to regulatory harmonization are being seriously considered (Hanks, 1991). One favors a system of *reciprocity* based on some substantially equivalent minimum threshold. Under this approach, national jurisdictions with roughly similar regulatory principles agree to accept each other's requirements as a condition for market access. The second approach favors the adoption of a *uniform* set of disclosure, accounting, and securities distribution standards. Recent discussion between the United States and Canada proposing mutual recognition of prospectuses in connection with certain types of offerings by certain classes of issuers is an example of the former approach. Support for international accounting standards by IOSCO, the International Organization of Securities Commissions, is an example of the latter.

Regardless of which of the foregoing approaches is settled on, the implication is clear. Harmonization of accounting and disclosure standards will move from the back burner to become a dominant theme in the 1990s. Moreover, it will be a theme that will find strong reinforcement in the work of the European Community in its efforts to create an integrated capital market. Financial managers and accountants who have a stake in the outcome must be prepared to actively participate in the promulgation process to assure that international accounting and disclosure standards that emanate from the process are palatable.

Internationalization of Capital Markets

Encouraged by recent advances in telecommunications and the gradual deregulation of national capital markets alluded to above, domestic investors are expanding their purchases of foreign debt and equity securities. Toward the end of the 1980s, for example, U.S. gross purchases and sales of foreign stocks exceeded $140 billion, a nine-fold increase over the flows at the beginning of the decade. Non-U.S. gross purchases and sales of U.S. purchases and sales of U.S. stocks exceeded $380 billion, a five-fold increase over the same time span (GAO, 1989). Motivating investor behavior are enhanced returns that are frequently available abroad, as well as the opportunity to reduce portfolio risk by diversifying internationally (Grubel, 1968; Solnik, 1988). In similar fashion, business enterprises interested in increasing the supply and reducing their capital costs are increasingly sourcing their external capital needs abroad, both in terms of new issues and listings on foreign stock exchanges. As a consequence, investment and corporate funding decisions have become international in scope.

In contrast, accounting and financial reporting practices have not kept pace. In Germany, for example, firms continue to follow accounting treatments considered ultra-conservative by international standards. While some of this conservative bias is attributed to financial reporting practices that are based on tax law, managements are allowed to use balance sheet reserves that enable managements to disguise true earnings. Thus, in early 1987 Volkswagen is reported to have uncovered a major foreign currency fraud committed by persons who falsified foreign exchange contracts and left the company exposed to dollar losses estimated at $260 million (approximately DM 473 million). While the company indicated that the loss was accounted for in its 1986 financials, its reported bottom line in that year of DM 580 million was virtually unchanged from that of the preceding year, this despite a lower earnings prediction by industry analysts. Was the cause an unprecedented increase in sales or a drastic reduction in operating expenses? Far from it. An examination of its shareholders' equity suggests that the loss was absorbed by contingency reserves which amounted to over DM 9 billion prior to the loss. Had Volkswagen adhered to international standards, its reported earnings for 1986 would have been virtually eliminated and prior years' results substantially higher (Schieneman, 1989).

As a consequence of such international accounting diversity, differences in reported profits of say, Bavarian Motor Werks, A.G. and Ford Motor Company could be due as much to differences in accounting measurement rules employed as to differences in real performance. This could lead to problems of interpretation and understanding when financial statements are read by foreign readers who may not be familiar with local accounting and reporting norms.

If accounting measurement rules were the only difference among countries, then straightforward transformation of figures (analogous to converting feet or yards to their metric equivalents) would be sufficient to enable accounting reports, assuming sufficient data were available to make the desired adjustments, to be universally understood and unambiguously interpreted. Unfortunately, countries also reflect substantial economic, institutional and cultural differences that preclude accounting figures from having the same interpretation even if they were generated using the same accounting principles. As one example, let us consider Eastern Europe, and in particular, the Soviet Union. As relations between Russia and the West continue to improve, foreign investors are increasingly pondering joint venture arrangements and security investments there. While the conversion of cash basis accounts, practiced by plants in the Soviet Union (Aaron, 1990), can be converted to an accruals basis and provide a better picture than first meets the eye, the reader must appreciate the objectives of financial reporting in an environment that has just begun to make the transition to a mixed economy. In an economy where all resources have previously been provided by the state and resource allocation decisions are largely beyond the control of enterprise managers, the notion of reporting to external investors and managing an enterprise with the external reporting effects of their actions in mind is a new development that will take many years to embrace fully. Hence, readers of Eastern European financial statements in particular, and all foreign statements in general, must attempt to discern to what extent reported accounting numbers are due to (a) accounting measurement differences, (b) environmental differences and (c) real differences in the attributes being reported on. In practice, this problem is made more difficult by the fact that certain accounting data are not disclosed in some countries. And, even where disclosures are similar, differences in auditing standards or practices may affect the reader's confidence in what is reported.

A major issue that international investors and corporate issuers will have to address in the 1990s is whether or not the juxtaposition of international financial decisions and divergent accounting practices—measurements, disclosure, auditing—leads to problems of understanding and interpretation on the part of foreign readers of accounting reports. And, if so, do these problems lead to capital market effects in terms of the location of market activity, the pricing of foreign securities and ultimately a firm's capital costs? In a recent study sponsored by Arthur Andersen and Salomon Brothers, a significant number of statement readers in major capital markets of the world report that they are bothered by accounting differences and that these differences are associated with capital market effects ranging from the location of market activity to the pricing of international securities (Choi and Levich 1990).

Additional empirical evidence regarding the capital market effects of international accounting differences will have significant implications for investors, corporate issuers and accountants. In making their investment picks, investors will need some mechanism, either implicit or explicit, for making cross-country comparisons. This problem is especially germane for those involved in cross-border mergers and acquisitions, as the reliance on firm-specific information is an integral part of such negotiations.

At the present time, large scale data bases which adjust local accounting data for accounting principles differences do not exist. For the segment of investors who find accounting diversity a barrier to cross-country comparisons, additional effort in improving accounting restatement algorithms or better application of existing algorithms may be worthwhile. On the other hand, those who make the effort to understand firms in a foreign country on their own terms, i.e., familiarize themselves with local environmental norms and develop skills in interpreting foreign accounts in their original form, may be least likely to encounter problems caused by accounting differences.

Firms attempting to raise funds abroad at reasonable costs face the choice of how much they wish to accommodate the information needs of investors who are used to providing capital on the basis of reports prepared according to local accounting and reporting norms. In attempting to court investors who may be less tolerant of accounting differences, management can opt to provide foreign readers with (1) accounts that have been restated to the accounting principles of the reader's country-of-domicile, (2) additional disclosure, (3) enhanced audits, or any combination of the above. Alternatively, they can provide investors with unadulterated financial statements, save for language and currency convenience translations, and host meetings or do road shows in which management meets with analysts to resolve accounting and other questions. In either event, management is faced with an optimization problem. To wit, one can model a firm's cost of capital as a function of financing cost, information preparation cost and competitive costs. While the provision of additional information is designed to lower the firm's financing cost, it may also reveal information that is valued by competitors. Measuring the cost and benefits of the various tradeoffs will confront management accountants with challenges of no small proportion.

CONCLUSIONS

There are a number of current trends that will significantly affect the internal and external reporting environment of multinational business entities during the 1990s. The forces of global competition, macroeconomic volatility, a deepening of financial technology and deregulation and integration of international capital markets will necessitate information categories and accounting measurements that transcend conventional accounting mores. Adjectives such as *futuristic, market-based, nonfinancial, on-line* and *international* will have to become an integral feature of multinational reporting systems. Financial managers and accountants who cling to the security blanket of "generally-accepted accounting principles" will find themselves being replaced by those who embrace the notion of "decision-relevance."

REFERENCES

Aaron, P. H., "The Securities Market in the Soviet Union," *Report # 39*. New York: Daiwa Securities America Inc., August 17, 1990, pp. 1–11.

Bartlett, C. and S. Ghoshal, *Managing Across Borders: The Transnational Solution*. Boston: Harvard Business School Press, 1989.

Choi, F.D.S.; H. Hino; S. K. Min; S. O. Nam; J. Ujiie; and A. I. Stonehill, "Analyzing Foreign Financial Statements: The Use and Misuse of International Ratio Analysis," *Journal of International Business Studies,* Spring/Summer 1983, pp. 113–31.

Choi, F.D.S. "Accounting and Taxation for Interest Rate Swaps," in Carl Beidleman (ed.), *Handbook of Interest Rate Swaps*. Chicago: Probus Publishing Company, 1990.

Choi, F.D.S. and R. M. Levich. *The Capital Market Effects of International Accounting Diversity*. Chicago: Dow Jones-Irwin, 1990.

Grubel, H. G. "International Diversified Portfolios: Welfare Gains and Capital Flows," *American Economic Review*, 58, 1968, pp. 1299–1314.

Hanks, S., "Globalization of World Financial Markets: Perspective of the United States Securities and Exchange Commission," in F.D.S. Choi (ed.), *Handbook of International Accounting*. New York: John Wiley & Sons, 1991.

Lessard, D., "Corporate Finance in the 1990s—Implications of a Changing Competitive and Financial Context," *Journal of International Financial Management and Accounting,* Fall 1989, pp. 209–31.

Levich, R. M. "Recent International Financial Innovations: Implications for Financial Management," *Journal of International Financial Management and Accounting,* Spring 1989, pp. 1–14.

Organization for Economic Cooperation and Development Secretariat, *New Financial Instruments: Disclosure and Accounting.* Paris: OECD, 1988.

Schieneman, G. "International Capital Markets: The Accounting Challenge," unpublished manuscript, 1989.

Smith, R. C. "Integration of World Financial Markets—Past, Present and Future," in F.D.S. Choi (ed.), *Handbook of International Accounting.* New York: John Wiley & Sons, Inc., 1991.

Solnik, B., *International Investments.* Reading, Massachusetts: Addison-Wesley Publishing Company, Inc., 1988.

Stewart, J. E. "The Challenges of Hedge Accounting," *Journal of Accountancy,* November 1989, pp. 48–50*ff.*

United Nations Intergovernmental Working Group of Experts on International Standards of Accounting and Reporting (ISAR), "Review of Important Current Developments At the Global Level in the Field of Accounting and Reporting by Transnational Corporations," *Programme of Work of the Intergovernmental Working Group of Experts on the International Standards of Accounting and Reporting.* New York: United Nations Economic and Social Council, E/C.10/AC.3/1990/2.

U.S. Securities and Exchange Commission, "Internationalization of the Securities Markets," *SEC Staff Report to the U.S. Senate Committee on Banking, Housing and Urban Affairs and U.S. House of Representatives Committee on Energy and Commerce.* Washington, D.C.: SEC, 1987.

Walter, I. "Competitive Positioning in International Financial Services," *Journal of International Financial Management and Accounting*, Spring 1989, pp. 15–40.

Warren, M. G., III. "The Global Harmonization of Securities Laws: The Achievements of the European Communities," unpublished paper presented at the Fifth Annual North American Securities Administrators Association Public Policy Conference, Washington, D.C., April 26, 1990.

CHAPTER 7

A NEW VIEW OF U.S. SAVING RATES

Paul Wachtel

Concern about the level and composition of saving in the United States is a pervasive topic of discussion among both economists and politicians. More often than not, these discussions take a cursory look at some standard measures of saving rates and assert that the levels of saving and capital formation in the U.S. are insufficient. However, the data are often presented in ways that are uninformative or even misleading. In this essay, I will suggest a new way of presenting the data on saving that facilitates an accurate understanding of the level of and trends in the American saving rate.[1]

Nevertheless, a more informative way of examining the data does not change the fundamental conclusions. Any examination of savings rates leads to two striking conclusions. First, both gross and net saving in the U.S. are low relative to other countries.[2] Second, there has been a substantial decline in the American saving rate. In particular, the rate of net national saving is much lower in the 1980s than in earlier decades.[3] I do not intend to take issue with these observations. However, I will suggest that informed discussion should not give undue emphasis to aggregate measures of saving. Instead, I propose an alternative form

Paul Wachtel is a Research Professor of Economics at Stern School of Business, New York University.

Research assistance was ably provided by Andrew Jolivet-Habiby, a 1989–90 Glucksman scholar at the Stern School. Support from the Glucksman Institute is appreciated.

of data presentation that highlights the diversity of activities covered by the rubric saving and should be helpful in understanding the nature and origins of the saving problem.

An aggregate measure of saving is comprised of a large number of disparate activities. Thus, an examination of trends in the aggregate saving rate does not tell us very much about the nature of changes. To illustrate this, Figure 7–1, shows three commonly cited ratios used in discussions of saving and capital formation—the personal savings rate (the ratio of personal savings to disposable personal income), the ratio of gross private domestic investment to GNP and the ratio of net national saving to GNP. There is no apparent trend in the ratio of gross investment to GNP. The personal saving rate had an upward trend until the mid-1970s and has trended down since. Finally, the net saving rate has declined dramatically since the mid-1970s. Clearly, there are movements in the components of saving and investment that warrant a closer look.

My purpose in this essay is to suggest a way of presenting the data

FIGURE 7–1
Saving Rates

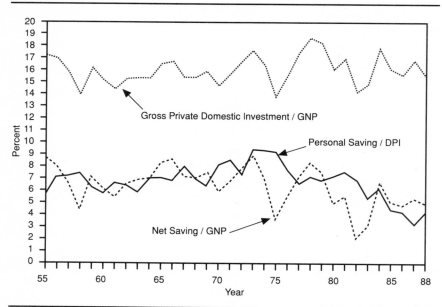

that facilitates an understanding of the sources of the movements in the aggregates. To do this, I will suggest a matrix presentation of the data on savings and investment which is informative without being overly complex. The matrix presentation provides a functional and sectoral breakdown of aggregate savings that enables us to see where changes in aggregate saving measures are coming from. The matrix form also provides an easy framework for examining the effects of changes in the definition of saving.

The first section of the paper presents the saving matrix. It uses data on savings and investment from the National Income and Product Accounts (NIPA). The standard and familiar data are reorganized to create a presentation that highlights the sources of changes in the saving rate. In the second section, we introduce adjustments to the NIPA definition of savings and also augment the data with some additional information. We then present saving matrices and saving rates with the augmented data.

THE SAVING MATRIX

The savings matrix draws upon the concepts used in the Flow of Funds accounting scheme. Flow of funds accounting presents financial flows for each type of financial instrument by sector of the economy. Our saving matrix provides instead data on the functional components of savings and investment from the NIPA by sector of the economy. To some extent it replicates information in the aggregate Flow of Funds matrix. However, the Flow of Funds data prepared by the Federal Reserve Board is not nearly as widely used or followed as the data from the NIPA. Our presentation uses the more familiar and generally more reliable NIPA data.

The functional components of saving in the income accounts are shown by the identity:

Gross Investment Expenditures – Depreciation (Capital consumption allowances and adjustments) + Sectoral Surplus = Net Saving.

All the elements except the sectoral surplus are NIPA data published by the Bureau of Economic Analysis (BEA). The sectoral surplus is therefore calculated as the residual. The sectoral breakdown found in the NIPA is simply:

personal, business, government, foreign and the discrepancy.

The sectoral allocation of saving in the NIPA is fraught with ambiguities. There are a number of instances where the production and saving generated by a particular activity are allocated to different sectors.[4] Nevertheless, the sectoral surplus is particularly interesting because it shows the extent to which a sector is absorbing resources from else-

TABLE 7–1
Matrix Scheme

Sector	Gross Investment	– Depreciation	+ Sectoral Surplus	= Net Saving
Personal	Residential (5.2.16)	(5.2.17)	*	Personal Saving (5.1.3)
Business	Nonresidential Fixed and change in inventories (5.2.7) + (5.2.28)	(5.2.28)	*	(5.1.2) – (5.1.3) – (5.2.2)
Government	0	0	(5.1.11)	(5.1.11)
Foreign	0	0	Net Foreign Investment – (5.1.17)	– (5.1.17)
Discrepancy	0	0	Statistical Discrepancy (5.1.18)	(5.1.18)
Total	Gross Private Domestic Investment (5.2.1)	(5.2.2)	0	*

	Total Net Saving	
+	Depreciation	(5.2.2)
+	Net Foreign Investment	(5.1.17)
=	Gross Investment	(5.1.15)
–	Statistical Discrepancy	(5.1.18)
=	Gross Saving	(5.1.1)

where in the economy or making resources available to the other sectors.

Table 7–1 presents the scheme of the savings matrix. The data sources are shown by reference to the standard NIPA table. The relationship of the matrix entries to the aggregate definitions is also shown. Several categories are by definition zero because the NIPA system does not allow for a government capital account or for a breakdown of foreign investment. Finally, the categories that are not defined explicitly in the accounts (denoted by an asterisk) can be derived from the adding up constraints of the matrix.

Tables 7–2a–d present decadal averages for the savings matrix. Each entry is the average ratio to GNP from the annual data. Tables are presented for 1950–59, 1960–69, 1970–79 and 1980–89. A glance at the four tables provides some interesting observations on trends in saving rates and the changes in the composition of saving:

- Business investment has been a fairly constant proportion of GNP—about 11 percent. However, larger depreciation charges (due to the changes in the composition of the capital stock toward more short-lived equipment) results in a decline in the net saving by the business sector from 3.5 percent of GNP in the 1960s to less than half as much in the 1980s.

- Personal saving was a much smaller fraction of GNP in the 1980s than in any earlier decade. It was almost 2 percentage points less than in the peak decade of the 1970s. However, since the level of housing expenditures as a percent of GNP declined as well from the 70s to the 80s, the decline in the personal sector surplus was not as large. In fact, the personal sector surplus in the 80s was as large as it was in the 1950s and 1960s. Thus, the fall in personal saving in the 1980s should be put in the context of abnormally large saving rates in the 1970s.

- Not surprisingly, a major feature that distinguishes the latest decade from the three previous post-war decades is the emergence of the large government and foreign deficits. The foreign sector became a net saver in the U.S. for the first time. The government sector deficit has grown from decade to decade and took a large leap from less than one percent of GNP in the 1970s to about 2.5 percent in the 1980s.

- Concern about overall levels of private capital formation in the 1980s are clearly warranted. The net saving of the business sector

TABLE 7–2a
NIPA Savings Matrix, 1950–59

Sector	Gross Investment	− Depreciation	+ Sectoral Surplus	= Net Saving
Personal	5.60%	2.12%	1.25%	4.73%
Business	10.58	6.54	−1.25	2.79
Government	0.00	0.00	−0.12	−0.12
Foreign	0.00	0.00	−0.13	−0.13
Discrepancy	0.00	0.00	0.24	0.24
Total	16.18	8.65	0.00	7.52

	Total Net Saving	7.52%
+	Depreciation	8.65%
+	Net Foreign Investment	0.13%
=	Gross Investment	16.31%
−	Statistical Discrepancy	0.24%
=	Gross Saving	16.06%

TABLE 7–2b
NIPA Savings Matrix, 1960–69

Sector	Gross Investment	− Depreciation	+ Sectoral Surplus	= Net Saving
Personal	4.64%	1.98%	1.96%	4.63%
Business	10.89	6.47	−0.93	3.48
Government	0.00	0.00	−0.26	−0.26
Foreign	0.00	0.00	−0.62	−0.62
Discrepancy	0.00	0.00	−0.16	−0.16
Total	15.53	8.45	0.00	7.08

	Total Net Saving	7.08%
+	Depreciation	8.45%
+	Net Foreign Investment	0.62%
=	Gross Investment	16.15%
−	Statistical Discrepancy	−0.16%
=	Gross Saving	16.31%

TABLE 7–2c
NIPA Savings Matrix, 1970–79

Sector	Gross Investment	– Depreciation	+ Sectoral Surplus	= Net Saving
Personal	4.88%	2.18%	2.81%	5.51%
Business	11.40	7.34	–1.62	2.44
Government	0.00	0.00	–0.94	–0.94
Foreign	0.00	0.00	–0.23	–0.23
Discrepancy	0.00	0.00	–0.03	–0.03
Total	16.29	9.52	–0.01	6.75

	Total Net Saving	6.75%
+	Depreciation	9.52%
+	Net Foreign Investment	0.23%
=	Gross Investment	16.51%
–	Statistical Discrepancy	–0.03%
=	Gross Saving	16.54%

TABLE 7–2d
NIPA Savings Matrix, 1980–89

Sector	Gross Investment	– Depreciation	+ Sectoral Surplus	= Net Saving
Personal	4.38%	2.39%	1.60%	3.59%
Business	11.01	8.61	–0.70	1.70
Government	0.00	0.00	–2.47	–2.47
Foreign	0.00	0.00	1.68	1.68
Discrepancy	0.00	0.00	–0.11	–0.11
Total	15.39	10.99	–0.01	4.38

	Total Net Saving	4.38%
+	Depreciation	10.99%
+	Net Foreign Investment	–1.68%
=	Gross Investment	13.70%
–	Statistical Discrepancy	–0.11%
=	Gross Saving	13.81%

peaked in the 1960s and the net saving of the personal sector peaked in the 1970s. Both saving rates are at their postwar lows in the 1980s.

The saving matrix gives emphasis to different concepts than those that are viewed as the most important in the NIPA. For example, NIPA emphasizes Gross Private Domestic Investment and Gross Saving, both of which appear in our matrix (see Table 7–1). However, the matrix presentation focuses attention on two different concepts. First, net saving and particularly net saving by sector, and second, the sectoral surpluses. With the exception of the fall off in Gross Saving in the 1980s, the movements in the gross aggregates in the NIPA are much less striking than those emphasized by the saving matrices.[5]

The individual sectoral surpluses are implied from the NIPA but do not appear in the official accounting schemes. They tell us which sectors are the sources and users of saving. A closer look at the individual sectoral surpluses will show how the patterns of saving and investment have changed in recent years. Time series plots of the four sectoral surpluses as a percent of GNP for 1950–89 are shown in Figures 7–2a–d. From the early 1960s to the early 1980s, the personal sector had a substantial surplus—usually more than 2 percent of GNP—which provided financing to the business sector where deficits were about the same order of magnitude. The personal sector surplus disappeared after 1984 and the business sector deficits became much smaller as well. Also, since 1982, large government deficits have been mirrored by similarly large and unprecedented foreign surpluses.

The use of our saving matrix as a context for examining capital formation trends has, so far, relied upon the accounting conventions embodied in the NIPA data. There are a large number of issues where alternative accounting definitions can reasonably be introduced. In the next section we will consider some expanded definitions of saving and examine how they affect our saving matrix.

EXPANDING AND CHANGING THE DEFINITION OF SAVING

In this section we will introduce some changes to the standard definition of saving and see how they affect our measures of saving. The first group of changes will reflect some alternative accounting conven-

FIGURE 7–2a
Business Sector Surplus, 1950–89 (Percent of GNP)

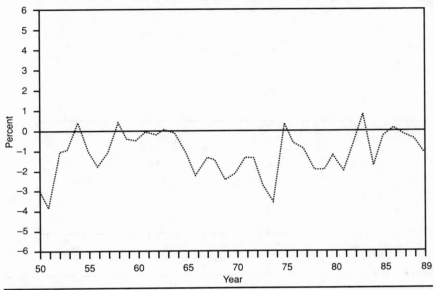

FIGURE 7–2b
Personal Sector Surplus, 1950–89 (Percent of GNP)

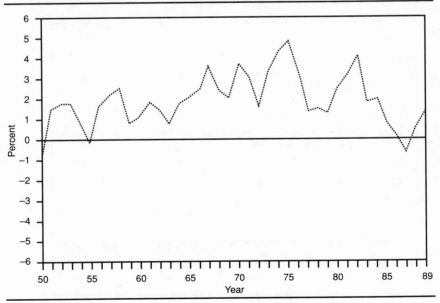

FIGURE 7–2c
Governmental Sector Surplus, 1950–89 (Percent of GNP)

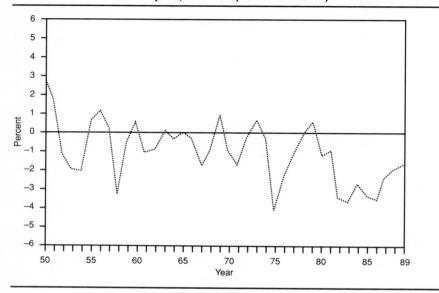

FIGURE 7–2d
Foreign Sector Surplus, 1950–89 (Percent of GNP)

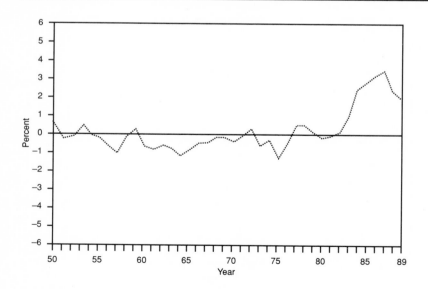

tions which will provide a better measure of saving. The second group will be changes in the definition on saving.

Alternative sectoral allocations. The Flow of Funds (FOF) accounts prepared by the Federal Reserve Board have several important accounting differences with the NIPA. We can use data from the FOF accounts to make some changes in the sectoral allocation of saving in our matrices. These changes do not alter the overall or aggregate saving rates.

Two alterations in the sectoral allocation of saving will be introduced:

a. The NIPA treatment of housing expenditure is a well known peculiarity. All housing expenditure is a business sector investment. For owner occupied housing, imputations are made for expenditures on rental services and for rental income. These are by far the largest imputations in the accounts. This fictional business treatment of owner occupied housing is inappropriate for our examination of the components of saving since such investments are personal and not business sector decisions. As a consequence, our NIPA saving matrix (Table 7–1) classifies all housing expenditures as gross investment by the personal sector. However, some part of it is truly a business sector activity and should remain in that sector.

The FOF individual's saving account can be used to isolate owner occupied housing from the rest (nonfarm, multifamily residential structures owned by businesses and some other minor categories). We use the FOF information to put all of the nonowner occupied housing expenditure and capital consumption back into the business sector. This results in a decrease in household investment and depreciation and increases for the business sector. Since overall outlays and income in each sector are unchanged by this reallocation, the sectoral net saving remains the same, although the sectoral surpluses change. The household surplus increases and the business sector surplus decreases. The changes are small but noticeable; nonowner occupied housing expenditures are usually less than 1 percent of GNP.

b. The NIPA treats private and public sector life insurance and pension fund reserves differently, while the FOF accounts treats them consistently. For the private sector, the net accumulation of reserves is considered to be part of personal savings. That is, the reserves accrue to the ultimate owners or beneficiaries. In the NIPA, public sector reserves are part of government saving. The inconsistency has become important in recent years as public sector pension reserves have grown rapidly.[6]

We will adopt the consistent FOF treatment of the public and private sectors. Public sector insurance and pension fund reserves will be moved from the government sector and added to personal sector saving. This has the consequence of increasing personal saving and reducing government saving.

Figures 7–3a–c show the sectoral surplus for the business, personal and government sectors after these two reallocations. Comparison with Figures 7–2a–d shows that the decline in the government surplus is more profound and the decline in the personal surplus is less profound than with the standard NIPA definitions.

Expanded Definition of Saving. We now introduce two important changes in the definition of saving. They involve areas where the NIPA do not capitalize expenditure. The first is expenditure on consumer durable goods which is treated as current expenditure in the NIPA, but as investment expenditure in the FOF accounts. The second is capital expenditures made by the government sector. Both U.S. accounting schemes treat all public expenditure as current expenditure, although it is common in many national accounts to capitalize public sector investment.

a. The largest difference between the NIPA and FOF views of saving is the treatment of consumer durable expenditures. The FOF accounts and many economists view durables as investment goods. Thus, personal sector gross investment expenditures should be increased because durable goods are a substantial part of consumer expenditures. Depreciation goes up as well and the impact on saving is small but not insignificant. The personal sector surplus is unaffected by this change.

b. In the U.S., it is not common to distinguish between government sector consumption and investment expenditures. However, increasing concern about our investment in public infrastructure is likely to focus attention on government capital formation.[7] Furthermore, data are available to make the distinction. The BEA prepares data on government stocks of capital, investment expenditures and depreciation. These data can be used to create capital account entries for the government sector and to adjust the government sector saving.

The adjusted government sector net saving adds net physical investment by the government to the previously measured surplus. The sectoral surplus is unchanged by the capitalization of government investment.

FIGURE 7–3a
Business Sector Surplus After Reallocations, 1950–89 (Percent of GNP)

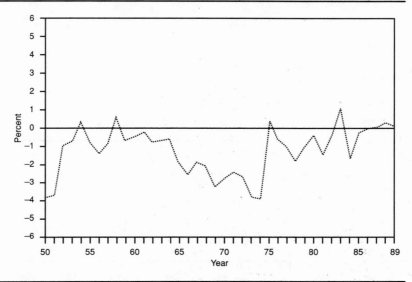

FIGURE 7–3b
Personal Sector Surplus After Reallocations, 1950–89 (Percent of GNP)

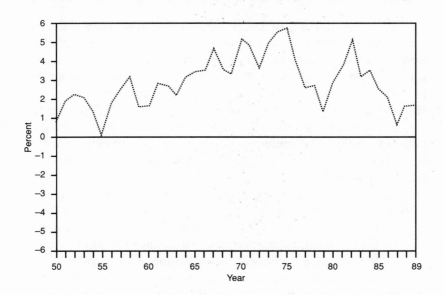

FIGURE 7–3c
Government Sector Surplus After Reallocations, 1950–89 (Percent of GNP)

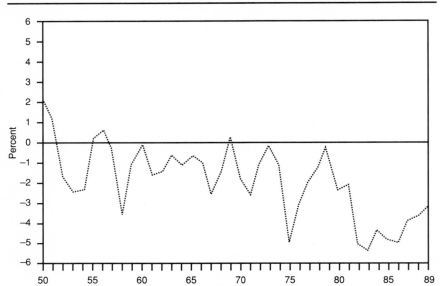

The capitalization of government investment raises a difficult issue because a substantial fraction of the government's capital formation is military structures and equipment.[8] Since such expenditures are for the most part not investments in infrastructure that contribute to productive activity, it is logical to exclude them from national saving. However, insofar as government capital goods provide the infrastructure required for growth in the private sector, they should be a part of national saving. The preferred treatment of government investment is to include only nonmilitary capital expenditures. This is the approach that we will take.[9]

Tables 7–3a–d show the decadal averages for the expanded saving matrices. These data reflect all the changes discussed in this section:

- the reallocation of nonowner occupied housing expenditures,
- the reallocation of government insurance saving,
- the capitalization of consumer durable goods, and
- the capitalization of nonmilitary government investment goods.

A comparison of Tables 7–3a–d with Tables 7–2a–d indicates some

TABLE 7–3a
Expanded Savings Matrix, 1950–59

Sector	Gross Investment	– Depreciation	+ Sectoral Surplus	= Net Saving
Personal	13.76%	7.72%	1.72%	7.76%
Business	11.36	7.39	–1.19	2.79
Government	3.32	1.66	–0.65	1.01
Foreign	0.00	0.00	1.68	1.68
Discrepancy	0.00	0.00	–0.13	–0.13
Total	28.44	16.76	0.00	11.68

Total Net Saving	11.68%
+ Depreciation	16.76%
+ Net Foreign Investment	0.13%
= Gross Investment	28.57%
– Statistical Discrepancy	0.24%
= Gross Saving	28.33%

TABLE 7–3b
Expanded Savings Matrix, 1960–69

Sector	Gross Investment	– Depreciation	+ Sectoral Surplus	= Net Saving
Personal	12.15%	7.70%	3.07%	7.52%
Business	12.01	7.15	–1.37	3.48
Government	3.50	1.57	–0.92	1.00
Foreign	0.00	0.00	–0.62	–0.62
Discrepancy	0.00	0.00	–0.16	–0.16
Total	27.66	16.43	0.00	11.23

Total Net Saving	11.23%
+ Depreciation	16.43%
+ Net Foreign Investment	0.62%
= Gross Investment	28.28%
– Statistical Discrepancy	–0.16%
= Gross Saving	28.43%

TABLE 7–3c
Expanded Savings Matrix, 1970–79

Sector	Gross Investment	− Depreciation	+ Sectoral Surplus	= Net Saving
Personal	12.78%	7.97%	4.05%	8.86%
Business	12.38	8.04	−1.90	2.44
Government	2.81	1.80	−1.91	−0.90
Foreign	0.00	0.00	−0.23	−0.23
Discrepancy	0.00	0.00	−0.03	−0.03
Total	27.96	17.81	−0.01	10.15

Total Net Saving	10.15%
+ Depreciation	17.81%
+ Net Foreign Investment	0.23%
= Gross Investment	28.18%
− Statistical Discrepancy	−0.03%
= Gross Saving	28.21%

TABLE 7–3d
Expanded Savings Matrix, 1980–89

Sector	Gross Investment	− Depreciation	+ Sectoral Surplus	= Net Saving
Personal	12.85%	8.22%	2.71%	7.35%
Business	11.31	9.39	−0.23	1.70
Government	2.14	1.68	−4.06	−3.61
Foreign	0.00	0.00	1.68	1.68
Discrepancy	0.00	0.00	−0.11	−0.11
Total	26.30	19.29	−0.01	7.01

Total Net Saving	7.01%
+ Depreciation	19.29%
+ Net Foreign Investment	−1.68%
= Gross Investment	24.61%
− Statistical Discrepancy	−0.11%
= Gross Saving	24.72%

important differences in the way we should view trends in saving behavior.

First of all, the role of the government deficits in the 1980s is even more striking in the expanded saving matrix. In 20 years the government sector has changed from a net saver (by 1 percent of GNP) to a large dissaver with a sectoral deficit or drain on the other sectors of 4 percent of GNP. Second, as business sector saving has declined, the sector has also become less of a drain on the other sectors. It is clear that the higher levels of business sector saving would require higher external financing (a smaller surplus) which is probably simply not available. Third, the decline in personal sector saving is not as large in the expanded data. Finally, the uniqueness of the 1980s is still apparent with the expanded data; net and gross saving are smaller than in any other decade.

CONCLUSION

The saving matrices introduced here are a suggested way of viewing data that are by and large already familiar. I have made the suggestion because these matrices are, I believe, both a more convenient and more informative way of looking at the data. The matrix structure draws upon Flow of Funds concepts to present NIPA data. The FOF accounts are conceptually admirable but are, in actuality, little used because the data are often viewed as unreliable. Our presentation here retains the familiar and trusted NIPA data and applies some of the useful conceptualizations from FOF.

Furthermore, the matrix framework allows for easy changes in the definition of saving. Thus, we have introduced some extensions to the definition of saving from the FOF data and additional BEA data which result in a better definition of saving and also change our view of saving behavior in the last 40 years.

Finally, the saving matrix is well suited for introducing additional definitional changes. For example, economists might prefer a very broad definition of saving which equates it with changes in the value of wealth. Thus, price changes leading to accrued capital gains and losses can be viewed as a component of saving broadly defined. A revaluation account could be easily added to our matrix. An additional column could show the revaluations to wealth for each sector and saving could be shown both net and gross of revaluations. Expansion of the basic framework is a topic for future work.

NOTES

1. An improved understanding of saving rates and capital formation is an apt topic for this conference. Arnold Sametz's interest in the topic has a long history which includes our collaborative work in the mid-1970s on the so-called "capital shortage." We concluded then that the discussions of capital shortages were more myth than reality and that a careful view of the data would dispel the myth. In fact, the form of data presentation suggested here draws on some of our earlier forecasts with Flow of Funds data; see Sametz, Wachtel and Shuford (1976) and Sametz and Wachtel (1977).
2. See Blades and Sturm (1982).
3. See Michael Boskin (1990), and Thomas Holloway (1989).
4. Clear examples are the activities of unincorporated businesses and government enterprises whose saving are in the personal and government sectors respectively.
5. The NIPA emphasis on the gross concepts is logical because the initial intent of these accounts is to provide a framework for measuring income and output. However, these aggregates are of lesser interest when our primary interest is the level and allocation of saving.
6. Holloway (1989) indicates that this reallocation is likely to be introduced in the next major revision to the NIPA.
7. See the Congressional Budget Office (1990) for a discussion of these issues.
8. In 1985, total (Federal, State and Local) government gross investment was $152 billion, of which 56 percent was military investment. In recent years, military investment has been a smaller proportion of total net investment (42 percent in 1985).
9. The data on government investment and depreciation are from *Fixed Reproducible Tangible Wealth in the United States, 1925-85* and updates in various issues of the *Survey of Current Business*. The investment data are from Tables B13 (Federal investment less military and State and Local investment) and B7 (government residential capital) and Tables A20 and A26 for depreciation.

REFERENCES

Blades, Derek, and Peter Sturm, "The Concept and Measurement of Saving: The United States and other Industrialized Countries," in *Saving and Government Policy*, pp. 1–30, Federal Reserve Bank of Boston Conference Series, No. 25, 1982.

Boskin, Michael, "Issues in the Measurement and Interpretation of Saving and Wealth," pp. 159–83 in Ernst Berndt and Jack Triplett (eds.), *Fifty Years of Economic Measurement: The Jubilee of the Conference on Research in*

Income and Wealth, Vol. 54, National Bureau of Economic Research Studies in Income and Wealth, University of Chicago Press, 1990.

Congressional Budget Office, U.S. Congress, *The Federal Deficit: Does It Measure the Government's Effect on National Saving?* March 1990.

Holloway, Thomas, "Present NIPA Savings Measures: Their Characteristics and Limitations," in Lipsey and Tice (1989), pp. 21–92.

Lipsey, Robert, and Helen Tice (eds.), The *Measurement of Saving, Investment and Wealth*, National Bureau of Economic Research Studies in Income and Wealth, Volume 52, University of Chicago Press, 1989.

Sametz, Arnold; Paul Wachtel; and Harry Shuford, "Capital Shortages: Myth or Reality?" *Journal of Finance, 31,* May 1976.

Sametz, Arnold, and Paul Wachtel (eds.), *Understanding Capital Markets, Volume II: The Financial Environment and the Flow of Funds in the Next Decade*, Lexington Books, 1977.

U.S. Department of Commerce, Bureau of Economic Analysis, *Fixed Reproducible Tangible Wealth in the United States, 1925-85*, U.S. Government Printing Office, 1987.

Wachtel, Paul, "Household Savings and Wealth in 1985: A Judgmental Forecast," in Sametz and Wachtel (1977), pp. 97–110.

Wachtel, Paul, "Comment" on Holloway in Lipsey and Tice (1989), pp. 93–100.

PART THREE

U.S. FINANCIAL INSTITUTIONS IN THE 1990s

CHAPTER 8

THE DISAPPEARING SYNDICATE

Ernest Bloch

During the decade of the 1980s, the century-old mechanism for issuing new corporate debt, the syndicate, has undergone a startling and fundamental change: It is disappearing. The purpose of this paper will be to spell out how, in the past, a large group of industry members was mobilized to spread the risk in floating a new issue; how the same group distributed the new bonds; and, finally, why such arrangements are no longer deemed to be necessary today even though the volume of bond flotations keeps growing.

The typical syndicate consists of a group of broker/dealer firms associated for a single, specific, bond flotation. Syndicates perform two functions: they buy the new issue from the *selling* corporation, which raises a large amount of new money in one batch at one time. Subsequently, the syndicate distributes the new issue to investors who are the ultimate *buyers* of the issue. The process, called *underwriting*, typically takes five business days: At the closing, the corporation receives a check (the "proceeds") from the syndicate manager for the full amount of the issue. By this process two risk-taking services are performed by the syndicate members:[1]

1. They take on the *flotation risk*, which consists of pricing the new

Ernest Bloch is the C. W. Gerstenberg Professor of Finance at Stern School, New York University. Support from the Yamaichi Curriculum Fund is gratefully acknowledged.

issue in a market in which a rise in rates can occur before the issue is fully distributed.
2. They take on *distribution risk*. Suppose that, during syndicate flotation, bonds don't sell (for any reason). Nevertheless, the issuing corporation will get its money whether the bonds are all sold or not.

Compensation to the syndicate members for taking on these risks comes from the difference between the (higher) price per bond paid by the public, and the (lower) price paid by the syndicate to the issuing corporation. From the point of view of that corporation, that difference (called the "gross spread") is its flotation cost. And during the time that the syndicate is maintained, the price to the public is fixed under U.S. rules. Below, the discussion will cover, first, how the process worked at the beginning of the 1980s. The second part of the paper will indicate how, and how much, the process has changed, and we will conclude with a discussion of the rationale for the change.

THE BEGINNING

The decade of the 1980s could be said to have begun with the first-ever $1 billion syndicate offering of industrial bonds. That was the IBM financing of October 4, 1979;[2] the syndicate consisted of 220 different firms (see Appendix 1). The securities were priced on October 4, and opened for trading on October 5. In an environment of continuing inflation, and even stronger inflationary expectations, sales began slowly and remained sluggish to the end of that week. During the weekend, the (then new) chairman of the Board of Governors of the Federal Reserve, Paul Volcker, announced that henceforward the Fed would execute monetary policy differently. Instead of setting and maintaining interest rate *levels*, (and thereby tending to stabilize new-issue prices), monetary policy targets would now be specified in the form of the money supply, allowing interest rates to float. In that inflationary environment money supply growth was tightened, and rates rose sharply; as a result, bond prices plummeted. On Monday, October 11, 1979, rate levels and the discount rate were sharply higher—and rising—and participants in the IBM bond syndicate with unsold bonds lost money. Indeed, with that Fed policy change, the age of rate volatility had begun and with it the decade of corporate-style and institutional-size investment banking.

THE CHANGING FINANCIAL ENVIRONMENT: RESPONSES TO MARKET VOLATILITY

The 1987 collapse of stock prices on October 19, the dramatic recovery the next day, and further sharp price fluctuations in 1989—both down and up—have called attention to stock market price volatility. Public perception of price volatility has focussed on equity markets although, as the following will show, fixed income securities have experienced a far greater rise in volatility during the 1980s than have equities.

Figures 8–1a and 8–1b below summarize a study done by the Federal Reserve Bank of Kansas City.[3] In that study, volatility is measured by annual standard deviations of monthly returns (for equities and for bonds). As the charts indicate, the volatility of *stock* returns since the outliers experienced during the Great Depression has remained within the same general range, including the decades of the 1950s, 60s, 70s and 1980s. By contrast, the volatility of bond returns has, since 1950, been widening, and by ever increasing amplitudes. Indeed, the greatest surge in volatility occurred during the years 1979–80. This was just prior to the period when shelf-registration was first authorized by the SEC (Rule 415) in March 1982 on a temporary basis. The rule was made permanent in March 1983.

The relevance of the shelf-registration mechanism to bond price volatility can be understood when considered from an issuer's point of view. Consider the preshelf mechanics required before an issue was declared "effective" by SEC—that is, before it was permitted to be sold to the public. Prior to March 1982, and the promulgation of SEC's rule 415, the customary examination process at the SEC of a new issue prospectus could take between four to six weeks (or longer) before an issue was declared "effective" for flotation. In an environment of stable interest rates, the expected cash proceeds from an issue of securities— or the expected interest rate or cost of capital—could be anticipated over such a period with some assurance. But as rate volatility surged in the late 1970s and early 1980s, and as monetary policy execution was changed, the four- to six-week wait imposed an unpredictable— and usually increasing—cost of capital over and above the expected interest rate. A mere market change, namely a rise in volatility, thus tended to increase the cost of capital and hence reduced the expected value of a publicly financed investment. That rise in volatility also raised flotation risks to underwriters.

FIGURE 8–1a
Volatility [a] **of Stock Returns, 1918–88**

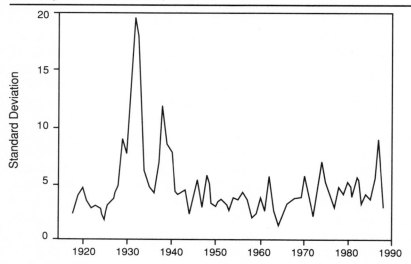

[a] In this chart, volatility is measured by the annual standard deviation of monthly stock returns.

Source: Center for Research in Security Prices.

FIGURE 8–1b
Volatility [a] **of Treasury Bond Yields, 1926–87**

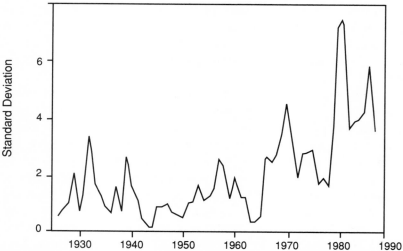

[a] In this chart, volatility is measured by the annual standard deviation of a 20-year Treasury bond index.

Source: Center for Research in Security Prices.

Consider the fact that prior to the 1980s' surge in volatility a normal fluctuation in rates over a six-week period would be placed at a 1/16 or a 1/32. Now, over lesser time periods, *rate* changes in long Treasuries would be calculated by 1/2 of a percentage point, or more. In the latter case, because of an unanticipated rate change, a project to be financed could be moved out of the positive present value group, and thus be no longer acceptable. But, meanwhile, the new issue would have been put through its necessary preliminaries by the managing underwriter and other members of the syndicate. This includes the required legal and accounting due diligence, as well as the preliminary marketing activities. The sunk costs already incurred when the issue is declared effective, at last, would make the issuer's ultimate decision—go or no go— a more difficult one at best. It was, in fact, the addition of the cost of uncertainty to the cost of capital that generated the demand for shelf registration.

To be sure, by reducing the risk to issuers by making shelf registration available, other costs were generated, costs that were not exactly foreseen. For example, opposition to shelf registration was based mainly on the difficulties anticipated with the shortness of the preissue period, and the anticipated reduction of due diligence efforts. This view was countered by actual experience that, when shelf registration was offered, it applied mainly to those large corporations whose full disclosure requirements (under the Securities Exchange Act) at all times for their already outstanding issues made "due diligence" for them a continuous process. In other words, for large firms, due diligence did not become operative only with a new-issue prospectus.[4]

DEBT VERSUS EQUITY FINANCING

In connection with shelf registration it is important to understand that most new financing comes as *debt* securities, and not as equities. As Figure 8–2 shows, in 1981 and in 1982 about $25 billion of new stock issues was placed in the US capital markets. In 1986 and 1987, in the great bull market, gross equity proceeds came to about $50 billion per year.[5] But during those same two years, bond proceeds were $300 billion each, an amount about six times greater than equity proceeds. In the earlier years of the 1980s, dollar bond proceeds were three to five times as great as equities. Thus we see that, despite a surge to a record in debt volatility and in interest rate levels that exceeded prior

FIGURE 8–2
Corporate Security Issues—Annual Totals of Gross Proceeds, 1950–1987

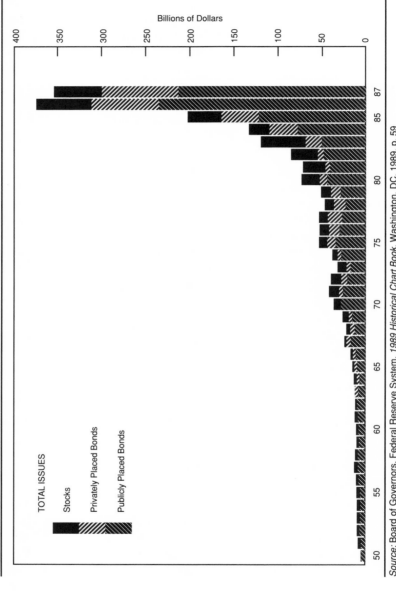

Source: Board of Governors, Federal Reserve System, *1989 Historical Chart Book*, Washington, DC, 1989, p. 59

history, while equity volatility remained in a roughly comparable range, the *volume* of debt flotation surged nonetheless in dollar value and in multiples of equity flotations.

CHANGES IN UNDERWRITING

For most outsiders, the quintessential investment banking activity is the flotation of new issues. And the major changes in the financial environment—greater institutionalization and greater variance—have led to a totally unanticipated result: the syndicate process is disappearing for bond issues. Consider the changes that took place in the underwriting agreement between the beginning of the decade and its end.

The $1 billion IBM flotation that initiated the decade of the eighties had *228* separate underwriting firms (see Appendix 1). The two managing underwriters for the IBM issue each signed up for about $125 million of securities. To indicate the "retail" orientation of that issue consider that more than 40 firms that signed the underwriting agreement each accepted a position—and thus were at risk for—*less* than $1/2 million bonds and notes in the offering. By contrast, in late October 1989, Ford Motor Credit Corp. floated a $3 billion issue of asset-backed certificates (of car installment sales contracts; see Appendix 2). The entire underwriting group consisted of five firms, as Table 8–1 indicates. Further, of those five firms, the two lead managers underwrote $2.9 billion out of the $3 billion. In short, First Boston and Goldman underwrote about 95 percent of the $3 billion Ford issue, whereas 10 years earlier Salomon and Merrill together only took down

TABLE 8–1
Underwriters of the Ford Credit Corporation 1989 Bond and Note Offering

Underwriters	Principal Amount of Certificates
The First Boston Corporation	$1,434,411,190,64
Goldman, Sachs & Co.	1,434,410,000.00
Merrill Lynch, Pierce, Fenner & Smith Inc.	59,000,000.00
Salomon Brothers Inc	59,000,000.00
Shearson Lehman Hutton Inc.	59,000,000.00
Total	$3,045,821,190.64

Source: See Appendix 2

about 25 percent of the IBM $1 billion issue. Another interesting side-light: the underwriting discount (or gross spread) for the IBM issue came to $7.5 million (on $1 billion raised), or 0.75 percent. On the $3 billion Ford issue, the gross spread came to about $6.9 million, or a bit above 0.2 percent (or 2/10 of 1 percent). These changes in syndicate structure and the decline in flotation costs will now be examined in a broader context.

Figure 8–3 covers flotation of fixed income securities by method of issue: nonsyndicated as a ratio to total flotations. In that context, nonsyndicated means flotation by lead-managers alone, without a syndicate. In the first two years shown, when shelf registration was not yet available, only a tiny fraction of securities sold was not syndicated (called non-U in Appendix 3). With the advent of shelf registration, however, in 1982, nearly a quarter of the sum of shelf-registered and nonshelf issues (by dollar value) was sold without syndicates. By 1983, that proportion had risen to about one third, and in the years 1984–87, the proportion sold without syndication held in the neighborhood of one half of total debt flotations. Over the last two years shown, the

FIGURE 8–3
Nonsyndicated Share of Value of U.S. Debt Underwritings

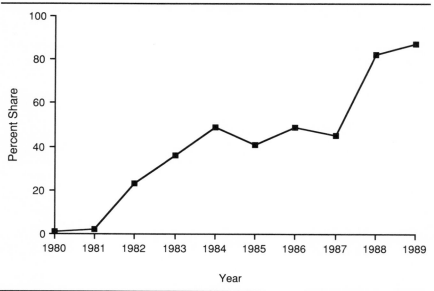

Source: Securities Data Co.

proportions sold solely by managers rose to 4/5 and to about 90 percent, respectively.

Table 8–2 and Figure 8–4 indicate that, for investment-grade debt, the decline in the use of syndicates was associated with declines in flotation costs.[6] Thus the ratio of fees paid (called gross spread) by investment grade borrowers to underwriters declined on average from about $8 per $1,000 bond in 1980 to about $4.50 per bond in 1989 (Table 8–2 and Figure 8–4). In other words, flotation costs fell for investment grade corporate borrowers. And this cost decline took place in step with the rise in the nonsyndicated proportion of bond flotations. Between 1980 and 1983, when the nonsyndicated proportion was held to a third or less, the underwriting fee ratio to bond proceeds was held to the neighborhood of 0.8 of 1 percent (for proportions of nonsyndicated flotations see Figure 8–3).

Now consider that, when the share of nonsyndicated flotations rose to about half of all new issues in the period 1984–87, the fee ratio dropped to between 0.6 percent and 0.7 percent.[7] In the last two years shown, when the nonsyndicated share rose to 80 and 90 percent, fee ratios fell further to 1/2 of 1 percent or less. And, as the last column of Table 8–2 indicates, the average size of investment grade issues kept on climbing during the decade.

TABLE 8–2
Flotation of Investment Grade Corporate Debt, Underwriting Spreads and Average Issue Size, 1980–89

Year	(1) Gross Spread ($ mill.)	(2) Gross Proceeds ($ mill.)	(3) Gross Spread Ratio [(1)/(2)] (%)	(4) Number of Issues Floated (#)	(5) Average Issue Size [(2)/(4)] ($ mill.)
1980	282	35,374	0.80	373	95
1981	270	33,864	0.80	346	98
1982	307	36,984	0.83	447	83
1983	234	30,032	0.78	334	90
1984	229	39,175	0.58	329	119
1985	410	62,173	0.66	515	121
1986	825	117,921	0.70	878	134
1987	549	89,683	0.61	686	131
1988	474	92,614	0.51	582	159
1989	486	108,793	0.45	645	169

Source: Securities Data Company, Inc.

FIGURE 8–4
Flotation Costs ª of Investment-Grade Bonds, 1980–89

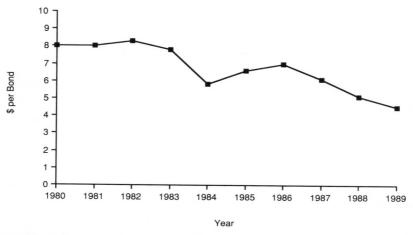

Year

ª Annual Gross Spread as percent of proceeds.

Source: Table 8–2, column 3

Why have the major investment banking firms accepted such seeming increases in flotation risks? And why have they done this in an environment of generally declining overall returns? And how have they been able to distribute such large amounts of bonds by themselves?

The answer has to be threefold:

1. The larger risks to managing underwriters of floating issues without using industry members to spread risk, or without syndicate support, can be managed by hedging risks in a futures (or options on bond futures) market, and at a reasonable cost.[8] In consequence, competition among the major firms to underwrite the maximum volume of securities has resulted in driving down gross spreads—that is, total flotation costs. Of course, the managing underwriters now collect the entirety of gross spread. But why is the competition (at declining spreads and at rising hedge costs) so intense?

2. In part the growing institutionalization on the *buy*-side (pension funds, insurance firms, mutual funds, etc.) and associated expansion of average trade size has reduced, if not eliminated, the usefulness of small securities firms as distributors for new bond

issues. Most selling groups today consist exclusively of major bracket firms.

3. Finally, and in a seemingly perverse way, the pressure to compete for underwriting business probably has intensified among special bracket firms as the total business volume of investment bankers contracts. This is so because declining volume reveals excess capacity and/or capital that needs to be employed to maintain the banker's own stock price. (Recall that today all but one of the major bracket firms are organized as *corporate* units.) For the bidder-underwriter it then becomes increasingly important to show as good a number as possible in the "league tables" (Appendix 4) of securities underwriting. And a good show in the league tables is believed by major securities firms to be an essential component of successful marketing schemes for mergers and acquisitions, large-scale secondary dealer trades, asset-backed securities, and all other transactions. From the *issuers'* point of view, that kind of competition has led to reduced flotation costs.

CONCLUSIONS

The foregoing has indicated that new-issue flotation, like other aspects of the investment banking business, has undergone a fundamental change in the decade of the eighties. That core component—new-issue bond financing—has now, in the 1990s, become a competitive oligopoly where the countervailing powers of the buy side—the institutional investors—and of the sell side—the large-scale issuers—press the much smaller number of intermediaries (the investment bankers) to provide fast and good service at declining flotation revenues to latter. The change in the underwriting process itself has substituted a hedging strategy by less than a handful of managing underwriters for the use of an industry-wide syndicate to spread risks. Likewise, the institutionalization of the marketplace requires *institutional* investment bankers to sell institution-sized pieces in each new issue. The broad-based syndicate has withered away.

What these changes have produced with respect to industry organization and structure is ironic: At the time when competition has sharply cut flotation costs to issuers and to buyers, the underwriters are closer to a true oligopoly than before. An oligopoly was, of course, the presumptive industry structure that led, in 1947, to a Department of Justice antitrust suit. (Ultimately, in 1953, that suit was dismissed by Judge Medina.) It is worth noting that the group thought to "monopolize" the new-issues business in 1947 consisted of 17 firms rather than the handful of investment bankers (literally) that provides 90 percent of flotation services today.

NOTES

1. Please note that none of the risks discussed refer to credit risks. Most new bond issues are investment grade.
2. The financing included $500 million of 9 1/2 percent notes and $500 million of 9 3/8 percent debentures. The prospectus date was October 4, 1979, and the issue became effective October 5, 1979.
3. S. Becketti and G. H. Sellon, Jr., "Has Financial Market Volatility Increased," *Economic Review,* Federal Reserve Bank of Kansas City, June 1989, pp. 17–30.
4. That is why many new-issue prospectuses under Rule 415 simply made reference to previously issued financials and presented only current data. Audited data covering previous five years thus were incorporated into the document "by reference" only. For further discussion, see E. Bloch, *Inside Investment Banking,* (2d edition), Dow Jones-Irwin, 1989, especially chapter 16.
5. Net equity proceeds, that is, gross issues less repurchases, were *negative.*
6. Only high-grade debt is discussed here to avoid the rise and fall of junk debt flotations that occurred in the second half of the decade. Junk debt issues carry much higher gross spreads.
7. In the period 1984–87, syndicates had shrunk to an intermediate position of including major bracket firms almost exclusively.
8. The following is a brief explanation of the hedge problem and of the hedging mechanism. The problem exists because, for the syndicate manager, the basic payoff is asymmetrical. Since the (new) security *must* be sold at the stated price to public, a rise in market prices results in an immediate sellout, with capital gains accruing to market investors *only.* If market prices fall, the syndicate is stuck with unsold bonds *that can be sold only at stated price* until the syndicate is formally dissolved. Only at that point can syndicate members individually decide to take their losses. If interest rates are a stochastic variable, hedging in futures market with matched duration could leave syndicate with the *uncovered* hedged position if rates fall. Perhaps the most rational hedge for bond syndicate is an option on Treasury bond futures developed in over-the-counter market. This latter set of ideas will be explored further in a subsequent paper.

APPENDIX 1 TO CHAPTER 8

IBM PROSPECTUS EXCERPTS

Prospectus

$1,000,000,000

International Business Machines Corporation

$500,000,000
9 ½% Notes Due 1986

$500,000,000
9 ⅜% Debentures Due 2004

Interest on the Notes is payable semi-annually on April 1 and October 1 beginning April 1, 1980. The Notes are redeemable on or after October 1, 1983 at the option of the Company, in whole or in part, at their principal amount plus accrued interest.

Interest on the Debentures is payable semi-annually on April 1 and October 1 beginning April 1, 1980. The Debentures are redeemable at any time at the option of the Company, in whole in part, at declining premiums. Prior to October 1, 1989, no such redemption may be made from or in anticipation of borrowed funds having an annual interest cost of less than 9.415%. In addition, a mandatory sinking fund beginning October 1, 1985 will be sufficient to retire at par 95% of the aggregate principal amount of the Debentures prior to maturity. The Company may increase its sinking fund payment in any year by an additional amount up to 150% of the mandatory sinking fund payment of that year.

The Notes and Debentures have been approved for listing on the New York Stock Exchange subject to official notice of issuance.

THESE SECURITIES HAVE NOT BEEN APPROVED OR DISAPPROVED BY THE SECURITIES AND EXCHANGE COMMISSION NOR HAS THE COMMISSION PASSED UPON THE ACCURACY OR ADEQUACY OF THIS PROSPECTUS. ANY REPRESENTATION TO THE CONTRARY IS A CRIMINAL OFFENSE.

	Price to Public(1)	Underwriting Discount	Proceeds to Company(1)(2)
Per Note	99.400%	.625%	98.775%
Total	$497,000,000	$3,125,000	$493,875,000
Per Debenture	99.625%	.875%	98.750%
Total	$498,125,000	$4,375,000	$493,750,000

(1) Plus accrued interest, if any, from October 16, 1979 to date of delivery.
(2) Before deducting expenses payable by the Company estimated to be $850,000.

The Notes and Debentures are offered when, as and if accepted by the Underwriters named herein, subject to prior sale or withdrawal, cancellation or modification of the offers without notice, and subject to the approval of certain legal matters by counsel. It is expected that delivery of the Notes and Debentures will be made at the office of Salomon Brothers, One New York Plaza, New York, New York, or through the facilities of The Depository Trust Company, on or about October 16, 1979.

Salomon Brothers   Merrill Lynch White Weld Capital Markets Group
Merrill Lynch, Pierce, Fenner & Smith Incorporated

The date of this Prospectus is October 4, 1979.

If an Event of Default shall have occurred and be continuing, the principal of all the Note or Debentures may be declared to be due and payable immediately by either the Trustee or the holders of 25% in principal amount thereof, but upon certain conditions such declaration may be annulled and past defaults (except continuing payment defaults and defaults in respect of certain covenants) may be waived by the holders of a majority in principal amount of the Notes or the Debentures then outstanding. (§§ 7-2 and 7-13 of the Indentures)

The holders of a majority in principal amount of the outstanding Notes or Debentures will have the right to direct the time, method and place of conducting any proceeding for any remedy available to the Trustee under the applicable Indenture, provided that they shall have offered to the Trustee reasonable indemnity against expenses and liabilities. (§§ 7-12 and 8-3 of the Indentures) Each Indenture will require the annual filing by the Company with the Trustee of a certificate as to compliance with the terms of such Indenture. (§ 5-4 of the Indentures)

Modification of the Indentures; Waiver of Covenants

With the consent of the holders of not less than 66⅔% in principal amount of the outstanding Notes or Debentures the Company may modify the applicable Indenture in any way except to change the due dates of principal or interest, or to reduce the amount of principal (or premium, if any) or interest, or to reduce the foregoing percentage. (§ 9-2 of the Indentures) The holders of a majority in principal amount of the outstanding Notes or Debentures may waive the Company's compliance with the covenants in the applicable Indenture limiting Secured Indebtedness and sale and leaseback transactions described under "Certain Covenants of the Company". (§ 5-7 of the Indentures)

The Trustee

Morgan Guaranty Trust Company of New York will be the Trustee under both Indentures. Mr. Frank T. Cary, Chairman of the Board and Chief Executive Officer of the Company, is a director of the Trustee. The Trustee is a depository for funds and performs other services for, and transacts other banking business with, the Company in the normal course of business. In addition, the Trustee is one of the banks with which the Company maintains a line of credit as described under "Use of Proceeds".

UNDERWRITING

Subject to the terms and conditions set forth in the Underwriting Agreement, the Company has agreed to sell to each of the Underwriters named below, and each of the Underwriters, for whom Salomon Brothers and Merrill Lynch, Pierce, Fenner & Smith, Incorporated are acting as Representatives, has severally agreed to purchase, the respective amount of Notes and Debentures set forth opposite its name below:

Underwriter	Principal Amount of Notes	Principal Amount of Debentures
Salomon Brothers	$62,175,000	$62,175,000
Merrill Lynch, Pierce, Fenner & Smith Incorporated	62,175,000	62,175,000
Morgan Stanley & Co. Incorporated	20,000,000	20,000,000
The First Boston Corporation	10,000,000	10,000,000
Goldman, Sachs & Co	10,000,000	10,000,000
Bache Halsey Stuart Shields Incorporated	7,500,000	7,500,000
Bear, Stearns & Co	7,500,000	7,500,000
Blyth Eastman Dillon & Co. Incorporated	7,500,000	7,500,000
Dillon, Read & Co., Inc.	7,500,000	7,500,000

7

Underwriter	Principal Amount of Notes	Principal Amount of Debentures
Donaldson, Lufkin & Jenrette Securities Corporation	$7,500,000	$7,500,000
Drexel Burnham Lambert Incorporated	7,500,000	7,500,000
E. F. Hutton & Company Inc.	7,500,000	7,500,000
Kidder, Peabody & Co. Incorporated	7,500,000	7,500,000
Lazard Frères & Co.	7,500,000	7,500,000
Lehman Brothers Kuhn Loeb Incorporated	7,500,000	7,500,000
Paine, Webber, Jackson & Curtis Incorporated	7,500,000	7,500,000
L. F. Rothschild, Unterberg, Towbin	7,500,000	7,500,000
Shearson Hayden Stone Inc.	7,500,000	7,500,000
Smith Barney, Harris Upham & Co. Incorporated	7,500,000	7,500,000
Warburg Paribus Pecker Incorporated	7,500,000	7,500,000
Wertheim & Co., Inc.	7,500,000	7,500,000
Dean Witter Reynolds Inc.	7,500,000	7,500,000
ABD Securities Corporation	3,500,000	3,500,000
Allen & Company Incorporated	3,500,000	3,500,000
A. E. Ames & Co. Incorporated	3,500,000	3,500,000
Atlantic Capital Corporation	3,500,000	3,500,000
Basle Securities Corporation	3,500,000	3,500,000
Alex. Brown & Sons	3,500,000	3,500,000
Daiwa Securities America Inc.	3,500,000	3,500,000
F. Eberstadt & Co., Inc.	3,500,000	3,500,000
A. G. Edwards & Sons, Inc.	3,500,000	3,500,000
EuroPartners Securities Corporation	3,500,000	3,500,000
Robert Fleming Incorporated	3,500,000	3,500,000
Hudson Securities, Inc.	3,500,000	3,500,000
Kleinwort, Benson Incorporated	3,500,000	3,500,000
Ladenburg, Thalmann & Co., Inc.	3,500,000	3,500,000
Moseley, Hallgarten, Estabrook & Weeden Inc.	3,500,000	3,500,000
New Court Securities Corporation	3,500,000	3,500,000
The Nikko Securities Co. International, Inc.	3,500,000	3,500,000
Nomura Securities International, Inc.	3,500,000	3,500,000
Oppenheimer & Co., Inc.	3,500,000	3,500,000
Scandinavian Securities Corporation	3,500,000	3,500,000
Stuart Brothers	3,500,000	3,500,000
Thomson McKinnon Securities Inc.	3,500,000	3,500,000
Tucker, Anthony & R. L. Day, Inc.	3,500,000	3,500,000
Wood Gundy Incorporated	3,500,000	3,500,000
Yamaichi International (America), Inc.	3,500,000	3,500,000
Advest, Inc.	1,400,000	1,400,000
Arnhold and S. Bleichroeder, Inc.	1,400,000	1,400,000
Bacon, Whipple & Co.	1,400,000	1,400,000
Robert W. Baird & Co. Incorporated	1,400,000	1,400,000

Underwriter	Principal Amount of Notes	Principal Amount of Debentures
Bateman Eichler, Hill Richards Incorporated	$1,400,000	$1,400,000
Sandford C. Bernstein & Co., Inc.	1,400,000	1,400,000
William Blair & Company	1,400,000	1,400,000
Blaut Ellis & Loewi Incorporated	1,400,000	1,400,000
Boettcher & Company	1,400,000	1,400,000
J. C. Bradford & Co.	1,400,000	1,400,000
Butcher & Singer Inc.	1,400,000	1,400,000
Dain Bosworth Incorporated	1,400,000	1,400,000
Dominion Securities Inc.	1,400,000	1,400,000
Greenshields & Co., Inc.	1,400,000	1,400,000
Janney Montgomery Scott Inc.	1,400,000	1,400,000
McDonald & Company	1,400,000	1,400,000
McLeod Young Weir Incorporated	1,400,000	1,400,000
Nesbitt Thomson Securities, Inc.	1,400,000	1,400,000
Piper, Jaffray & Hopwood Incorporated	1,400,000	1,400,000
Wm. E. Pollock & Co., Inc.	1,400,000	1,400,000
Prescott, Ball & Turben	1,400,000	1,400,000
Rauscher Pierce Resfsnes, Inc.	1,400,000	1,400,000
Richardson Securities Inc.	1,400,000	1,400,000
The Robinson-Humphrey Company, Inc.	1,400,000	1,400,000
Rotan Mosle Inc.	1,400,000	1,400,000
Stephens Inc.	1,400,000	1,400,000
Stone & Youngberg	1,400,000	1,400,000
Sutro & Co. Incorporated	1,400,000	1,400,000
Wheat, First Securities, Inc.	1,400,000	1,400,000
American Securities Corporation	900,000	900,000
Bruns, Nordeman, Rea & Co.	900,000	900,000
Burns Fry and Timmins Inc.	900,000	900,000
The Chicago Corporation	900,000	900,000
Crowell, Weedon & Co.	900,000	900,000
Eppler, Guerin & Turner, Inc.	900,000	900,000
Fahnestock & Co.	900,000	900,000
First Bavarian Capital Corporation	900,000	900,000
First of Michigan Corporation	900,000	900,000
First Southwest Company	900,000	900,000
Folger Nolan Gleming Douglas Incorporated	900,000	900,000
Foster & Marshall Inc.	900,000	900,000
Freeman Securities Company, Inc.	900,000	900,000
Howard, Weil, Labouisse, Friedrichs Incorporated	900,000	900,000
Interstate Securities Corporation	900,000	900,000
Johnston, Lemon & Co. Incorporated	900,000	900,000
Josephithal & Co. Incorporated	900,000	900,000

Underwriter	Principal Amount of Notes	Principal Amount of Debentures
Keefe Bruyette & Woods, Inc.	$900,000	$900,000
Cyrus J. Lawrence Incorporated	900,000	900,000
Legg Mason Wood Walker, Incorporated	900,000	900,000
Montgomery Securities	900,000	900,000
The Ohio Company	900,000	900,000
Parker/Hunter Incorporated	900,000	900,000
Underwood, Neuhaus & Co. Incorporated	900,000	900,000
Burton J. Vincent, Chesley & Co.	900,000	900,000
Birr, Wilson & Co., Inc.	400,000	400,000
Craigie Incorporated	400,000	400,000
Davis, Skaags & Co., Inc.	400,000	400,000
R. G. Dickinson & Co.	400,000	400,000
Doft & Co., Inc.	400,000	400,000
Elkins, Stroud, Suplee & Co.	400,000	400,000
First Albany Corporation	400,000	400,000
Furman Selz Mager Dietz & Birney Incorporated	400,000	400,000
Gruntal & Co.	400,000	400,000
Herzfeld & Stern	400,000	400,000
J. J. B. Hilliard, W. L. Lyonds, Inc.	400,000	400,000
Johnson, Lane, Space, Smith & Co., Inc.	400,000	400,000
Laidlaw Adams & Peck Inc.	400,000	400,000
Midland Doherty Inc.	400,000	400,000
Morgan, Keegan & Company, Inc.	400,000	400,000
Neuberger & Berman	400,000	400,000
New Japan Securities International Inc.	400,000	400,000
Newhard, Cook & Co. Incorporated	400,000	400,000
Nippon Kangyo Kakumaru International, Inc.	400,000	400,000
Phillips, Appel & Walden, Inc.	400,000	400,000
Robertson, Colman, Stephens & Woodman	400,000	400,000
Rodman & Renshaw, Inc.	400,000	400,000
Sanyo Securities America Inc.	400,000	400,000
Scudder Stephens & Clark	400,000	400,000
Stern Brothers & Co.	400,000	400,000
Stifel, Nicolaus & Company Incorporated	400,000	400,000
Arthurs, Lestrange & Short	300,000	300,000
Baker, Watts & Co.	300,000	300,000
Burdge, Daniels & Company, Inc.	300,000	300,000
Colin, Hochstin Co.	300,000	300,000
Cunningham, Schmertz & Co., Inc.	300,000	300,000
Davenport & Co. of Virginia, Inc.	300,000	300,000
Shelby Cullom Davis & Co.	300,000	300,000
Dominick & Dominick, Incorporated	300,000	300,000

10

Underwriter	Principal Amount of Notes	Principal Amount of Debentures
Ferris & Company Incorporated	$300,000	$300,000
Gallagher & Jensen, Inc.	300,000	300,000
J. A. Glynn & Co.	300,000	300,000
Hambrecht & Quist	300,000	300,000
Frank Henjes & Company, Inc.	300,000	300,000
Jesup & Lamont Securities Co., Inc.	300,000	300,000
Kirkpatrick, Pettis, Smith, Polian Inc.	300,000	300,000
Lepercq, de Neuflize & Co., Incorporated	300,000	300,000
A. E. Masten & Co. Incorporate	300,000	300,000
The Milwaukee Company	300,000	300,000
Moore & Schley, Cameron & Co.	300,000	300,000
Morgan, Olmstead, Kennedy & Gardner Incorporated ..	300,000	300,000
Printon, Kane & Co.	300,000	300,000
Wm. C. Roney & Co.	300,000	300,000
R. Rowland & Co., Incorporated	300,000	300,000
Scott & Stringfellow, Inc.	300,000	300,000
Silberberg, Rosenthal & Co.	300,000	300,000
Thomas & Company, Inc.	300,000	300,000
Ultafin International Corporation	300,000	300,000
Wagenseller & Durst, Inc.	300,000	300,000
Wedbush, Noble, Cooke, Inc.	300,000	300,000
Wiley Bros., Inc.	300,000	300,000
Anderson & Strudwick, Incorporated	200,000	200,000
George K. Baum & Company Incorporated	200,000	200,000
Black & Company, Inc.	200,000	200,000
Burgess & Leith Incorporated	200,000	200,000
The Cherokee Securities Company	200,000	200,000
B. C. Christopher & Co.	200,000	200,000
City Securities Corporation	200,000	200,000
C. C. Collings and Company, Inc.	200,000	200,000
Daniels & Bell, Inc.	200,000	200,000
A. Webster Dougherty & Co., Incorporated	200,000	200,000
Ehrlich-Bober & Co., Inc.	200,000	200,000
Equitable Securities Corporation	200,000	200,000
Ernst & Co.	200,000	200,000
Evans & Co., Incorporated	200,000	200,000
First Equity Corporation of Florida	200,000	200,000
First Mid America Inc.	200,000	200,000
First Harlem Securities Corporation	200,000	200,000
Gabelli & Company, Inc.	200,000	200,000
Hanifen, Imhoff & Samford, Inc.	200,000	200,000
Wm. P. Harper & Son & Company	200,000	200,000

Underwriter	Principal Amount of Notes	Principal Amount of Debentures
Howe, Barnes & Johnson, Inc.	$200,000	$200,000
The Illinois Company Incorporated	$200,000	$200,000
Kolb & Company	$200,000	$200,000
Kormendi, Byrd Brothers, Inc.	$200,000	$200,000
Manley, Bennett, McDonald & Co.	$200,000	$200,000
John Muir & Co.	$200,000	$200,000
W. H. Newbold's Son & Co., Inc.	$200,000	$200,000
J. A. Overton & Co.	$200,000	$200,000
Raffensperger, Hughs & Co., Inc.	$200,000	$200,000
Ross Stebbins Inc.	$200,000	$200,000
John J. Ryan & Co.	$200,000	$200,000
Scharff & Jones Incorporated	$200,000	$200,000
Schneider, Bernet, & Hickman, Inc.	$200,000	$200,000
Seasongood & Mayer...	$200,000	$200,000
Securities Corporation of Iowa	$200,000	$200,000
Seidler, Arnett & Spillane Incorporated	$200,000	$200,000
I. M. Simon & Co.	$200,000	$200,000
Stix & Co. Inc.	$200,000	$200,000
Sweney Cartwright & Co.	$200,000	$200,000
Henry F. Swift & Co.	$200,000	$200,000
Wm. Sword & Co., Incorporated	$200,000	$200,000
Traub and Company, Inc.	$200,000	$200,000
Van Kasper & Company Incorporated	$200,000	$200,000
Edward A. Viner & Co., Inc.	$200,000	$200,000
Wako Securities California Inc.	$200,000	$200,000
Young, Smith & Peacock, Inc.	$200,000	$200,000
Abu Dhabi Investment Company	1,250,000	1,250,000
Banco de la Nación Argentina	1,250,000	1,250,000
Banco do Brasil S.A.	1,250,000	1,250,000
Banco Nacional de Mexico, S.A.	1,250,000	1,250,000
Bank of Tokyo and Detroit (International) Limited	1,250,000	1,250,000
Banque Française du Commerce Extérieur.....................	1,250,000	1,250,000
Banque Nationale de Paris	1,250,000	1,250,000
Bayerische Landesbank Girozentrale	1,250,000	1,250,000
Berliner Handels- und Frankfurter Bank	1,250,000	1,250,000
Caisse des Dépôts det Consignations	1,250,000	1,250,000
Hambros Bank Limited	1,250,000	1,250,000
Hill Samuel & Co. Limited	1,250,000	1,250,000
IBJ International Limited	1,250,000	1,250,000
Kredietbank N.V.	1,250,000	1,250,000

Underwriter	Principal Amount of Notes	Principal Amount of Debentures
B. Metzler seel. Sohn & Co.	$1,250,000	$1,250,000
Samuel Montagu & Co. Limited	1,250,000	1,250,000
Morgan Grenfell & Co. Limited	1,250,000	1,250,000
Nippon Credit International (HK) Ltd.	1,250,000	1,250,000
Orion Bank Limited	1,250,000	1,250,000
Société Général de Banque S.A.	1,250,000	1,250,000
Vereins- und Westbank Aktiengesellschaft	1,250,000	1,250,000
Westdeutsche Landesbank Girozentrale	1,250,000	1,250,000
Total	$500,000,000	$500,000,000

In the Underwriting Agreement, the several Underwriters have agreed, subject to the terms and conditions set forth therein, to purchase all the Notes and all the Debentures offered hereby if any Notes or Debentures are purchased.

The Company has been advised by the Representatives that the several Underwriters propose initially to offer the Notes and Debentures to the public at the public offering prices set forth on the cover page of this Prospectus, and to certain dealers at such prices less a concession not in excess of .375% of the principal amount in the case of the Notes and not in excess of .500% of the principal amount in the case of the Debentures. The Underwriters may allow and such dealers may reallow a concession not in excess of .250% of the principal amount in the case of the Notes and not in excess of .250% of the principal amount in the case of the Debentures to certain other dealers. After the initial public offering, the public offering prices and such concessions may be changed.

The Underwriting Agreement provides that the Company will indemnify the several Underwriters against certain liabilities, including liabilities under the Securities Act of 1933, or contribute to payments which the Underwriters may be required to make in respect thereof.

LEGAL OPINIONS

The validity of the Notes and Debentures offered hereby will be passed upon for the Company by Messrs. Cravath, Swaine & Moore, One Chase Manhattan Plaza, New York, N. Y., and for the Underwriters by Messrs. Cleary, Gottlieb, Steen & Hamilton, One State Street Plaza, New York, N. Y.

EXPERTS

The consolidated financial statements included in the Annual Report of the Company on Form 10-K incorporated by reference in this Prospectus have been so incorporated in reliance on the report of Price Waterhouse & Co., independent accountants, as experts in auditing and accounting.

INFORMATION INCORPORATED BY REFERENCE

The Company's definitive Proxy Statement dated March 21, 1979, the Annual Report of the Company on Form 10-K for the fiscal year ended December 31, 1978, and the Quarterly Reports of the

APPENDIX 2 TO CHAPTER 8

FORD CREDIT PROSPECTUS EXCERPTS

PROSPECTUS

$3,045,821,190.64

Ford Credit 1989-A Grantor Trust

8.70% Asset Backed Certificates

Ford Motor Credit Company

Seller, Servicer, and Limited Guarantor

Principal, and interest at the Pass-Through Rate of 8.70% per annum, will be distributed to Certificateholders on the 15th day of each month (or the next following business day if such 15th day is not a business day), beginning November 15, 1989. Each Certificate offered hereby will represent a fractional undivided interest in the Ford Credit 1989-A Grantor Trust (the "Trust") to be formed by Ford Motor Credit Company ("Ford Credit"). The property of the Trust will include a pool of retail installment sale contracts originated on or after January 1, 1989 secured by new automobiles and light trucks (the "Receivables"), certain monies due thereunder on or after October 1, 1989, security interests in the vehicles financed thereby, and Ford Credit's limited guaranty of payments under the Receivables. The final scheduled payment date of the Certificates will be October 17, 1994.

The Certificates initially will be represented by Certificates registered in the name of Cede & Co., the nominee of The Depository Trust Company ("DTC"). The interests of beneficial owners of the Certificates will be represented by book entries on the records of DTC and participating members thereof. Definitive Certificates will be available only under limited circumstances.

There is currently no secondary market for the Certificates and there is no assurance that one will develop. The First Boston Corporation and Goldman, Sachs & Co. expect, but are not obligated, to make a market in the Certificates. There is no assurance that any such market will continue.

THE CERTIFICATES REPRESENT INTERESTS IN THE TRUST AND DO NOT REPRESENT INTERESTS IN OR OBLIGATIONS OF FORD CREDIT OR ANY AFFILIATE THEREOF, EXCEPT TO THE EXTENT OF THE LIMITED GUARANTY DESCRIBED HEREIN.

THESE SECURITIES HAVE NOT BEEN APPROVED OR DISAPPROVED BY THE SECURITIES AND EXCHANGE COMMISSION NOR HAS THE COMMISSION PASSED UPON THE ACCURACY OR ADEQUACY OF THIS PROSPECTUS. ANY REPRE-SENTATION TO THE CONTRARY IS A CRIMINAL OFFENSE.

	Price to Public(1)	Underwriting Discount(2)	Proceeds to Ford Credit(1)(3)
Per Certificate	99.59375%	0.22500%	99.36875%
Total	$3,033,447,542.05	$6,853,097.68	$3,026,594,444.37

(1) Plus accrued interest at the Pass-Through Rate from October 1, 1989.
(2) Ford Credit has agreed to indemnify the Underwriters against certain liabilities under the Securities Act of 1933.
(3) Before deducting expenses payable by Ford Credit estimated at $948,164.

The Certificates are offered by the Underwriters when, as, and if issued and accepted by the Underwriters and subject to their right to reject orders in whole or in part. It is expected that the Certificates will be delivered in book-entry form only on or about October 31, 1989 through the facilities of DTC.

The First Boston Corporation   **Goldman, Sachs & Co.**

The date of this Prospectus is October 25, 1989.

(3) The Certificates acquired by the Benefit Plan have received a rating at the time of such acquisition that is in one of the three highest generic rating categories from either Standard & Poor's Corporation, Moody's Investors Service, Inc., or Duff & Phelps Inc.

(4) The sum of all payments made to each Underwriter in connection with the distribution of the Certificates represents not more than reasonable compensation for underwriting the Certificates. The sum of all payments made to and retained by the Seller pursuant to the sale of the Receivables to the Trust represents not more than the fair market value of such Receivables. The sum of all payments made to and retained by the Servicer represents not more than reasonable compensation for the Servicer's services under the Agreement and reimbursement of the Servicer's reasonable expenses in connection therewith.

In addition, it is a condition that the Benefit Plan investing in the Certificates be an "accredited investor" as defined in Rule 501(a)(1) of Regulation D of the Securities and Exchange Commission under the Securities Act of 1933.

The Exemption does not apply to the aquisition and holding of Certificates by Benefit Plans sponsored by the Seller, the Underwriters, the Trustee, the Servicer, any obligor with respect to Receivables included in the Trust constituting more than 5% of the aggregate unamortized principal balance of the assets in the Trust, or any affiliate of such parties (the "Restricted Group"). As of the date hereof, no obligor with respect to Receivables included in the Trust constitutes more than 5% of the aggregate unamortized principal balance of the Trust. Moreover, the Exemption provides relief from certain self-dealing/conflict of interest prohibited transactions, only if, among other requirements (i) a Benefit Plan's investment in Certificates does not exceed 25% of all of the Certificates outstanding at the time of the acquisition and (ii) immediately after the acquisition, no more than 25% of the assets of a Benefit Plan with respect to which the person who has discretionary authority or renders investment advice are invested in Certificates representing an interest in a trust containing assets sold or serviced by the same entity.

UNDERWRITING

Subject to the terms and conditions set forth in the Underwriting Agreement, Ford Credit has agreed to sell to each of the Underwriters named below, and each of the Underwriters has severally agreed to purchase the principal amount of Certificates set forth opposite its name below:

Underwriters	Principal Amount of Certificates
The First Boston Corporation	$1,434,411,190.64
Goldman, Sachs & Co.	1,434,410,000.00
Merrill Lynch, Pierce, Fenner & Smith Incorporated	59,000,000.00
Salomon Brothers Inc	59,000,000.00
Shearson Lehman Hutton Inc.	59,000,000.00
Total	$3,045,821,190.64

Ford Credit has been advised by the Underwriters that they propose initially to offer the Certificates to the public at the prices set forth herein, and to certain dealers at such prices less a concession not in excess of 0.135% of the Certificate amounts. The Underwriters may allow and such dealers may reallow a concession not in excess of 0.100% of the Certificate amounts to certain other dealers. After the initial public offering, the public offering prices and such concessions may be changed.

Ford Credit has agreed to indemnify the Underwriters against certain liabilities, including civil liabilities under the Securities Act of 1933, or to contribute to payments which the Underwriters may be required to make in respect thereof.

The Disappearing Syndicate **175**

APPENDIX 3 TO CHAPTER 8

Yearly Flotation of U.S. Debt Issues, Non-Shelf and Shelf, Using Syndicates (U) and Without Syndicates (Non-U), 1980–89 (in billions of dollars and percent)

Lines	1980	1981	1982	1983	1984	1985	1986	1987	1988	1989
(1) Non-Shelf Total	41.6	40.3	27.8	25.6	31.6	45.4	80.8	79.6	111.1	179.8
(2) Non-Shelf Non-U	0.3	0.9	5.2	11.9	19.1	27.4	61.6	56.8	97.2	166.6
(3): (1) − (2) = U	41.3	39.4	22.6	23.7	12.5	18.0	19.2	22.8	13.9	13.2
(4) Shelf Total	–	–	16.0	26.3	27.8	59.3	146.9	139.8	125.7	94.3
(5) Shelf Non-U	–	–	4.8	6.8	14.6	16.0	51.1	42.0	96.1	71.7
(6): (4) − (5) = U	–	–	11.2	19.5	23.2	43.3	95.8	97.8	29.6	22.6
(7): (5) + (2) = Non-U	0.3	0.9	10.0	18.7	33.7	43.3	112.7	98.8	193.3	238.3
(8) Grand Total (1) + (4)	41.6	40.3	43.8	51.9	69.4	104.7	227.7	219.4	236.8	274.1
(9) % Non-U (7) / (8)	1%	2%	23%	36%	49%	40%	49%	45%	82%	87%

Source: Securities Industry Association and Securities Data Co.

APPENDIX 4 TO CHAPTER 8

THE CORPORATE UNDERWRITING LEADERS

A summary of the top firms according to full credit to lead manager.

1988	1989		$ Volume (millions)	Number of Issues
1	1	Merrill Lynch	$45,985.0	428
2	2	Goldman Sachs	42,910.6	491
4	3	First Boston	37,765.1	418
3	4	Salomon Brothers	31,605.3	403
6	5	Morgan Stanley	30,136.0	294
5	6	Shearson Lehman Hutton	24,745.3	342
9	7	Bear Stearns	18,186.0	424
7	8	Drexel Burnham Lambert	16,804.9	224
8	9	Prudential-Bache	16,426.1	349
10	10	Kidder Peabody	8,799.0	196
14	11	Donaldson, Lufkin & Jenrette	4,843.7	106
11	12	PaineWebber	4,745.3	114
21	13	UBS Securities	2,830.7	89
12	14	Smith Barney, Harris Upham	2,808.8	79
18	15	Dean Witter Reynolds	2,572.5	24
20	16	Alex. Brown & Sons	2,384.8	37
13	17	Citicorp	1,918.2	59
17	18	BT Securities	1,829.1	49
19	19	Dillon Read	1,521.2	15
16	20	Chemical Securities	1,510.2	14
15	21	Wheat First Butcher & Singer	1,082.3	15
31	22	Nomura Securities	776.5	34
22	23	L.F. Rothschild	738.7	22
–	24	Greenwich Capital Markets	719.6	12
–	25	Lazard Frères	694.9	6

RANKING THE CORPORATE UNDERWRITERS

These rankings include all firmly underwritten taxable debt or equity deals offered during the period January 1 through December 31, 1989. Figures are reported at the net, not the principal, amount. "Lead manager" is defined as the book runner. All other managers are considered co-managers.

In the full-credit-to-lead-manager table, the lead manager is given full credit for the deal. In the full-credit-to-each-manager table, each manager is given full credit.

Data and rankings supplied by IDD Information Services. New York.

CHAPTER 9

THE THEORY OF FINANCIAL REGULATION IN THE NEW ENVIRONMENT OF LIBERALIZATION

Lawrence J. White

INTRODUCTION

The financial services sector is a very heavily regulated area in most economies. This extensive overlay of government regulation is no accident. Financial services play a central role in any economy. Credit and finance are ubiquitous inputs for all other sectors. Deposits and other liabilities created through the financing process are, in turn, important financial assets for these other sectors. Banks usually provide a payments mechanism for the economy. Financial institutions are often relatively large in an economy and are often perceived to wield great economic, social, and political power. And finance and financial transactions are often complicated, unfamiliar to many of the transactors, and heavily laden with uncertainties and incomplete information.

This chapter will provide an overview of financial services regula-

Lawrence J. White is the Arthur E. Imperatore Professor of Economics and Chairman of the Economics Department at Stern School of Business, New York University.

An earlier version of this paper was presented at the World Bank Seminar on Financial Sector Liberalization and Regulation, June 11, 1990, at Harvard University.

tion: its forms, purposes, functions, and effects. The two major theories that have been offered to explain regulation in general (and financial services regulation in particular) will be explored. And special attention will be given to the U.S. experience in deregulating a number of its industries, including the savings and loan industry, and the lessons that can be learned from this experience for financial services deregulation and especially for banks.[1]

There will be one theme that will surface repeatedly in this chapter: Government regulation of financial services is a multifaceted phenomenon. It has many forms and functions; it has multiple objectives; and there are multiple means by which it can be implemented. There are overlaps among these facets. For example, a specific type of regulation that is intended to deal with one set of goals may well have consequences for other goals. Still, an understanding of these distinctions is essential for an understanding of the changes in regulation and deregulation that are occurring in the financial sectors of many countries and the consequences they have for those economies. It is also useful for understanding how and why liberalization or deregulation of one aspect of regulation could be good public policy, while the continued vigorous application of another aspect of regulation (toward the same firms) could also be sensible.

DEFINITIONS AND DISTINCTIONS

Types of Financial Services Firms

The financial services sector—and the web of financial services regulation—encompasses a broad range of firms and services. All are involved (directly and indirectly) in the process of helping channel resources from savers to the users of the savings and thereby creating financial assets for the former and financial obligations for the latter. (The latter may be companies that use the savings to invest in real assets, but it also includes governments that borrow to finance current consumption.)

One useful distinction among financial services firms is between financial services intermediaries and other financial services firms.[2] The former group of firms *intermediate* by collecting the funds from savers (or from other intermediaries), issuing their own liabilities to those savers, and in turn investing the collected funds primarily in financial assets. Banks, savings institutions, credit unions, other depositories, insurance companies, pension funds, mutual funds, and industrial and consumer finance companies are the primary institutions in this area.

The other group of firms include entities that do not directly intermediate but instead facilitate the direct flow of resources from savers to users and the creation of the financial assets and obligations. This group encompasses underwriters, brokers, dealers, market makers, and advisors.

Types of Regulation

Just as there are useful distinctions to be made among financial services firms, so also are there useful distinctions to be made among types of financial services regulation. Three generic types stand out.

First, *economic* regulation focuses on prices (e.g., interest rates), entry (e.g., limitations on who can organize or own a bank, what activities a bank can undertake, and where a bank can operate), and/or profits. Economic regulation is often intended to deal with perceived problems of monopoly (i.e., market power) or social or political problems (e.g., the perceived social or political power of large financial institutions or the consequences of their being owned by foreigners).

Second, *safety and soundness* (or prudential) regulation focuses on maintaining the financial health of financial firms. It usually encompasses net worth (capital) standards, asset type and composition limitations, liability type and composition limitations, and/or activity limitations, as well as character standards for who can own the institution. It is intended to avoid the consequences of the insolvency of financial institutions.

Third, *information* regulation focuses on perceived inadequacies in the provision of the information that accompanies financial transactions. It usually involves specific requirements for information that must accompany specific products or services (e.g., disclosure requirements on securities offerings or interest rate information on mortgage originations or deposit offerings).

The interconnections among these types of regulation should be mentioned immediately. Some forms of economic regulation have safety and soundness justifications and consequences. For example, economic regulation that limits competition among financial services firms may create a franchise value that becomes an additional off-balance-sheet or intangible asset that is not formally registered as an asset or as part of net worth for the firm; it is thereby an extra protection for the liability holders of the firm.[3] Similarly, entry limitations with respect to the activities that a financial firm can undertake may also affect the overall riskiness of that firm.

THEORIES OF REGULATION AND THEIR APPLICATION TO FINANCIAL SERVICES

Theories of regulation (including financial services regulation), because they encompass the interaction of governments and firms, fall into the arena of political economy. There are two major theoretical approaches to explaining regulation.[4] The first is frequently described as the "public interest" theory of regulation. It sees regulation primarily as a response to market failures, but it also includes regulation as a response to purely social or political concerns that are outside of the market failure paradigm. The second approach is often described as the "public choice" theory or "economic" theory of regulation.[5] It hypothesizes that government policymakers, who are concerned with re-election or other support from affected parties, will respond to the pressures of interest groups that care deeply about the regulatory issues. Though these groups' membership numbers may be relatively small, their depth of concern and involvement will cause them to mobilize energies and resources to mold policies that favor themselves; larger groups (e.g., the general public), who are adversely affected in a broader but less intense fashion, are likely to find the mobilization of opposition to these policies to be too costly and not worthwhile.

In this section we will examine the application of the three main types of regulation to the financial services sector in the light of these alternative explanations. Examples from U.S. financial regulation will illustrate some of the points.

Economic Regulation

Since the tools of economic regulation are primarily designed to deal with problems of market power or other perceived social power problems, a "public interest" theory would predict that financial regulation in this area would be aimed at these types of problems; the "public choice" theory would look instead to the interest groups that benefit.

The experience of the United States indicates that both approaches have explanatory power. Let us begin with banks. American populism has had a strain of deep suspicion of banks as wielders of economic and social power. One indicator of this suspicion has been the strong tradition of localism applied to banks: Banks generally have been confined in their physical locations to individual states, and many states have further restricted bank branching to smaller geographic areas within their state boundaries. This tradition began to erode only in the 1980s and is still quite powerful. Another indicator of the suspicion has been the limitations on the activities that a bank or its holding company can undertake. Also, concerns about the perceived market power of banks have led some states, at various times, to impose usury ceilings on the interest rates charged on loans.

Though the localism and activities limitations might originally have been motivated by true social concerns, favored parties have been quick to recognize the advantages that flow from these limitations and to use their political weight to oppose alterations of these arrangements. The localism tradition has clearly *protected* local banks from competition from banks headquartered elsewhere and *created* (rather than ameliorated) market power problems.[6] The limitations on banks' activities have protected firms in these other activity areas, and the latter have vociferously opposed relaxation of these limitations.

A similar picture emerges in the instances in which economic regulation tools have been used to deal with perceived safety and soundness problems. In the early 1930s, after the failures of thousands of banks in the U.S., many policymakers believed that "excessive competition" had caused banks to make excessively risky loans and subsequently to fail.[7] Others believed that commercial banks' involvements in investment banking (especially underwriting) had contributed to their failures (and to the stock market crash).[8] As a consequence, the banking legislation of the 1930s placed limits on the interest rates that banks could pay on checking accounts and other deposits (Regulation Q), imposed tighter entry standards for those who wished to organize a bank *de novo*, and separated commercial banking from investment banking (the Glass-Steagall Act). In 1966, to deal with the solvency problems of U.S. savings and loan (S&L) institutions, legislation extended the coverage of Regulation Q to those institutions as well.

But once these restrictions were in place, the beneficiaries fought their removal. Banks and S&Ls opposed the elimination of the Regulation Q interest ceiling (and a zero interest ceiling still applies to commercial checking accounts today). And the investment banking community has vigorously resisted the incursions of commercial banks into corporate securities underwriting and related securities areas.

The insurance industry in the U.S. fits a similar pattern. The tradition of localism has led to exclusive regulation by the individual states. And price ceiling regulation by some states on some product lines (e.g., automobile insurance) has been directed at perceived market power problems. But the regulatory structures of the states have often encouraged collusion and price-fixing and reduced competition among insurance companies, thereby *creating* market power.[9]

In the securities area, the major feature of economic regulation until the 1970s was the federal government's tolerance of the New York Stock Exchange's system of fixed commission rates on stock brokerage transactions—a practice that would have been forbidden under the U.S. antitrust laws in any other industry. Though the origins of the government's tolerance of this practice are unclear,[10] the NYSE's vigorous (but ultimately unsuccessful) defense of this practice was clear indeed.[11]

Safety and Soundness Regulation

This type of regulation has been applied primarily to specific types of financial intermediaries.[12] It is especially associated with banks and other depositories, but it applies also to insurance companies and pension funds.

Safety and soundness regulation is designed to preserve the solvency and viability of a financial intermediary. The primary beneficiaries of this type of regulation are the firm's borrowing customers (who thereby enjoy a continuing business relationship with the intermediary and do not have to search for alternative sources of credit), its liability holders (who thereby face reduced likelihoods of losses), and its owners (who enjoy a special status and face less likelihood of bankruptcy—but they may also be more constrained in their activities).

The "public interest" theory would ask about market failures or other types of problems associated with the financial transactions of these intermediaries; the "public choice" theory would ask about the interest groups involved.

A closer examination of the financial transactions of intermediaries and of the specific application of safety and soundness regulation—in the U.S., for example, it applies most vigorously to banks and other depositories, insurance companies, and pension funds and only mildly to mutual funds and finance companies—indicates that it is the nature of the *liabilities* of these intermediaries that generates the greatest safety and soundness concern. Depositories are special institutions: They offer deposit liabilities that are expected to be liquid and redeemable at par; the deposits are used as money or near-money and are the major means of payment in the economy, as well as a significant form of household wealth. At the same time, banks' assets are substantially less liquid. Monitoring of these institutions' solvency and liquidity by depositors may be extremely difficult, and the institutions are always subject to the possibility of depositor runs.[13] Similarly, the liability holders of these other financial intermediaries—life insurance beneficiaries, property and casualty insurance claimants, and present and future pension holders—are usually in a poor position to protect their interests and control the managers of the institutions.

Safety and soundness regulation is a reasonable response to the special character of these institutions and their liabilities; it is thus consistent with the "public interest" approach. It is worth noting that the existence of an explicit governmental guarantee or insurance arrangement is not a necessary ingredient for the concern about and protection of these liability holders. In the U.S., federal safety and soundness regulation of national banks preceded by 70 years the institution of a formal federal deposit insurance program in 1933.[14]

An alternative interpretation for the existence of safety and soundness regulation, but one that reaches the same conclusion, would start by assuming that the social goal of protecting the value of the deposit liabilities is important enough to warrant an explicit or implicit insurance (or guaranty) arrangement for depositors. The safety and soundness regulation can then be interpreted as the rules and other procedures that protect the deposit insurer.[15]

"Public choice" issues, though, have not been absent. The S&L industry was an ardent advocate of relaxed safety and soundness regulation during the early 1980s, which occurred in an extremely unfortunate conjunction with the economic deregulation of the industry.[16]

Information Regulation

A "public interest" approach to this type of regulation would ask about informational deficiencies in the market and the problems of "asymmetric information".[17] The "public choice" approach would ask whether some interest groups are favored over others.

Information regulation is pervasive throughout the U.S. financial services sector—banking, securities, insurance, and pensions. Transactions in these areas often are complex and subject to problems of asymmetric information and the lack of sophistication by some transactors. A "public interest" framework does seem to explain the intent behind this type of regulation, though the efficiency of some of it can be questioned.[18] It is also worth noting, however, that there are usually economies of scale in the provision of this type of information, so that smaller firms are at a greater disadvantage in providing it than are larger firms; the latter usually protest less vigorously when new informational requirements are suggested or introduced.

In sum, a rough-and-ready review indicates that both theoretical approaches have value in understanding financial services regulation. We can neither assume that financial services regulation is always dealing exclusively with specific market failure problems nor that financial services regulation is solely the result of special interest groups. Reality, as usual, is more complex, and distinctions among types of regulation are especially important here.

THE LESSONS FROM THE ECONOMIC DEREGULATION EXPERIENCE IN THE U.S.

As the previous sections have made clear, distinctly different types of regulation have been applied to the financial services sector (and to other sectors of the U.S. economy as well). The "environment of liberalization" that has occurred or is contemplated by many countries applies primarily to *economic* regulation. The experiences of the U.S. in undergoing substantial economic deregulation during the 1970s and 1980s in a number of sectors—airlines, trucking, rail, natural gas, securities brokerage commissions, banking, and savings institutions (S&Ls)—provide important lessons that have wide applicability for any future financial services deregulation.

We will first review the general lessons from the deregulation experiences. We will then turn specifically to the S&L deregulation episode, to see briefly the pitfalls of an ill-designed deregulation experience. Finally, we will draw together the lessons for financial services deregulation and more specifically for banking.

The General Lessons

There are two major and general lessons that can be gleaned from the U.S. experience.[19] First, economic deregulation in these industries has generally been a boon to increased competition and efficiency in the previously regulated sectors. Economic regulation had clearly been largely (if not entirely) impeding competition rather than dealing with market power problems. With the advent of deregulation, prices have generally decreased, wider varieties of services (and prices) have appeared, and resources have been used with greater efficiency. Services have been bundled and unbundled in new forms, and new technologies have appeared.[20]

Secondly, economic deregulation has generally been accompanied by increased turnover and failure rates among firms. This is exactly what would be expected in the transition from a protected environment to a more competitive environment. Firms that were expert at doing business under the regulation regime would not necessarily be the most efficient in a deregulated, more competitive environment. New, more efficient firms could enter, and some incumbents could expand at the expense of other incumbents. *Judgments about the success or failure of economic deregulation should not be based on the failure rates of incumbents (or of entrants either).*

This second lesson has important implications for the deregulation of the financial services sector. To the extent that economic deregulation occurs among depositories, insurance companies, or pension funds—the type of firms that are subject to safety and soundness regulation, because of the special nature of the liabilities of these firms—there are likely to be failures (insolvencies) among these firms. *Heightened safety and soundness regulation as a simultaneous requirement is vital for heading off and ameliorating the consequences of these failures.* This is one of the important lessons from the ill-fated S&L deregulation experience. Even with heightened safety and soundness regulation, however, some failures are probably inevitable, and some liability holders will thereby be put at risk. If these liabilities really are special, then governments will have to devise some way for keeping their holders whole. Again, this probably ought to be an explicit accompaniment to the deregulation actions.

The U.S. S&L Deregulation Experience

The experience of the U.S. in deregulating the S&L industry in the early 1980s is especially instructive for understanding the vital link between safety and soundness regulation and economic deregulation.[21]

Because S&Ls had previously been forced into a pattern of lending in the form of fixed-interest-rate thirty-year residential mortgages and funding this lending through short-term deposits—in short, S&Ls were borrowing short and lending long—they were especially vulnerable financially to sharp increases in interest rates. When interest rates rose in the late 1970s and early 1980s, S&Ls began to hemorrhage.

The response by the Congress and by many individual states was to provide *economic* deregulation of S&Ls: wider lending and investment powers (to allow S&Ls to diversify their lending portfolios) and an end to Regulation Q's ceilings on deposit interest rates. The Congress also (in 1980) increased the insured deposit amount to $100,000 (from its previous level of $40,000).

These were basically sensible actions. Academics and advisory commissions had been recommending these deregulation actions for the previous decade.[22] The increase in the insured amount is now considered a controversial action, but at the time it attracted little notice. And in this author's view, it too was sensible, because increases in the insured amount reduce the likelihood of runs.

But this economic deregulation needed to be accompanied by stepped-up safety and soundness regulation and/or increased attention to economic incentives (e.g., risk-based insurance premiums) in the S&L regulatory system. This was true because the actions of the Congress and the states increased the *opportunities* for taking risk (wider asset powers) and enhanced the *capabilities* for funding that risk-taking (S&Ls could now pay market rates of interest on deposits and collect those deposits in larger insured amounts). And this occurred at a time when many S&Ls' *incentives* for risk-taking were heightened because their net worth (capital) had been reduced or eliminated by the high interest rate environment and their heavy losses.

Unfortunately, exactly the opposite occurred. Net worth standards were *lowered*, not raised, in the early 1980s. Changes in accounting practices and the liberal creation of goodwill as an asset allowed reported net worth levels to be artificially buoyed. And the numbers of the field-force regulators—the examiners and supervisors—were actually *reduced* between 1981 and 1984. A generally more relaxed attitude toward safety and soundness pervaded the regulatory system.

These actions in the safety and soundness arena can only be described as perverse. Unfortunately, too many people in Washington did not understand the distinction between economic regulation and safety and soundness regulation, and they believed that the general concept of "deregulation" applied indiscriminately.[23]

Hundreds of S&Ls took advantage of the enhanced opportunities, capabilities, and incentives for risk-taking in the environment of relaxed safety and soundness regulatory control. They grew rapidly, investing in many new, non-traditional types of assets. All too often, the executives of these rapidly growing thrifts were careless, ignorant, excessively optimistic, deliberately risk-prone, and/or fraudulent and criminal in their lending and investing behavior. The decline in the price of oil in the 1980s and changes in the U.S. tax laws in 1981 (which made real estate a tax-favored investment) and in 1986 (which reversed course) together compounded what was already destined to be an extremely serious problem.

After a lag of a few years, the S&L regulatory system did tighten substantially—but too late. The bad loans and investments had already been made and were on the S&Ls' books.

The costs to the U.S. Government from this episode will be huge.

The Lessons for Financial Services Deregulation

The economic deregulation of the financial services sector can be economically beneficial. It can bring greater competition, lower prices, better services, and improved efficiency. But it is also likely to bring failures for some of the firms in this sector. For financial intermediaries, it is likely to increase the opportunities for risk-taking and the capabilities for funding that risk-taking. Further, to the extent that the economic deregulation causes the net worths of financial intermediaries to decline, either because of explicit losses or because of the lower implicit value of the franchise, it will also increase the incentives for risk-taking. And, unless otherwise curbed, this increased risk-taking will inevitably lead to yet greater (and more deeply insolvent) levels of failures by some of these intermediaries.

For the intermediaries with special types of liabilities—banks and other depositories, insurance companies, and pension funds—these potential failures raise issues of genuine social concern. Accordingly, any significant economic deregulation of these intermediaries (e.g., decontrolling prices or interest rates, permitting new activities, permitting new entrants) must be accompanied by *heightened* efforts at safety and soundness regulation. The following are the elements of a strong safety and soundness regulatory system that specifically applies to banks and that would be consistent with economic deregulation;[24] the same precepts would apply to other intermediaries:

1. An overall regulatory framework that stresses prudence and fiduciary responsibility.
2. An adequate number of well-paid and well-trained examiners and supervisors.
3. An accounting system that is based on the *market value* of all assets, liabilities, and off-balance sheet items.

   The existing accounting framework that applies to depository institutions is not adequate, because it is based on historical book (cost) values rather than on current market values. Only the latter can provide a representation of current economic reality. Anything else provides misleading information to the regulators (and to the firm itself).[25]

4. Net worth (capital) requirements that are based on the market value accounting system, that are risk-based, and that are high enough to keep the likelihood of insolvency at an acceptably low level.

   Net worth is like a deductible clause in a standard insurance arrangement; the higher is net worth, the greater can be the decline in the value of the assets before the deposit liability holders (or their guarantor) are exposed to loss. A high net worth level not only provides direct protection for the depositors, but it provides indirect protection as well: With a higher level of net worth, the owners of a bank have more at stake, and they are less likely to be careless or risk-prone.

   The so-called BIS or Basel agreement on international net worth standards is a welcome step in the right direction, but it is nevertheless wholly inadequate. First, it is based on existing cost-based accounting frameworks rather than a market value accounting framework. Second, the Basel approach ignores portfolio effects and the co-variance of returns among assets. Third, it wholly ignores interest rate risk. And fourth, the relative risk categories and absolute net worth levels have no empirical foundation.

5. Risk-based deposit insurance premiums.

   If governments are de facto not prepared to see depositors lose money, those guarantees should be made explicit, and risk-based premiums should be levied in return. Risk-based premiums and risk-based net worth standards are not perfect substitutes, since the actual net worth level of the bank should be one of the elements of risk on which premiums should be based. Risk-based premiums can thereby provide an incentive for banks to operate with *higher* net worth levels than the bare-bones minimum requirements.

6. Strong powers of early intervention and rapid disposal.

   Bank regulators need to be able to intervene and take control of a bank *before* it becomes insolvent; waiting until insolvency almost always means waiting too long, with large consequent costs. And insolvent or near-insolvent banks should be placed with an acquirer or liquidated rapidly. Delay is costly.

7. Specify the activities of the bank and its owners (e.g., a holding company) and the permitted financial relationships between them.

   The activities of a bank should be restricted to those that regulators can monitor and for which they can comfortably set risk-based net worth levels and premiums; in essence, they are activities that can be examined and supervised. All other activities should be in a holding company or its non-bank subsidiaries, and financial transactions between the bank and its holding company (or owners generally) must be tightly restricted and closely monitored, because it is too easy to "loot" the bank through improper transactions (e.g., excessive dividends or loans that are backed by inadequate collateral or that are made at excessively low interest rates).

CONCLUSION

Financial services regulation still has a powerful role to play in an environment of liberalization. But policymakers must understand the distinctions among the various types of regulation that apply to the financial services sector and must be careful to allow deregulation of the type that will be most beneficial (i.e., *economic* deregulation) while retaining the type (*safety and soundness* regulation) that is vital for protecting the special groups of liability holders toward which governments have legitimate concerns. The lack of proper attention and care in this respect has already been shown to have huge costs. But a careful program of sensible deregulation *and* regulation can surely have substantial benefits.

NOTES

1. Generally in this paper references to "banks" will encompass other depository institutions as well.

2. This distinction is made by Campbell (1988, ch.12).
3. See Keeley (1989).
4. See, generally, Stigler (1970), Posner (1974), and Peltzman (1976).
5. The "capture" theory of regulation is a hybrid of the two.
6. See, for example, Gilbert (1984), Weiss (1989), and Berger and Hannan (1989a; 1989b).
7. See Peltzman (1965) and Edwards and Edwards (1974).
8. See Walter (1985) and E. White (1989).
9. For an example in the area of title insurance, see White (1984).
10. See Baxter (1970), West and Tinic (1971), and Mann (1975).
11. See Mann (1975), Stoll (1979), and Stoll (1981).
12. In the U.S., however, securities firms (which are not intermediaries) also have net worth requirements.
13. See Diamond and Dybvig (1983).
14. As Calomiris (1989a; 1989b) points out, the involvement of individual states with deposit insurance began in 1829.
15. See White (1989).
16. See Phelan (1989), Pizzo, Fricker, and Muolo (1989), Pilzer (1989), and Adams (1990).
17. See, for example, Ackerlof (1970) and Jensen and Meckling (1976).
18. See, for example, Stigler (1964) and Benston (1973; 1975); see also Friend and Herman (1964) and Friend and Westerfield (1975).
19. This section draws heavily on Stoll (1979; 1981), Tinic and West (1980), Meyer et al. (1981), Keeler (1981), Morrison and Winston (1986), Kaplan (1986), White (1986), Moore (1986), and MacDonald (1989).
20. For example, the U.S. airlines' "hub-and-spokes" technology of scheduling flights had not appeared during the period of economic regulation.
21. This section draws heavily on White (1990b; 1990c; 1991a); see also Brumbaugh and Carron (1987), Strunk and Case (1988), Brumbaugh (1988), Kane (1989), Brumbaugh and Litan (1989), and Brumbaugh, Carron, and Litan (1989).
22. See, for example, Jacobs and Phillips (1972) and Phillips and Jacobs (1983).
23. See Pizzo, Muolo, and Fricker (1989, ch. 22) and Adams (1990, chs. 11 and 13).
24. This section draws heavily on White (1989; 1991a, ch. 11).
25. On this topic see White (1988a; 1988b; 1990a; 1990c; 1991b); see also Benston (1989) and Berger, Kuester, and O'Brien (1989).

REFERENCES

Ackerlof, George A., "The Market for 'Lemons': Quantitative Uncertainty and the Market Mechanism," *Quarterly Journal of Economics*, 84 (August 1970), pp. 488–500.

Adams, James R., *The Big Fix: Inside the S&L Scandal*. New York: John Wiley & Sons, 1990.

Baxter, William F., "NYSE Fixed Commission Rates: A Private Cartel Goes

Public," *Stanford Law Review*, 22 (April 1970), pp. 675–712.

Benston, George J., "Required Disclosure and the Stock Market: An Evaluation of the Securities Exchange Act of 1934," *American Economic Review*, 63 (March 1973), pp. 132–55.

Benston, George J., "Required Disclosure and the Stock Market: Rejoinder," *American Economic Review*, 65 (June 1975), pp. 473–77.

Benston, George J., "Market Value Accounting: Benefits, Costs, and Incentives," in Federal Reserve Bank of Chicago, *Banking System Risk: Charting a New Course*. Chicago: 1989, pp. 547–63.

Berger, Allen N., and Timothy H. Hannan, "Deposit Interest Rates and Local Market Concentration," in Leonard W. Weiss (ed.), *Concentration and Price*. Cambridge, MA: MIT Press, 1989a, pp. 255–65.

Berger, Allen N., and Timothy H. Hannan, "The Price-Concentration Relationship in Banking," *Review of Economics and Statistics*, 71 (May 1989b), pp. 291–99.

Berger, Allen N.; Kathleen A. Kuester; and James M. O'Brien, "Some Red Flags Concerning Market Value Accounting," in Federal Reserve Bank of Chicago, *Banking System Risk: Charting a New Course*. Chicago: 1989, pp. 515–46.

Brumbaugh, R. Dan, Jr., *Thrifts Under Siege: Restoring Order to American Banking*. Cambridge, MA: Ballinger 1988.

Brumbaugh, R. Dan, Jr., and Andrew S. Carron, "Thrift Industry Crisis: Causes and Solutions," *Brookings Papers on Economic Activity* (1987, no. 2), pp. 349–77.

Brumbaugh, R. Dan, Jr.; Andrew S. Carron; and Robert E. Litan, "Cleaning Up the Depository Institutions Mess," *Brookings Papers on Economic Activity* (1989, no. 1), pp. 243–83.

Brumbaugh, R. Dan, Jr., and Robert E. Litan, "The S&L Crisis: How to Get Out and Stay Out," *Brookings Review*, 7 (Spring 1989), pp. 3–13.

Diamond, Douglas W., and Philip H. Dybvig, "Bank Runs, Deposit Insurance, and Liquidity," *Journal of Political Economy*, 91 (June 1983), pp. 401–19.

Edwards, Linda N., and Franklin R. Edwards, "Measuring the Effectiveness of Regulation: The Case of Bank Entry Regulation," *Journal of Law & Economics*, 17 (October 1974), pp. 445–60.

Friend, Irwin, and Edward S. Herman, "The SEC Through a Glass Darkly," *Journal of Business*, 37 (October 1964), pp. 382–405.

Friend, Irwin, and Randolph Westerfield, "Required Disclosure and the Stock Market: Comment," *American Economic Review*, 65 (June 1975), pp. 467–72.

Gilbert, R. Alton, "Bank Market Structure and Competition: A Survey," *Journal of Money, Credit and Banking*, 16 (November 1984), pp. 617–45.

Gorton, Gary, "Public Policy and the Evolution of Banking Markets," in Federal Reserve Bank of Chicago, *Banking System Risk: Charting of New Course*. Chicago: 1989, pp. 233–52.

Jacobs, Donald P., and Almarin Phillips, "Overview of the Commission's Philoso- phy and Recommendations," in Federal Reserve Bank of Boston, *Policies for a More Competitive Financial System.* Boston: 1972.

Jensen, Michael C., and William H. Meckling, "Theory of the Firm: Managerial Behavior, Agency Costs, and Ownership Structure," *Journal of Financial Economics,* 3 (October 1976), pp. 305–60.

Kane, Edward J., *The S&L Insurance Mess: How Did it Happen?* Washington, D.C.: Urban Institute Press, 1989.

Kaplan, Daniel P., "The Changing Airline Industry," in Leonard W. Weiss and Michael W. Klass (eds.), *Regulatory Reform: What Actually Happened.* Boston: Little, Brown, 1986, pp. 40–77.

Kaufman, George G., "The Truth about Bank Runs," in Catherine England and Thomas Huertas (eds.), *The Financial Services Revolution: Policy Directions for the Future.* Boston: Kluwer, 1988, pp. 9–40.

Keeler, Theodore E., "The Revolution in Airline Regulation," in Leonard W. Weiss and Michael W. Klass (eds.), *Case Studies in Regulation: Revolution and Reform.* Boston: Little, Brown, 1981, pp. 53–85.

Keeley, Michael C., "Deposit Insurance, Risk, and Market Power in Banking," in Federal Reserve Bank of Chicago, *Banking System Risk: Charting a New Course.* Chicago: 1989, pp. 101–16.

MacDonald, James M., "Railroad Deregulation, Innovation and Competition: Effects of the Staggers Act on Grain Transportation," *Journal of Law & Economics,* 32 (April 1989), pp. 63–95.

Mann, H. Michael, "The New York Stock Exchange: A Cartel at the End of Its Reign," in Almarin Phillips (ed.), *Promoting Competition in Regulated Markets.* Washington, D.C.: Brookings Institution, 1975, pp. 301–27.

Meyer, John R., and Clinton V. Oster (eds.), *Airline Deregulation: The Early Experience.* Boston: Auburn House, 1981.

Moore, Thomas G., "Rail and Trucking Deregulation," in Leonard W. Weiss and Michael W. Klass (eds.), *Regulatory Reform: What Actually Happened.* Boston: Little, Brown, 1986.

Morrison, Stephen, and Clifford Winston, *The Economic Effect of Airline Deregu- lation.* Washington, D.C.: Brookings Institution, 1986.

Peltzman, Sam, "Entry in Commercial Banking," *Journal of Law & Economics,* 8 (October 1965), pp. 11–50.

Peltzman, Sam, "Toward a More General Theory of Regulation," *Journal of Law & Economics,* 19 (August 1976), pp. 211–40.

Phelan, Richard J., *Record of the Special Outside Counsel in the Matter of Speaker James C. Wright, Jr.,* Committee on Standards of Official Conduct, U.S. House of Representatives. Washington, D.C.: U.S. Government Printing Office, February 21, 1989.

Phillips, Almarin, and Donald P. Jacobs, "Reflections on the Hunt Commission," in George J. Benston (ed.), *Financial Services: The Changing Institutions and Government Policy*. Englewood Cliffs, NJ: Prentice-Hall, 1983, pp. 235–65.

Pilzer, Paul Z., *Other People's Money: The Inside Story of the S&L Mess*. New York: Simon and Schuster, 1989.

Pizzo, Stephen; Mary Fricker; and Paul Muolo, *Inside Job: The Looting of America's Savings and Loans*. New York: McGraw-Hill, 1989.

Posner, Richard A., "Theories of Economic Regulation," *Bell Journal of Economics and Management Science*, 5 (Autumn 1974), pp. 335–58.

Stigler, George J., "Public Regulation of the Securities Markets," *Journal of Business*, 37 (October 1964), pp.117–42.

Stigler, George J., "The Theory of Regulation," *Bell Journal of Economics and Management Science*, 2 (Spring 1971), pp. 3–21.

Stoll, Hans R., *Regulation of Securities Markets: An Examination of the Effects of Increased Competition*. Monograph Series in Finance and Economics no. 1979–2, New York University Solomon Center, Leonard N. Stern School of Business, 1979.

Stoll, Hans R., "Revolution in the Regulation of Securities Markets: An Examination of the Effects of Increased Competition," in Leonard W. Weiss and Michael W. Klass (eds.), *Case Studies in Regulation: Revolution and Reform*. Boston: Little, Brown, 1981, pp. 12–52.

Strunk, Norman, and Fred Case, *Where Deregulation Went Wrong: A Look at the Causes Behind Savings and Loan Failures in the 1980s*. Chicago: U.S. League of Savings Institutions, 1988.

Tinic, Seha M., and Richard R. West, "The Securities Industry Under Negotiated Brokerage Commissions: Changes in the Structure and Performance of the New York Stock Exchange Member Firms," *Bell Journal of Economics*, 11 (Spring 1980), pp. 29–41.

Walter, Ingo (ed.), *Deregulating Wall Street: Commercial Bank Penetration of the Corporate Securities Market*. New York: John Wiley & Sons, 1985.

Weiss, Leonard W., "A Review of Concentration-Price Studies in Banking," in Leonard W. Weiss (ed.), *Concentration and Price*. Cambridge, MA: MIT Press, 1989, pp. 219–54.

West, Richard R., and Seha M. Tinic, "Minimum Commission Rates on New York Stock Exchange Transactions," *Bell Journal of Economics and Management Science*, 2 (Autumn 1971), pp.577–605.

White, Eugene N., "Commercial Banks and Securities Markets: Lessons of the 1920s and 1930s for the 1980s and 1990s," in Federal Reserve Bank of Chicago, *Banking System Risk: Charting a New Course*. Chicago: 1989, pp. 258–66.

White, Lawrence J., "The Title Insurance Industry, Reverse Competition, and Controlled Business—A Different View," *Journal of Risk and Insurance*, 15 (Summer 1984).

White, Lawrence J., "The Partial Deregulation of Banks and Other Depository Institutions," in Leonard W. Weiss and Michael W. Klass (eds.), *Regulatory Reform: What Actually Happened.* Boston: Little, Brown, 1986, pp. 169–209.

White, Lawrence J., "Mark to Market is Vital to FSLIC and Valuable to Thrifts," *Outlook of the Federal Home Loan Bank System*, 4 (January/February 1988a), pp. 20–24.

White, Lawrence J., "Market Value Accounting: An Important Part of the Reform of the Deposit Insurance Systems," in Association of Reserve City Bankers, *Capital Issues in Banking.* Washington, DC: 1988b, pp. 226–42.

White, Lawrence J., "The Reform of Federal Deposit Insurance," *Journal of Economic Perspectives*, 3 (Fall 1989), pp. 11–29.

White, Lawrence J., "Mark-to-Market: A (Not So) Modest Proposal," *Financial Managers' Statement*, 12 (January/February 1990a), pp. 27–37.

White, Lawrence J., "The S&L Debacle: How it Happened and Why Further Reforms are Needed," *Regulation*, 13 (Winter 1990b), pp. 11–16.

White, Lawrence J., "Problems of the FSLIC: A Former Policy Maker's View," *Contemporary Policy Issues*, 8 (April 1990c), pp. 62–81.

White, Lawrence J., "Market Value Accounting: It's the Only Answer," *Secondary Mortgage Markets*, 7 (Summer 1990d), pp. 2–4

White, Lawrence J., *The S&L Debacle: Public Policy Lessons for Bank and Thrift Regulation.* New York: Oxford University Press, 1991a.

White, Lawrence J., "The Value of Market Value Accounting for the Deposit Insurance System," *Journal of Accounting, Auditing, and Finance*, 6 (April 1991b).

CHAPTER 10

WILL SMALL BANKS SURVIVE? SMALL BANKS AND THE THEORY OF FINANCIAL INTERMEDIATION

Gregory F. Udell

INTRODUCTION

One often gets the impression reading the New York financial press that conventional commercial banking as we've come to know it is fast becoming an anachronism. Securitization and loan sales seem to have transformed much of the asset side of commercial banking into loan origination. Moreover, the exodus of the Fortune 500 borrower and the upper middle market borrower from the intermediated market would appear to leave commercial banks with a residual clientele composed of a smaller and riskier customer. Competition in this market appears to be intense as the emerging mega-regional banks are basing their explosive growth on this remaining customer base and simultaneously devouring small banks along the way. On the retail side, financial innovation would seem to have created a national market for investment and credit products, including the money market mutual fund and an increasing list of nationally issued credit cards. On the surface, it would appear that these changes suggest a

Gregory F. Udell is an Associate Professor of Finance at Stern School of Business, New York University. He would like to thank Allen Berger and Mitchell Berlin for helpful comments.

much diminished role for small commercial banks. The purpose of this paper is to assess the prospects for the small commercial bank in the next decade.

There is a growing literature which attempts to theoretically motivate the existence of the banking firm. This literature offers a variety of explanations of the economic role of commercial banks. We use this as a starting point in assessing the future of small banks. Some of these theories offer brighter prospects for the small bank than others. In the following section of this chapter we examine each of these theories and what they imply, if anything, about the role of the small bank. An important factor in assessing the future of the small bank (and one which is often ignored in much of the more recent information-based literature on the theory of the banking firm) is the presence of economies of scale in banking. The third section addresses the economies of scale issue both as an empirical issue and its relationship to the theory of the banking firm. The fourth section concludes.

THE THEORY OF FINANCIAL INTERMEDIATION AND ITS IMPLICATIONS FOR SMALL BANKS

Recently there has been much interest in applying information economics to the theory of financial intermediation. Beginning with Leland and Pyle (1977), these papers have focused on the importance of information problems in explaining the existence of the banking firm. To some extent these information-based models have come to represent the "contemporary view" on the subject, and, therefore, represent a good starting point for this exercise. A major implication of many of these models is the importance of diversification in rationalizing an economically significant role for the banking firm. Diamond's (1984) model is representative of this view. His model of the banking firm is one in which a bank emerges endogenously as the optimal organizational solution in an economy in which contracting is made problematic because of differentially informed agents. The bank monitors its borrowers in order to solve an information problem which arises because borrowers have an informational advantage with regard to ex post project returns. Funds are provided by depositors, although this engenders a concomitant problem associated with delegating monitoring responsibility to an agent (the bank). Diamond's insight was to demonstrate that diversification reduces this delegation cost to zero by facilitating a deterministic payoff when the agent who serves as an intermediary bears an infinitely large number of independent risks.

It would seem that the direct empirical implication of the Diamond model is that banks should be very large in order to obtain the benefits of diversification.[1] The prevalent view seems to be that this comports well with reality (i.e., what we observe in the commercial banking market in the U.S.). However, a more critical analysis casts some doubt on whether banks actually exhibit the kind of diversification suggested by Diamond. Diversification in the Diamond model is simplified to the case of forming a portfolio of independent and identical risks. Depositors are symmetrically informed as to the expected return and variance of each loan given monitoring by the bank. In the real world, however, this type of diversification is complicated by the fact that loans are not devoid of systematic risk nor are loans by any means homogeneous securities. The systematic component of individual loan risk is (most certainly) not only unknown to depositors but also unknown to the bank, both because the loans are generally nontraded assets and because the risk assessment techniques employed by banks are relatively unsophisticated [see Dickerson (1987) and Udell (1989) for discussions of commercial loan portfolio analysis and loan review]. More importantly, it is not at all clear that U.S. commercial banks exhibit the kind of diversification required in Diamond-type models of financial intermediation.

For the most part, we know relatively little about the degree of diversification in commercial banking. Information about bank portfolios is in a great part private. Call report data provide only a very broad categorization of loans and, therefore, provide virtually no information on the correlation among asset returns. It is interesting to note that the new risk-based capital requirements completely ignore diversification as a component in setting capital requirements. This is a direct consequence of having inadequate quantitative information on the degree of portfolio diversification as well as unresolved issues relating to the measurement of diversification. What limited information we do have about bank portfolio diversification suggests that banks may not be all that diversified. Keeton and Morris (1987) analyzed loan losses in the Tenth Federal Reserve District and discovered that well over half of the variation in loan losses across banks was related to local market conditions and specialization in specific categories of lending (i.e., over half of the variation was related to a lack of diversification).

One could argue that any lack of diversification in bank portfolios, such as that evidenced in the Keeton and Morris study, would be more an artifact of regulatory constraints than the natural tendency of banks to pursue Diamond-type diversification. That is, geographic restrictions and other regulatory constraints have artificially produced a banking market characterized by a large number of small banks (of which the Tenth Federal Reserve District is particularly representative). Large money center banks, on the other hand, may be more representative of the natural evolution of banks into large well-diversified financial intermediaries. However, there is some evidence which suggests that large is not necessarily synonymous with diversified even with respect to large money center banks. Some of the big bank failures of the 1980s suggest that at least some large banks are anything but diversified. Continental Illinois Bank is a good example. At the time of its bailout Continental was heavily exposed to the oil industry, in great part through its purchase of loan participations from Penn Square Bank. Moreover, regulators also discovered that the bank's aggressive lending policies in the late 1970s (for which Continental had become widely regarded as one of the nation's premier commercial lenders) had resulted in Continental's becoming disproportionately exposed to some of the worst credits of the 1980s—often as the lead bank. In addition, Continental, like many other U.S. money center banks, had an enormous exposure to LDC debt. More recently, the failure of large regional banks in Texas and problems with many large New England banks also suggest a lack of diversification in relatively large banks. It is important to note that increases in bank size need not necessarily lead to more diversification. In fact, the binding constraint on the maximum size of commercial loans is the legal lending limit which necessarily rises *proportionately* with bank capital. If the average loan size in the commercial loan portfolio increases with bank size, then large banks may not be any more diversified than small banks—at least with respect to the commercial loan portfolio, which is the asset category most affected by information problems.

So what can we conclude from Diamond-type information models with respect to the prospects for small banks? Certainly from a theoretical point of view the Diamond model suggests that small banks should disappear. As noted above, however, the empirical prediction of the model that banks will become well-diversified has not been verified—nor, for that matter, has it been rejected. In part this is because of a lack of data. In addition, it stems from the fact that it is extremely difficult to econometrically control for the effect of regulation. In particular, the moral hazard problem inherent in fixed rate deposit insurance introduces a strong disincentive to minimize risk through diversification. Numerous studies [for example, Keeton and Morris (1987), Marcus and Shaked (1984), Ronn and Verma (1986) and Saunders, Strock, and Travlos (1987)] indicate that moral hazard-induced risk-taking is evident in commercial bank behavior, including that of the large money centers. Therefore, at this point in time the diversification prediction of the Diamond model must be regarded only as a theoretical possibility—which may or may not be offset by other factors not included in the model.

It is worth noting at this juncture that not all information-based models of the banking firm generate a diversification argument which implies that banks will necessarily be very large. For example, Boot, Thakor, and Udell (1990) develop a model of the banking firm based on the role of banks as credible issuers of off-balance sheet claims. In their model, loan commitments solve a moral hazard problem which occurs because banks cannot observe borrower action in the first period of a two period world. Banks emerge as credible issuers of loan commitments because there is an incentive for individual commitment issuers to renege on commitments (in takedown states) because the probability of doing so with impunity is sufficiently high. Banks, on the other hand, cannot renege on their commitments because the probability of being caught unjustifiably reneging becomes unacceptably high due to the fact that banks issue many commitments. However, unlike in the Diamond model, in the Boot, Thakor, and Udell model the optimal bank size is not infinitely large; the bank need only be large enough to make it incentive-compatible to issue loan commitments credibly. Therefore, their model specifically allows for the possibility that banks may be relatively small.

In another information-based approach, Berlin (1990) develops a model in which banks indigenously emerge to permit optimal rescheduling of loans. Banks may dominate individual lenders because revenues from one part of the portfolio are used to finance rescheduling of loans in the rest of the portfolio. Banks, however, need not be infinitely large because firms have available alternative forms of financing (i.e., firms can sell alternative forms of debt).

While the emphasis in recent years has been to justify the existence of banks on the basis of information economics, other more traditional approaches are still being used in modeling the banking firm; these include the liquidity transformation approach, the risk sharing approach and the transaction (or brokerage) approach. The implications of each of these more traditional approaches of the future of small banks are discussed below.

The liquidity transformation approach argues that the role of the depository institution is to create a liquid instrument (a deposit) on the right hand side of the balance sheet and invest in an illiquid instrument (a loan) on the left hand side. This approach is the one, for instance, taken by Diamond and Dybvig (1983). Liquidity in deposits of course means that some random fraction of depositors will withdraw (or deposit) funds from their accounts in the short run. The solution to this liquidity problem in part involves spreading the withdrawal risk over a sufficiently large number of accounts. Systematic withdrawals, on the other hand, motivate the existence of a central bank as lender of last resort. While the liquidity transformation approach seems to suggest that very small banks may be suboptimal, it is difficult to take this argument too far given today's institutional landscape: an extensive interbank loan market, a highly developed market for securitized assets, deposit insurance and the presence of the Federal Reserve discount window.

Another approach to modeling the banking firm is to motivate the existence of banks through optimal risk sharing. In this approach, a risk neutral (or at least less risk averse) bank contracts with a risk averse borrower in order to facilitate improved risk sharing [e.g., James (1981) and Thakor and Udell (1987)]. For example, banks might offer borrowers long term fixed rate loan contracts in which the bank absorbs the interest rate risk [as in Thakor and Udell (1987)]. Or banks might offer loan commitments in which the bank insures against changes in borrower credit risk [as in Avery and Berger (1990)]. There is some limited empirical evidence for this insurance view of banks. Berger and Udell (1990) suggest that the well-documented stickiness in the commercial loan interest rate [see, for example, Goldfeld (1966), Jaffee (1971) and Slovin and Shushka (1983)] is more likely the result of bank-borrower risk-sharing than credit rationing.

Risk-sharing, as a *raison d'être* for the existence of banks, would seem to be relatively silent on the issue of bank size. The necessary condition for banks to act as facilitators of risk sharing is that bank owners are either risk neutral or that they are otherwise well-diversified. While this condition does not necessarily imply anything about bank size, one could argue that it is more likely to be met in the case of large widely held publicly traded banks. If this is the case, then movement from a regulatory regime in which small banks have been protected from competition to one in which they are not would likely lead to a significant decline in the number of small banks.

The transactions cost approach represents yet another alternative to motivating the existence of banks. Here banks exist because of transactions costs associated with bringing together relatively small borrowers and lenders. The bank provides a mechanism for reducing search costs [see Benston and Smith (1976)] by assuming a brokerage function. A more extensive form of this approach incorporates the micro market structure literature in viewing the bank much as a broker-dealer [see Ho and Saunders (1981)]. This view suggests that banks whose "inventory risk" is smaller can afford to charge a smaller spread. We address the overall issue of economies of scale in banking in the next section.

So what can we conclude about the prospects for small banks based on the extant theory of the banking firm? In some sense this is an unfair demand upon the theory. Much of the contemporary literature on the existence of banks is motivated by a desire to put our "theoretical house in order."[2] That is, the foundations upon which much of modern financial theory rests essentially assume away an economically meaningful role for financial intermediaries. Specifically, in a Modigliani and Miller world banks exist only as an anomaly. Recent work on the theory of the banking firm has primarily focused on reconciling the existence of financial intermediaries by relaxing the assumptions behind M&M. As noted above, relaxing the assumption of symmetric information has been the approach which has garnered the most recognition. This work amounts to establishing a set of conditions which deviate from M&M under which financial intermediaries emerge endogenously. In this regard, this body of literature has been quite successful. At the very least it has provided us with a powerful framework with which to view the contribution of financial intermediation to overall economic activity and with which to analyze various regulatory issues. However, it has not (nor, in some sense was it intended to) provided us with a complete theory of the banking firm. The information models (as well as the more traditional models) for the most part ignore important organization issues in the Williamson sense which should place specific limits on the nature of the banking firm. For example, Ramakrishnan and Thakor (1984) assume away all such problems when they assume that information producers who coalesce to form a financial intermediary observe costlessly the efforts of all others in the coalition. In reality, these issues of internal organizational control may impose significant costs on the financial intermediary which have a direct impact on its optimal size.[3] Indeed, there is some evidence that these types of contracting problems are quite important in banking. Udell (1989) provides evidence that the organizational structure of a commercial bank can be likened to a tiered set of agency problems in which contracting is characterized by moral hazard at each level. The commercial borrower contracts with the commercial loan officer; the commercial loan officer contracts with the bank's senior management; the senior management contracts with the stockholders; and the stockholders contract with the regulator. Udell (1989) specifically examines the contracting problem between the loan officer and the bank (i.e., the bank's senior management). He provides empirical evidence that banks use loan review as an internal enforcement mechanism to insure that loan officers devote sufficient time and energy to monitoring the loans for which they have account responsibility. For a variety of reasons, loan officers may otherwise have an incentive to shirk this responsibility, including a disutility for effort, the perceived stigma associated with having made a bad loan and (in a worst case scenario) discovery of insider dealings between the borrower and the loan officer. Other types of internal control problems might also bound the size of the organization including the simultaneous management of heterogeneous tasks.

Which of the above paradigms best describes the banking firm is probably at this point in time anybody's guess. Banks tend to be rather more complicated creatures than the models we have constructed to explain their existence. Because these views are not generally mutually exclusive, it is quite possible that each of them applies and the true model of the banking firm is one which integrates them all. Unfortunately, this makes it very difficult to draw any meaningful prediction from the theory about the prospects for small banks. Fortunately, however, a great deal has been done empirically on the more focused issue of whether the bank production function exhibits economies of scale and scope. This literature will enable us to say something a bit more concrete about the question of small banks. We turn to this in the next section.

SMALL BANKS AND ECONOMIES OF SCALE AND SCOPE

While it is difficult to draw any definitive prediction from the theoretical literature on bank existence, the extensive empirical work on economies of scale and scope in banking affords a more clear basis on which to make some comment about the likely prospects for small banks. Empirical examination of the cost structure of banks began in earnest in the 1950s.[4] As noted by Shaffer (1989), there is general agreement in this literature that there exists some minimum size level below which banks are relatively inefficient. On the other hand, there is no consensus on what that level is, nor is there consensus about what happens at larger size levels.

In his study of the challenges facing small banks, Shaffer (1989) elaborates on the significance of this minimum threshold level. He notes that there is widespread agreement that banks with less than $25 million in assets are, on average, below the threshold level and banks with more than $200 million in assets are, on average, above the threshold level. At first blush it would appear that this difference is relatively small. After all, we measure the differences in money center banks in the tens of billions of dollars—not in the tens of millions. However, Shaffer points out that the difference between $25 million and $200 million is quite significant when talking about the survival of small banks. This can be seen by looking at the distribution of banks by size below $500 million in assets as shown in Table 10–1.

Table 10–1 demonstrates that as deregulation of banking (and in particular the elimination of geographic barriers) proceeds, the impact on the number of banks affected depends very much on where the threshold barrier is. Based on Table 10–1, Shaffer concludes that if the threshold level is $25 million in assets, then at least 1,535 banks would be eliminated—if all banks less than $25 million recombined with each other to form banks of $25 million in asset size each. However, if each and every one of these banks were absorbed by banks greater than $25 million in assets, then all 3,948 banks would disappear. On the other hand, if the

TABLE 10–1
Number of Banks by Asset Size in 1988

Size	No. of Banks
$0–25M	3,948
$25–50M	3,380
$50–100M	2,730
$100–300M	1,845
$300–500M	331

Source: Shaffer (1989)

threshold level is $50 million, then at least 3,680 banks would be elimi-
nated with the maximum possible eliminations due to inefficiency being
7,328 (i.e., the total number of banks with assets less than $50 million)![5]

There is another problem associated with making predictions based
on the empirical evidence suggesting a minimum size level for bank
efficiency (other than identifying the threshold level itself). This problem
involves interpretation of economies of scale in small banks. An empirical
finding that very small banks are inefficient could be construed in two
ways. It could be interpreted to mean that small banks are inherently
inefficient because of the nature of the bank production function (i.e., a
straightforward economy of scale argument). Alternatively, it could be
driven by the fact that a significant subset of small banks are inefficiently
run simply because, relative to large banks, they are managed by less
competent executives. This latter interpretation, however, would still be a
form of economies of scale if (small) size itself precludes these banks
from obtaining competent management. On the other hand, if managerial
inefficiency (or inefficiency in general) in small banks is not scale related,
then it is quite possible that competently run small banks may continue to
exist in the coming deregulated era.

Examination of bank performance data provides some interesting
evidence on the relative efficiency of small banks. Shaffer (1989) analyzed bank performance by size category against five alternative measures: percentage of failing banks, return on assets, return on equity,
percentage of noncurrent loans, and percentage of net charge-offs. As of
1988 he found that performance monotonically improves with size for
every performance measure using the size categories in Table 10–1.[6] Performance data alone, however, do not tell us whether these inefficiencies
stem from economies of scale or from nonscale inefficiencies. A recent
study by Berger and Humphrey (1990) addresses this issue. While Berger
and Humphrey confirm the presence of scale economies in small banks,
they also find that these scale economies are dominated by differences in
firm-specific inefficiencies that are not related to scale. Specifically, they
find that these inefficiencies dominate all measured scale, product mix,
input price, branching network and purchased funds effects. Their results
indicate that for most banks nonscale inefficiencies are on the order of 25
percent of costs, which far outweighs the impact of scale economies which
are generally 5 percent or less of costs. This difference is even greater for
small banks.

What can we conclude then from the empirical literature on bank efficiency? First, it generally supports the notion that the challenge to small bank survival is great. Second, the challenge comes not only from scale economies but also from the fact that it appears that many banks are simply inefficiently run *given their size*. Third, the empirical literature tends to suggest that while managerial control issues may be important, they appear to be outweighed by other factors in the production function for small banks.[7] It should also be noted that even though the evidence confirms the presence of economies of scale for small banks, this cannot necessarily be interpreted as strong empirical support for a Diamond-type diversification argument. Aside from the fact that some studies find a U-shaped average cost function {see, for example, Gilligan, Smirlock, and Marshall (1984), and Gilligan and Smirlock (1984)], interpreting empirical economies of scale in banking as evidence of a diversification-produced reduction in delegation costs is not justified in light of the problems associated with measuring diversification (and the fact that diversification may not be positively related to bank size).

CONCLUSION

Interest in the theory of financial intermediation has yielded a wealth of provocative papers in recent years. It is difficult, however, to draw specific predictions about the evolution of the financial services industry from this literature. To date we do not have an integrated model of the banking firm which encompasses its many-faceted features. A complete model of the bank, for instance, would have to explain the simultaneous existence of banks and the wide variety of other nondepository financial intermediaries (i.e., accounting firms, rating agencies, venture capital firms, broker/dealers)—along with the existence of other nonintermediated securities—as well as the role of banks as both producers of off-balance sheet and on-balance sheet activities, etc. While clearly some papers have succeeded in examining banks in a more general setting [see, for example, Diamond (1989)], it is unrealistic to expect that a complete model of the banking firm is likely to appear in the near future! In the absence of such a model we will not find the answer to our question about the survival of small banks in the theoretical literature (although the extant theory may be useful in identifying some of the factors which affect small bank survival). The relatively rich empirical literature on bank efficiency, on the other hand, offers a less ambiguous view. The nearly total agreement in that literature that at least the very small bank is inefficient on average suggests powerfully that we are likely to see a substantial consolidation in the banking industry.

NOTES

1. Other models of financial intermediation based on information economics also imply that financial intermediaries should be very large in order to enjoy the benefits of diversification; for example, Boyd and Prescott (1986) and Ramakrishnan and Thakor (1984). The former paper models banks while the latter models nonbank financial intermediaries.
2. I owe this quote to Mitchell Berlin.
3. See Williamson 1967 for a discussion of these costs in a nonfinancial intermediary setting.
4. There have been a number of excellent surveys of the literature on the economies of scale and scope in banking. In particular, see Gilbert (1984), Mester (1987) and Clark (1988).
5. Several other studies suggest that industry consolidation could be even more dramatic [see Kaufman et al. (1983) and Miller (1988)].
6. This monotonicity generally held true for all five measures for 1984 through 1987.
7. This conclusion is much more difficult to draw with respect to large banks. Studies which indicate that the average cost function displays a U-shape [such as Gilligan, Smirlock, and Marshall (1984), and Gilligan and Smirlock (1984)] might be construed as evidence that the cost of managerial control in the Williamson sense increases with bank size. A recent study of large banks by Mester (1990) suggests the possibility of diseconomies of scope in jointly producing loans for portfolio funding and loans for loan sales. One possible reason for this diseconomy of scope is the possibility that joint production of these products requires another layer of management which could be avoided if these products were produced separately in different organizations.

REFERENCES

Avery, R., and A. Berger, "Loan Commitments and Bad Risk Exposure," *Journal of Banking and Finance*, (1990).

Benston, G., and C. Smith, "A Transactions Cost Approach to the Theory of Financial Intermediation," *Journal of Finance* (May 1976), pp. 215–31.

Berger, A., and D. Humphrey, "The Dominance of Inefficiencies Over Scale and Product Mix Economies in Banking," Federal Reserve Board working paper (November 1990).

Berger, A., and G. Udell, "Some Evidence on the Empirical Significance of Credit Rationing," New York University working paper (December 1990).

Berlin, M., "Loan Reschedulings and the Size of the Banking Sector," New York University working paper (May 1990).

Boot, A.; A. Thakor; and G. Udell, "Credible Commitments, Contract Enforcement Problems and Banks: Intermediation as Credibility Assurance," New York University working paper (July 1990).

Boyd, J., and E. Prescott, "Financial Intermediary Coalitions," *Journal of Economic Theory* 38 (1986), pp. 211–32.

Campbell, T., and W. Krakaw, "Information Production, Market Signalling and the Theory of Financial Intermediation," *Journal of Finance* (September 1980), pp. 863–82.

Diamond, D., "Financial Intermediation and Delegated Monitoring," *Review of Economic Studies* (July 1984), pp. 393–414.

Diamond, D., "Monitoring and Reputation: The Choice Between Bank Loans and Directly Placed Debt," University of Chicago working paper (January 1989).

Diamond, D., and P. Dybvig, "Bank Runs, Deposit Insurance and Liquidity," *Journal of Political Economy* (June 1983), pp. 401–19.

Dickerson, C., *Current Approaches to Grading Commercial Loans*, Philadelphia: Robert Morris Associates (1987).

Fama, E., "Banking in the Theory of Finance," *Journal of Monetary Economics* (January 1980), pp. 39–57.

Gilligan, T., and M. Smirlock, "An Empirical Study of Joint Production and Scale Economies in Commercial Banking," *Journal of Banking and Finance* (1984), pp. 67–77.

Gilligan, T.; M. Smirlock; and W. Marshall, "Scale and Scope Economies in the Multi-Product Banking Firm," *Journal of Monetary Economics* (1984), pp. 393–405.

Goldfeld, S., *Commercial Bank Behavior and Economic Activity*, Amsterdam: North-Holland Press (1966).

Ho, T., and A. Saunders, "The Determinants of Bank Interest Rate Margins: Theory and Empirical Evidence," *Journal of Financial and Quantitative Analysis* (November 1981), pp. 581–600

Jaffee, D., *Credit Rationing and the Commercial Loan Market*, New York: John Wiley & Sons (1971).

James, C., "Self-Selection and the Pricing of Bank Services: An Analysis of the Market for Loan Commitments and the Role of Compensating Balance Requirements," *Journal of Financial and Quantitative Analysis* (December 1981), pp. 742–46.

Kaufman, G; L. Mote; and H. Rosenblum. "Implications of Deregulation for Product Lines and Geographic Markets of Financial Institutions," *Journal of Bank Research* (1983), pp. 8–12.

Keeton, W., and C. Morris, "Why Do Banks' Loan Losses Differ?" *Economic Review*, Federal Reserve Bank of Kansas City (May 1987), pp. 3–21.

Leland, H., and D. Pyle, "Informational Asymmetries, Financial Structure and Financial Intermediation," *Journal of Finance* (May 1977), pp. 371–87.

Marcus, A., and I. Shaked, "The Valuation of FDIC Deposit Insurance Using Option-pricing Estimates," *Journal of Money, Credit and Banking* (November 1984, Part 1).

Mester, L., "Efficient Production of Financial Services: Scale and Scope Economies," *Business Review*, Federal Reserve Bank of Philadelphia (January/February 1987), pp. 15–25.

Mester, L., "Traditional and Nontraditional Banking: An Information-Theoretic Approach," Federal Reserve Bank of Philadelphia working paper (1990).

Miller, S., "Counterfactual Experiments of Deregulation on Banking Structure," *Quarterly Review of Economics and Business* (1988), pp. 38–49.

Ramakrishnan, R.T.S., and A. Thakor, "Information Reliability and a Theory of Financial Intermediation," *Review of Economic Studies* (1984), pp. 415–32.

Ronn, E., and A. Verma, "Pricing Risk-Adjusted Deposit Insurance: An Option Based Model," *Journal of Finance* (September 1986), pp. 871–95.

Santomero, A., "Modeling the Banking Firm: A Survey," *Journal of Money, Credit and Banking* (November 1984, Part 2), pp. 576–602.

Saunders, A.; E. Strock; and N. Travlos, "Ownership Structure, Deregulation and Bank Risk-Taking," New York University working paper (October 1987).

Shaffer, S., "Challenges to Small Banks' Survival," *Business Review*, Federal Reserve Bank of Philadelphia (September/October 1989), pp. 15–27.

Slovin, M., and M. Shushka, "A Model of the Commercial Loan Rate," *Journal of Finance* (December 1983), pp. 1583–96.

Thakor, A., and G. Udell, "An Economic Rationale for the Pricing Structure of Bank Loan Commitments," *Journal of Banking and Finance*, (June 1987), pp. 271–89.

Udell, G., "Loan Quality, Commercial Loan Review and Loan Officer Contracting," *Journal of Banking and Finance* (1989), pp. 367–82.

Williamson, O. E., "Hierarchical Control and Optimum Firm Size," *Journal of Political Economy*. (April 1967), pp. 123–38.